W9-ABE-901

OPERATION DEVIL HORNS

OPERATION DEVIL HORNS

The Takedown of MS-13 in San Francisco

MICHAEL SANTINI AND RAY BOLGER

ROWMAN & LITTLEFIELD
Lanham • Boulder • New York • London

Published by Rowman & Littlefield
An imprint of The Rowman & Littlefield Publishing Group, Inc.
4501 Forbes Boulevard, Suite 200, Lanham, Maryland 20706
www.rowman.com

Unit A, Whitacre Mews, 26-34 Stannary Street, London SE11 4AB

British Library Cataloguing in Publication Information Available

Library of Congress Cataloging-in-Publication Data

Names: Santini, Michael (Special agent, Homeland Security Investigations), author.
Title: Operation Devil Horns : the takedown of MS-13 in San Francisco / Michael Santini and
  Ray Bolger.
Description: Lanham : Rowman & Littlefield, [2018] | Includes index.
Identifiers: LCCN 2018013695 (print) | LCCN 2018014646 (ebook) | ISBN 9781538115640
  (Electronic) | ISBN 9781538115633 (cloth : alk. paper)
Subjects: LCSH: MS-13 (Gang) | Gangs—California—San Francisco—Case studies. | Organized
  crime investigation—California—San Francisco—Case studies. | Undercover operations—
  California—San Francisco—Case studies.
Classification: LCC HV6439.U7 (ebook) | LCC HV6439.U7 S277 2018 (print) | DDC
  364.106/60979461—dc23
LC record available at https://lccn.loc.gov/2018013695

♾™ The paper used in this publication meets the minimum requirements of American National
Standard for Information Sciences—Permanence of Paper for Printed Library Materials, ANSI/
NISO Z39.48-1992.

Printed in the United States of America

Dedicated to HSI Special Agent Edward J. Smith
January 23, 1968–October 15, 2012
"Every time we see a star, it is Ed shining down on us."

Contents

PART II

Acknowledgments

To our mutual friend and colleague, Steve Olivera, we owe a sincere debt of gratitude for recognizing the potential of this project and encouraging us to collaborate in authoring the story of Operation Devil Horns. Without his creative soundboarding, logistical problem solving, and tenacious shepherding, this book would not exist.

There are a few people whose support demands public recognition. Laura Gwinn, lead prosecutor in the Operation Devil Horns investigation, lent her expertise and keen eye to the manuscript. Retired US Attorney Joseph Russoniello shared a well-seasoned perspective of the bureaucratic turf battles between federal, state, and local agencies in San Francisco during the time the story occurred. Jaxon Van Derbeken, an award-winning police and courts reporter for the *San Francisco Chronicle*, offered his savvy insights on the case, which he covered as the bloody saga unfolded. The dedicated law enforcement and public relations professionals of Homeland Security Investigations vetted certain technical aspects of the book. Jessica M. Vaughan of the Center for Immigration Studies provided invaluable statistics and context for understanding the controversies swirling around sanctuary city policies, locally and nationally, which continue to this day.

Thank you to editor John Paine, who provided an experienced hand in honing the book chapters into shape. So did writer Rafael Alvarez, who suffered nobly all the way through an early rough draft. Literary agent Michael Wright shared his broad knowledge of the publishing industry and media markets. Early guinea-pig readers who gave generously of their time and intelligence also include Kathleen McCaffrey Friedman, as well as Laura and James McGinty. Thank you to Kathryn

Knigge and the editorial and library boards at Rowman & Littlefield for recognizing the merits of this book.

Most of all, we would like to thank our immediate families, without whose love, support, and encouragement this project would never have been completed.

This is a true story. Some names have been changed to protect certain individuals involved with the case. Quoted dialogue is transcribed directly from original recordings in some instances, while some has been written based on firsthand recollections and is not necessarily verbatim.

Prelude

San Pedro Sula, Honduras
Christmas Eve, 2004

MAKING ITS WAY ALONG THE DARK, WINDING, POTHOLED ROAD BETWEEN the suburbs of San Isidro and Ebenezer, an old yellow passenger bus was standing-room-only inside, full of textile workers on their way home from Christmas shopping. Small children rocked and slept in their mothers' laps as the bus driver tried his best to negotiate the lurching vehicle around the street's gaping potholes and busted pavement.

On the most deserted stretch of road the bus traveled that night, alongside a dark, vacant soccer field, the driver was suddenly cut off by a small pickup truck coming in the opposite direction. It swerved and came to a stop, blocking both lanes. Two men with AK-47s hopped out of the truck, while behind the bus two other cars pulled up, blocking it from the rear. Several more armed men emerged from these vehicles.

The bus driver and his fare collector could only hope it was a robbery by some gang *mareros* who would demand a "tax," take all the money and valuables from them and their passengers, and let them go on their way. But even this was too much to hope for. The armed men did not make any demands. At once, they raised their weapons and began firing into the bus from all directions, the bullets penetrating and raking everyone inside with an estimated eight hundred rounds.

Screams and cries of anguish, fear, and pain echoed inside the bus over the flash and din of automatic guns. Women, children, and men trapped inside the vehicle wept and pled for mercy, gasping and dying in a sudden hellhole filled with gunpowder fumes and the coppery smell of fresh blood. The few passengers who could bolt out the rear emergency door and make a run for their lives were shot dead in their tracks.

When the killers stopped firing, one of them, an MS-13 gang leader known as *Culiche*, or Tapeworm, stepped onto the bus. He methodically made his way down the aisle, stepping over bleeding bodies, calmly poking and prodding the dead and dying. "Are you still alive?" he asked those who still moved or moaned—a question or complaint he followed up with point-blank shots to the head and face.

Described by US law enforcement agencies as intelligent, articulate, and highly mobile, Culiche was approximately thirty years old, with a round face, dark eyes, and large ears. Born in Honduras, he was an early member of the Normandie Locos, a Los Angeles–based clique of MS-13. He was arrested at least eight times in California, accused of drug trafficking, aggravated assault, burglary, writing bad checks, and driving without a license. Culiche had a record of carrying fake IDs and using multiple cell phones, and had thirty-eight known aliases, according to Honduran authorities and the FBI.

When he finally stopped the slaughter and stepped back off the bus, twenty-eight of its occupants were dead, including the driver and fare collector. The youngest murder victim was a fourteen-month-old child and the oldest was sixty-eight years old. Another twenty-eight victims were seriously wounded, among them a sixteen-year-old factory worker who was shot sixteen times—once for each year of his young life, like birthday candles from Satan himself.

On the windshield of the bullet-ridden bus, Culiche and his band of MS-13 killers posted a note claiming responsibility for the attack. It was bogusly signed by the Cinchonero People's Liberation Movement, a group that had not been active for more than a decade—not since the region's civil wars ended in 1992. The note warned Honduran authorities about similar repercussions if they passed a new law that would introduce the death penalty for violent crimes, a measure to bring the hammer down harder on gangs metastasizing in the country.

Before driving away from the slaughter, the gunmen attached a second note to the windshield of the bus.

It read, *Feliz Navidad.*

Merry Christmas.

PART I

Operation Card Shark

San Francisco

WALKING THROUGH THE MISSION DISTRICT, WEARING A TRACKSUIT TOP and a pair of jeans and running shoes, Michael Santini was a handsome man in his prime, built low to the ground, with a trim, powerful upper body from years of lifting weights and fitness training. Tattooed full sleeve on his right arm was a dragon, and under that a koi fish fighting against the current of a rushing waterfall. Considered in traditional Chinese culture the most powerful-swimming fish, koi represented strength of character. Rewarded for their perseverance here on Earth, in the afterlife they were transformed into dragons. On the back of Santini's left shoulder, an inked scorpion (his astrological sign) coiled its stinger-tipped tail.

It was a chilly, Saturday morning with torrential rain coming down, and the special agent with Homeland Security Investigations (HSI) had ventured from his apartment for a desperately needed cup of coffee. Under the weather after a late night partying, without a rain jacket or umbrella, he ignored the downpour while stepping around the sidewalk's flooded potholes. At the Java House on Valencia Street, he bought himself a steaming cup of joe.

He was headed home with the coffee when he suddenly spotted the red Nissan he had been hunting for over two weeks. It was parked at the curb halfway up a steep hill near the corner of 22nd and Fair Oaks Streets. Just a block from his house. The car belonged to "Jose," the leader of a criminal counterfeit identification document production and distribution ring known as the Miceros, comprised mostly of native Mexicans. The Miceros were by definition a gang, but lacked a propensity for violence unless their counterfeit ID business was threatened. They maintained a presence on every corner of Mission Street, from the 8th Street BART station, down to Glen Park.

The batteries on a vehicle tracker Santini and a team of HSI agents surreptitiously attached to the car a few weeks back had recently gone dead before he could trace the vehicle to the location of the network's main counterfeit ID production lab. He had been monitoring the movements of the vehicle for days with GPS-enabled software from his desktop computer and believed he had located the lab. He just needed evidence from the tracker data to lock down the probable cause for a warrant.

Santini shook his head and thought, *A special agent is never—ever—off duty.* He stood by the parked car in the heavy rain and scanned the streets to see if anyone was watching, then set down his coffee cup on the curb. From a crouched position, he dropped to the ground and slipped under the Nissan on his back. The tracker device was stuck to the undercarriage with a magnet and easily detached, but its long, wire antenna was strung the length of the frame, attached by technicians with a gooey, tarlike putty.

Lying on his back and struggling with the sticky mess, Santini's hands became covered in black tar. A torrent of water running downhill through the street gutter gushed through his jeans and out the neck of his T-shirt. The rushing rainwater flowed in such volume it blew up his clothes like a water balloon, as he struggled to yank off the tracker and antenna. Finally, he was able to rip it off and stuff the mess of wires down his pants.

He crawled out from under the vehicle and stood up, checking to see if anyone spotted him. Satisfied no one had, he bent down and grabbed the cup of coffee, which stuck fast to the tarry mess all over his hands. Walking slowly back to the apartment, he turned the corner of his street, where he almost bumped right into a Latino man heading in the opposite direction, reading a rain-soaked newspaper as he went. It was Jose, the Miceros' boss, owner of the Nissan. Another few seconds under the vehicle and Santini would have been caught red-handed.

When he arrived home, he glanced in the hallway mirror and couldn't help but burst out laughing. He was drenched with rainwater and covered in tar, with a tracking device crammed into his pants. His soaked condition sparked memories of his time with the US Border Patrol, not so long ago . . .

When the rains from El Niño hit the Southern California desert, the two-mile-wide patrol zone north of the international boundary turned into a sea of mud. Even the agents' four-wheel drive vehicles couldn't tackle the slippery slopes and fields north of the fence when the deluge came. Under those conditions, the border patrol essentially ceded control of the zone to Mexico, while holding the line at the Otay Mesa Freeway.

When the patrol fell back, the population of Tijuana jumped the line into the United States like a swollen river cresting its banks. Santini and his fellow border agents were forced to hike on foot into the San Ysidro hillsides to stem the northward flow of humanity, but to little avail. Groups of sometimes hundreds of migrants sneaked across together and set up camp on the US side, waiting for darkness to fall so they could creep farther north and hitch rides with the smugglers who cruised Route 905.

The strenuous and seemingly futile work was offset by an enviable off-duty beach party life for Santini in San Diego. The sunny days were replete with booze and beautiful women, attracted to Santini's cohort of border agents and naval officer buddies on shore leave. Then the 9/11 terrorist attack happened and life took on a more serious tone. Suddenly the southern border was viewed as more than just an out-of-control situation involving migrant Mexican and Central American laborers. If *they* could get across and into the country so easily, who else could? Bin Laden's minions from the Middle East? Carrying what types of weapons of mass destruction?

He took a second glance at himself in the mirror, a ridiculous image. A lot of water had passed under the bridge between his days on the border and now, standing in a Mission District apartment, covered in tar. He chuckled to himself and headed for the kitchen, trading his cup of coffee for a can of beer.

Santini and his team soon reinstalled the tracker with fresh batteries and followed the red Nissan back to the Miceros' main ID production lab, which was ensconced in an upscale apartment across from Dolores Park. Still, he didn't have enough hard evidence for a search warrant. To acquire it, the agent's assigned assistant US attorney advised him to take advantage of a recently enacted police power under the Patriot Act that permitted a surreptitious entry, or "sneak and peak" search, without a warrant.

He assembled a team for a sneak-and-peak visit to the lab, shielded by a squad of agents posing as home movers. A common investigative technique, ruses were used by feds for everything from fake phone calls to undercover purchases of illegal contraband. Santini believed the "moving company" ruse would ensure he wasn't surprised by the Miceros while searching the lab. As night fell, the undercover agents arrived in a truck and unloaded moving equipment and containers into the apartment building's hallway, creating obstacles to slow down the Miceros, in case they showed up unexpectedly while Santini was snooping around inside the apartment. The team spent an hour or so after the pre-operation brief, folding together various sizes of empty boxes and securing them with packing tape to complete the deception.

With the entrances and hallways to the building blocked and covered by agents, Santini and some of the team members pulled into the rear alleyway with a truck and extension ladder. They stood up the ladder atop the bed of a pickup truck and leaned it against the wall under a window to the Miceros' apartment. With his partners steadying the ladder, Santini scrambled up the rungs and found the window unlocked, slid it open, and climbed inside.

The unit's rooms were all dark and he was a little tense. His team had been keeping the apartment under regular surveillance, and they believed no one was inside now. But they couldn't be 100 percent certain. Alone inside, he needed to clear the darkened rooms before focusing on whatever evidence there might be. With gun drawn, he switched on his flashlight and cleared the rooms, one by one. To his relief nobody was home. Free to survey the apartment, he discovered a trove of document-making equipment and supplies. It was all there, everything somebody needed to make convincing fake IDs: printers, laminators, the whole works. Santini was certain this lab was supplying dozens of Miceros the fake IDs they were peddling to the masses in the Mission District.

With warrants in hand, Santini and his team watched and waited until Jose and his primary lab technician were in the apartment together before paying another visit, this time to bust the men and their equipment in one swoop. They surrounded the apartment, ready to raid the lab, which had been spared damage from a recent fire that left gaping holes and charred rafters across a portion of the building's roof.

When the team of agents made their move inside, the Miceros' boss was standing in the hallway, presumably heading back out to check on his street operation. He saw the cops coming and bolted out of sight, prompting a frantic building-wide search. With his gun in hand, Santini raced upstairs after him to the top floor, which the fire had rendered a scorched mess, filled with the smell of smoked wood, scattered with burnt lumber and the debris of ruined apartment dwellings. Plenty of places to hide in the dark.

Wary his target might have a gun, Santini crept through the burnt mess, trying to stay covered, straining to see in the dark, listening for him. And there he was, the glint of his eyes peering out from a hiding place among the scorched debris.

"Levanta tus manos! Raise your hands!" Santini ordered him.

The raid ended without injury, and the documents lab was hauled away for evidence. Later that afternoon, before word was out to the larger contingent of street-dealing Miceros that the lab had been busted, Santini and his team of HSI agents swept a segment of Mission Street, arresting about fifteen of the counterfeit ID peddlers associated with the lab. The criminal network was diminished and Operation Card Shark was a success.

For his efforts, Santini gained a good deal of respect from his colleagues at both HSI and the US Attorney's Office. Over a dozen crooks were put in federal prison for between five and fifteen years. He proved he had the crime fighting chops to take down bad guys, using federal resources to target not just street-level dealers, but the leadership structure as well.

CHAPTER 2

Diego Gets Arrested

DESPERATE TO AVOID SCRUTINY FROM AN SFPD COP DRIVING PAST HIM on routine patrol, Diego Cruz-Vasquez cut across the street before he reached the corner at the busy intersection of Eddy and Larkin streets in the Tenderloin District—a jaywalking infraction, technically. Over his shoulder, he caught a glimpse of the officer's side view mirror and could see the cop's squinting left eye giving him a hard look.

Diego was accustomed to this stare, except in his home country of Honduras the consequences could be much more severe. The same type of glare from a cop in San Pedro Sula could mean a physical beating, a few years in jail, or even an impromptu death sentence meted out by the ultra-corrupt Honduran National Police. He picked up his pace and quickly ducked into the First Coin Laundry on Eddy Street.

In the United States illegally, Diego had good reason to be concerned. He had only been in San Francisco for a few weeks, arriving after an arduous journey that included jumping freight trains through Mexico and hopping buses all the way to Houston. He was desperate to avoid deportation. If picked up by local law enforcement and sent back home, his chances of survival would not be good.

The customers washing and folding their clothes barely noticed him step inside the busy self-service laundry. He paced nervously a few moments before deciding it was safe to peek outside. He pushed the smudged glass storefront door ajar and looked right, then left. And there was the cop again. The patrolman had circled back around the block in his cruiser.

Diego slid back into the laundry and made a critical error. Attempting to blend in with the Tenderloin's recovering drug addicts and working-class Latino women doing their loads of wash, he stripped off his jacket and tossed it into a dryer. He dropped three quarters into the coin slot and stood motionless, staring intensely at the machine's spinning drum, sweating and nervous.

In his sleeveless shirt, all could see now that Diego's upper body was covered in tattoos that screamed his gang affiliation: *MS-13*. Around him, the laundry customers stole furtive glances at his inked-up torso. There was a time his gang tats had proclaimed proudly to the world that Diego was a serious *marero*, a man to be feared and respected. Now, they felt like targets on his back.

The gang—his gang, although now he was on the run from them—prided themselves on committing acts of extreme violence, much of it committed against their own members who had fallen out of favor with MS-13's leaders. Within the gang, members were made to understand if they ever failed to abide by the rules of La Mara, if they disobeyed an order from MS-13's top shot callers, the "Big Homies," they were as good as dead.

Several weeks earlier, Diego had failed in an assignment from the Big Homies to smuggle hand grenades into a Honduran prison to use against their 18th Street gang rivals. Suspecting that Diego had stolen the money intended to purchase the explosives, the gang had "green-lighted" him for death. Now, Diego believed, a notorious psychopathic killer and MS-13 assassin named Culiche was hot on his trail. Summoned by the Big Homies to kill Diego, Culiche must be somewhere between Honduras and the United States.[1]

Diego pulled his jacket from the dryer and put it back on, wincing as the hot zipper singed his bare skin. He peeked out the door of the laundry again and was relieved to see the coast was clear. He exited the building onto the sidewalk, making his way around the corner and heading for the nearest underground BART station.

As he rounded the corner, the same SFPD cop was standing on the sidewalk, staring at him with arms crossed over his chest. Diego attempted to walk past.

"Excuse me, sir!" the officer barked.

"Sí, oficial?" Diego responded, after an awkward pause.

"I observed you jaywalking earlier at the intersection of Eddy and Larkin," the cop said. "Can I see some identification, please?"

Diego, looking confused, fumbled through his pockets, groping for his wallet. He knew he was in real trouble now and considered making a run for it, but the officer was young and fit, a US Marine type. In broken English, Diego admitted, "No ID, sir."

He slumped in resignation against a wall of the closest building. The SFPD cop immediately began barraging him with questions, most of which he did not understand. He asked where Diego was from and what he was doing in San Francisco. The officer tried switching to rudimentary Spanish, which didn't improve the level of communication much. He asked about Diego's tattoos, pointing to the obvious "MS" on his left ear and "13" on his right. The officer indicated he had observed Diego through the laundry's windows and seen his arm tattoos. He asked if Diego had any others on his body.

"Sí, officer," the Honduran replied. "Tengo mas."

"Are you a member of a gang?" the cop asked.

"No, not anymore, but in a past life," he answered.

The officer pushed Diego up against the wall and frisked him for weapons, pulling a wallet from his rear pocket. He inspected an immigration card tucked inside, detecting immediately that it was a fake, likely purchased from the Miceros gang in the Mission District, which was widely known as the Bay Area's black market bazaar for forged IDs.

The cop told Diego to relax while he made a series of phone and radio calls. Diego heard him say the one word he prayed he wouldn't: *immigration*. He reconsidered running for it, but was too drained from stress. The officer hung up the phone and the two of them stood together in silence for several minutes, the brisk San Francisco wind blowing a cold chill.

His phone rang back and he answered, "Uh-huh, okay, I'll do that ASAP. Thanks again," and hung up. The officer ordered Diego to turn around, indicating he was under arrest for jaywalking.

Diego quickly found himself in the backseat of the patrol car with his hands secured behind his back, thinking about the deadly greeting he'd receive from his gang upon returning to San Pedro Sula. That's if he made it alive past screening by the Honduran National Police, who were always stationed at the Tegucigalpa airport.

At that moment, there was no way for Diego to realize that his inside knowledge of MS-13 and his ability to survive on the street represented valuable assets for a certain federal agent. His ride in the patrol car was not the first leg of a trip back to Honduras, but merely the beginning of a grueling, four-year odyssey of an investigation, involving one of the biggest takedowns of a criminal street gang in American history.

MS-13 was founded in Los Angeles in the early 1990s by Central Americans fleeing brutal civil wars in their home countries and crossing into the United States illegally. Most of the refugees originally settled in L.A., where the Salvadoran population expanded tenfold during the next twenty years, from thirty thousand to three hundred thousand. Criminologist observers of the gang considered its initial formation as a response by some of the younger male Salvadorans to defend themselves against violent African American and Mexican gangs already established in the city.

Many of the Central Americans were experienced in paramilitary or guerrilla warfare. As the MS-13 founders demonstrated their killing prowess on the streets of L.A., the gang's reputation grew and its membership expanded with various street criminal types from El Salvador, Honduras, and Guatemala.

The name MS-13 stands for Mara Salvatrucha, in which the first word of the moniker, *mara*, refers to a fierce, tenacious species of Central American ant, while *Salva* stands for El Salvador and *trucha* is slang for "reliable and alert." Thirteen is the position of the letter 'M' in the alphabet, a sign of respect among the gang for the Mexican Mafia with whom they allied inside US prisons. MS-13 also cooperated with Mexican gangs south of the border in various smuggling operations and violent crime.

By the turn of the twenty-first century, MS-13 was spreading rapidly across North America through a network of cliques, or *clicas*, comprised mainly of illegal immigrants who traveled back and forth across the southern US border with seeming impunity. According to Immigration and Customs Enforcement (ICE) statistics, of the six thousand six hundred Central American gangsters arrested in the United States between February 2005 and September 2007, at least 75 percent had entered the country by crossing the border illegally.[2]

MS-13 cliques spawned among larger enclaves of Salvadoran transplants across much of the United States, most of whom were illegal immigrants but otherwise honest, hardworking folks. Once established, leaders of the new cliques reported back up their chain of command to the gang's top leaders in El Salvador, known as the Big Homies. Even though many of the senior gang members lived behind bars thousands of miles away, they managed to call shots on the streets of Detroit, Philadelphia, Houston, Chicago, Baltimore, Los Angeles, San Francisco, and dozens of other cities and towns. From the corrupt and dysfunctional prisons in Central America, they used cell phones, the Internet, human couriers, and the US mail to convey their orders across borders and through the gang's rank and file.

By 2004, the FBI estimated MS-13 had 10,000 members in the States, responsible for a growing number of violent crimes and murder. Dead bodies were beginning to show up on the streets of Northern Virginia, where many of the FBI's and DOJ's top leadership lived with their own families. A highly publicized case at the time in the Washington, D.C., area involved a young gang informant named Brenda Paz, viciously murdered in the Shenandoah National Park. Her badly mutilated body, several months pregnant, was discovered in an isolated fishing spot on the park's riverbank.

To the extent MS-13 had a coherent, unifying ideology, it was imbued with an allegiance to *el diablo*, the devil, whom they referred to among themselves as The Beast. Their signature hand salute was the index and pinky fingers extended outward to form *la gara*, or devil horns. Many of the thugs had devil faces or horns tattooed somewhere on their bodies.

When MS-13 members committed some atrocity that shocked moral, law-abiding society, it seemed to be the devil that made them do it. For example, a group of gang members might chop off the limbs and disembowel a victim, or leave a corpse with a couple dozen kitchen knives stuck in it like pins in a voodoo doll. Such acts were performed in ritualistic fashion for the satanic glory of La Mara, as well as to intimidate their adversaries and potential snitches.

The gang members' duty to La Mara was codified in a set of regulations, or *reglos*, which sometimes varied slightly from clique to clique, all demanding a strict commitment to further the gang's interests and keep its secrets. Above all, the rules of MS-13 emphasized that if anyone in the gang violated his oath of secrecy, if he turned rat and cooperated with the cops, he was dead. No matter how fast or far the rat ran, whether to an American city or rural town, or some village in Mexico or Central America, La Mara would hunt him down and exact its vicious revenge.

First Collaboration with SFPD

THE ANGST OVER NATIONAL SECURITY VULNERABILITIES AS A RESULT OF lax immigration policies and enforcement that surrounded the 9/11 terrorist attacks, on top of reported noncooperation and "stovepiping" of intelligence between various agencies in the United States, led to the formation in 2002 of the Department of Homeland Security. The massive new federal conglomerate was patched together with eighty-seven federal agencies, including Customs and Border Protection (CBP), US Coast Guard, Secret Service, FEMA, and the new TSA.

As part of the huge overhaul of federal agencies and resources, the US Customs Service and the Immigration and Naturalization Service (INS) were combined into one agency as Immigration and Customs Enforcement (ICE). Included within ICE were the investigative and intelligence resources of the customs service and the criminal investigation resources of the INS and the US Federal Protective Service. The functions and jurisdictions of several border and revenue enforcement agencies were also consolidated into ICE. With over seventeen thousand employees, ICE became the largest investigative arm of the Department of Homeland Security, and the second largest contributor to the United States' joint terrorism task force, after the FBI.

With the overhaul of his agency, Santini, who had been slogging through the mud in the Border Patrol, pursuing illegal immigrants crossing the southern border, was tapped to serve as a criminal investigator, or special agent, in the San Francisco office of the newly formed ICE Office of Investigations. Under the Homeland Security Act, the new office was empowered with broad legal authority to investigate and combat a range of national security threats—over four hundred federal laws and statutes including those addressing violent gangs, human trafficking, narcotics, weapons, and other types of smuggling, including weapons of mass destruction, as well as financial crimes, terrorism, cybercrimes, and import-export enforcement issues.

The marriage of once separate federal law enforcement agencies, predictably, did not always go smoothly. Interagency rivalries and resentments sometimes bubbled to the surface as agents from INS and the customs service, for example, were forced to work and train side by side following the merger. For decades, these agents had shared interagency rivalries and viewed one another with disdain. After 9/11, literally overnight, longtime veteran customs agents were told to show up for work at INS offices, pointed to an empty desk, and told their new badges would be ready in a few weeks. Indignation and resentment among the ranks was palpable.

And then there was the FBI, which for decades had been the preeminent federal police agency, the subject of innumerable popular movies, books and TV shows. The "G-men" had been the ones with all the juice, seemingly forever, since the early days of J. Edgar Hoover's reign. Now, all of a sudden, there was a new kid on the block, ICE, with new combined powers of investigation and leverage in criminal cases involving citizens as well as anyone in the country who wasn't a citizen. There were more than ten million such people in the United States, counting just those from south of the border, who were in the country without legitimate papers and subject to ICE's "big hammer"—the threat of deportation, with the added authority to hold someone in custody indefinitely for alleged immigration violations. It was a power that even the FBI did not yet possess.

Quietly, without a lot of public awareness of what had happened, a new "super agency," had been created in the form of ICE, along with its Homeland Security Investigations (HSI) branch, Santini's employer. The HSI's new investigative powers weren't even completely understood in house, at first. It would take a real-life case, like the one Santini would pursue against the MS-13 gang in the Mission District—under the supervision of the US Attorney's Office—to realize just how potent these new legal powers could be when put into practice.

Despite Santini's recent takedown of the Miceros' counterfeit ID distribution network in the Mission District, the neighborhood's streets were edgy as ever. Blanketing the sides of buildings and alley walls, amid examples of fine Latino folk murals, crude gang graffiti marked the turf of MS-13's 20th Street clique on one side and their sworn enemies on the other—the Norteños. The two gangs' territories were demarcated by 23rd Street running east and west, and Van Ness Avenue running north and south.

Santini walked west along 19th, then took a right at Linda Street, heading into Mission Playground. Ahead, he spied several 20th Street members, who were posting up at their usual spot. With an approximate head count of one hundred in San Francisco, the street gang was considered by SFPD as among the most dangerous network of criminals in the city, prone to vicious acts of violence, from rape to homicide.

He exited Mission Playground and took a left on 20th Street. A block ahead, loitering outside the Ritmo Latino record store, three more MS-13 gang homies stood scrutinizing the sidewalk traffic passing by. The agent was sure he had seen at least one of them recently, a beefy, shaved-headed *payaso* with plenty of arm and neck tattoos. He wore an oversized pair of Dickie's work pants, partly hanging down his butt. The MS-13 thug was smiling at something one of his gang "homies" just told him and watching the backside of a sweet young *chica caliente* as she strolled past, pushing a baby stroller.

Santini wondered where he had seen the gangbanger before—and his brain made the connection. It was in the Skylark, a neighborhood bar just a few blocks away where Santini sometimes drank on weekend nights. Just as the thug's focus was wandering from the young woman's ass and turning toward Santini, the agent averted his face, pretending to look at something across the street. He kept his back to the MS-13 homies and walked away down Mission Street.

Living in the same neighborhood where he was beginning to target the gang was getting too dicey. He needed to find a new pad, in a different section of the Bay Area. Beyond that, he was going to need help getting his investigation off the ground, and it needed to come from the local cops. They were the ones who encountered the gang members on a regular basis, knew their faces and street names, and had access to their criminal records.

Despite the local politics, Santini was determined to enlist the cooperation of at least a couple SFPD officers. As with the recent Card Shark investigation of the Miceros, he understood that the eyes and ears of cops who spent the majority of their workday on the streets making contact with thugs was a critical component to a successful federal investigation. Santini could roam around the Mission everyday watching MS-13, but he needed gang cops to make real progress.

One local gang cop whom Santini had already encountered during the Miceros investigation, Ricardo Cabrera, was the perfect candidate to recruit for his new project, he thought. Cabrera, originally from El Salvador, was probably the most knowledgeable police officer about MS-13 in San Francisco.

During his operation to bust the Miceros, Santini discovered that Cabrera, in an undercover capacity, was renting a fleabag hotel room with a view of Mission Street for conducting surveillance. It was an effective way to get photo and video surveillance of gang activity on the streets, and in a comfortable setting to boot. Santini badgered Cabrera relentlessly to gain access to the room for his own investigation, because it offered a perfect view of the Miceros selling IDs to patrons walking the street. Santini wanted to observe them from the hidden vantage to analyze the tricks they used to avoid police patrols, as well as gather video evidence of hand-to-hand dealing of counterfeit IDs to buyers.

Time and again, Cabrera refused to share access to the hotel room without providing a precise explanation why. Santini pressed and pressed and finally, exasperated, Cabrera just gave him the hotel key, but completely stopped using the room himself. Without saying it outright, Cabrera made it clear he did not want to be perceived within SFPD as cooperating even in the slightest with an HSI agent in violation of the city's sanctuary policy.

———

It was six p.m. now, and all around the Mission, residents were straggling back home from work. Behind the wheel of an unmarked gray Chrysler parked at a curb, Cabrera sat watching and waiting.

A husky man with a large head, flat nose, dark eyes, and light brown complexion, Cabrera was staking out the residence of a known Norteño gang member. The thug was wanted for recently kidnapping and raping his ex-girlfriend, who was also the mother of his child. The suspect was living with a new girlfriend and her mother in the home Cabrera was staking out, anticipating the gangbanger could show up any minute from his day job as a construction laborer.

The 20th Street homies considered Cabrera a traitor. They hated him for being a gang cop, originally born and raised in El Salvador, as they were. He knew all about their culture, what it was like to arrive in the United States as a Central American transplant who didn't speak the local tongue or fully understand American customs. He had been making life in the Mission more difficult for the 20th Street thugs for years, always nosing around the parks and alleyways, hassling them. Every time they turned around, there was Cabrera, scolding them about how they were messing up their lives and disgracing their families and native country. To the gangsters, Cabrera did not seem to know to leave the homies well enough alone to take care of their illicit business on the streets.

Which is why they wanted him dead.

Through the car's windshield, Cabrera spotted Santini approaching on foot. The SFPD cop was expecting him. After weeks of Santini's persistent requests for a meet-up to discuss the current situation with MS-13 in the Mission, Cabrera had finally agreed—but only after Santini contacted his lieutenant, who in turn gave Cabrera the okay for the meeting. The HSI agent simply refused to go away.

The two men nodded to each other through the windshield and Cabrera flipped the car's automatic door lock open. Santini slid into the backseat and immediately began to pump Cabrera with questions about the 20th Street clique.

"Almost every day the crew is stabbing or shooting or robbing somebody," Cabrera said. He described how living conditions for Mission District residents were destabilized by 20th Street, who Cabrera said were at least as violent as the most ruthless African American gangs based in the city's Hunters Point neighborhood. "I know of a dozen or more recent cases of serious violence in the Mission alone—many homicides—that 20th Street was probably behind," he said.

From memory, he rattled off an impressively long litany of details about recent stabbings, clubbings, and shootings in the Mission that he suspected 20th Street had committed. Cabrera indicated the gang was well established, with over ten years of presence on the streets.

"Man, that's a hell of a lot of dirt to keep track of," Santini said, trying to scratch notes on a small pad. "How do you remember all that?"

Cabrera shrugged.

He reached for a small piece of paper tucked into a dashboard slot and handed it back to Santini. It was a funeral card with a photo of the deceased—a thirteen-year-old boy named Brian Martinez. At the bottom was a plea for information about who had committed the murder.

"His father is posting these all over the neighborhood," Cabrera said. "The kid was just walking down the sidewalk and somebody drove by and put a bullet in him. He wasn't even involved with a gang."

The photo showed a smiling, sweet-faced kid, still full of boyish optimism. Snuffed out forever now by a senseless, random murder. Cabrera explained that he had interviewed the family after the murder and was hard-pressed to obtain information about the perpetrators. Likely another murder orchestrated by MS-13.

"You know the FBI is already targeting these guys, right?" Cabrera said, as Santini got ready to hop out of the car and leave him to continue the solitary stakeout. "They've already got a task force assigned to MS-13 in the city."

Cabrera could tell from Santini's obvious double-take that the FBI's investigation was news to him. "No," he said. "I didn't know about the Bureau."

What Santini did know was that the FBI and US Attorney's Office in San Francisco had recently burned through an estimated $60 million on a RICO case targeting two African American gangs in the city, including the Big Block crew.

Working in conjunction with the Bureau of Alcohol, Tobacco, Firearms and Explosives, along with SFPD, the FBI had publicly trumpeted the investigation as a major victory for law enforcement. The reality was the case fizzled badly when it went to trial. Only a couple individuals received minimal jail time, while some extremely violent gang members who cooperated with the investigation as informants were already back on the streets, free and clear, thanks to their generous plea bargains.

"Well, Ricardo," Santini said, "I really appreciate the meet and I hope you and I and the GTF [Gang Task Force] can work together to tackle this MS-13 plague. If you can stop hiding from me, that is!" Santini laughed.

"Seriously," he added, "I know about your restrictions with policy, but I can assure you that this is going to be strictly a federal criminal investigation, not an immigration caper."

Cabrera smiled. "With the lieutenant's blessing, the GTF will be full speed ahead with you," he said.

"Absolutely," Santini said over his shoulder, as he climbed out of the unmarked car. "Thanks again for all the 411."

In his rear-view mirror, Cabrera watched Santini walk away. There goes another federal crusader, he thought. These guys come and go, always looking to make a big name for themselves, move up the chain, and on to their next big post somewhere else in the country. Meanwhile, SFPD answered the 911 calls, interviewed the victims' families, watched the next crop of neighborhood kids recruited into gang life, ruined.

Nothing ever seemed to change. But Cabrera sensed Santini might be different.

In an SFPD conference room full of city, state, and federal police officers, Santini tried his best to conceal his impatience as the Mission Station captain stood in front, reciting San Francisco's City of Refuge ordinance word for word, straight off the page: "Executive directive zero-seven-dash-one states that no department, agency, commission, officer or employee of the City and County of San Francisco shall use any city funds or resources to assist in the enforcement of federal immigration law or to gather or disseminate information regarding the immigration status of individuals in the City and County of San Francisco. . . ."

Because of his successful takedown of the Miceros, Santini had already made a splash as an investigator in the city. Most of the San Francisco gang cops knew who he was, although a few of them didn't appreciate his aggressive approach. A few others applauded his success. SFPD had been grappling with problems associated with the Miceros crew for years and Santini had rolled in and dismantled the entire organization in slightly over a year, utilizing a unique mix of federal authorities, including immigration enforcement. Street cops working the Mission appreciated the results, but anything beyond expressing basic professional courtesy for an HSI special agent risked career-crushing retribution from the city's highly politicized bureaucracy, which enforced the sanctuary policy with a vengeance. HSI was part of ICE, which represented a big problem for the local police.

This was San Francisco, world-renowned Mecca for aging hippies, activist gays, and assorted die-hard lefties, who were instinctively inclined to side with the dispossessed and downtrodden of society. Enforcing bedrock principles of social justice, as they defined them, trumped any effort to target a distinctly ethnic criminal gang from south of the border.

Santini thought the local cops in the pre-op briefing mostly looked nervous about rubbing up against the sanctuary policy, but they also seemed eager and willing at the same time. They knew firsthand the kind of serious threat to public safety that the 20th Street gang posed.

He glanced across the briefing room at Cabrera and his partner Sean Gibson, a tall redhead who had grown up in working-class San Francisco, with the big shoulders and slight paunch of a former football player sliding gently into middle age. For years, Cabrera and Gibson were warned to steer clear of federal immigration law enforcement. Now, they were receiving a slightly modulated message. There appeared to be some official wiggle room that might allow them to swing a bigger club in their fight against MS-13 through an alliance (although limited) with the feds from Homeland Security.

For Santini and his HSI colleagues, this interagency political education session was an exercise that had to be endured for the sake of Operation Mission Possible, Santini's plan to flood the Mission District's streets with an overwhelming number of local cops, state troopers, and federal agents all at once. They planned to cut off all escape routes and round up gang members to gather intelligence and bust them on whatever they could—everything except immigration violations, as far as SFPD's official cooperation was concerned.

Adopted in 1989, San Francisco's "City of Refuge" ordinance was intended to protect refugees of vicious civil wars in Central America from deportation. The idea was simple: Leave the poor folks alone, let them build new lives for themselves, free from police harassment and the threat of being sent back to the violent hellholes their home countries had become. According to proponents of sanctuary policy, if local police cooperated with federal immigration law enforcement it would result in a "chilling effect" on crime victims or witnesses in the city who were illegal immigrants. Such individuals would be hesitant to report crimes or provide testimony to the cops for fear of being arrested and deported, creating an environment in which crime could flourish due to lack of trust between the community and police. Or so the argument went.

Opponents of sanctuary city policies claimed there was no evidence to support the claim it led to less cooperation with police. On the contrary, they argued, the policy merely left huge loopholes in the legal system for repeat serious offenders to game the system and remain on American city streets.

In a previous series of meetings with Jim Sawyer, head of SFPD's Gang Task Force, Santini persuaded him to obtain approval for the operation from higher-ups in the local police department. Sawyer was in good standing with his department and had earned some collateral credit for the recent disruption of the Miceros. Sawyer's superiors in SFPD granted their okay for Operation Mission Possible, with the strict caveat there would be absolutely no immigration enforcement involved.

CHAPTER 3

Despite SFPD's official policy, while Santini kept quiet about it during the pre-op briefing, he was holding the immigration enforcement option in his back pocket. He had a bigger plan than just Mission Possible brewing in his mind. If hooking and booking the MS-13 crew on immigration charges could somehow further a potentially larger criminal case against them, he was determined to use HSI's enforcement authority.

Recently, he had run across an article published in the FBI *Law Enforcement Bulletin* titled "Enterprise Theory of Investigation," which succinctly laid out how to apply the federal (RICO) statute, designed to systematically dismantle a criminal network. The RICO approach had been used effectively by the FBI against the Gambino crime family, by the DEA against the Colombian Cali Cartel, and by the ATF against the Hells Angels outlaw motorcycle gang.

A successful RICO case usually entailed close cooperation between federal and state or local law enforcement, attacking a criminal organization at every possible level of its structure, with the goal of taking down its leaders. Instead of treating criminal acts as isolated crimes, the enterprise theory of investigation attempted to demonstrate that the targeted individuals committed crimes "in furtherance of the criminal enterprise itself."

Implementing the investigative attack plan for a RICO case often took a relatively long time—a luxury that local police, who were constantly reacting to 911 calls, didn't have. But Santini did. He knew MS-13 was proving difficult for the local cops to combat, largely due to the gang's insularity as a Spanish-speaking criminal subculture. SFPD cops, constrained by the city's sanctuary city policy, were practically fighting the gang with both hands tied behind their backs.

The most common strategy for criminal investigators to take down a gang entailed flipping inside informants in exchange for money or lessened sentences. SFPD's Gang Task Force had succeeded in arm-twisting small bits of intelligence from a few desperate 20th Street members here and there over the years, but the local cops were clearly losing the war. To defeat the gang in San Francisco, it would take a much more prolonged and better resourced attack, which was precisely what Santini intended to do—with whatever help he could muster from SFPD.

In developing the plan for Mission Possible, Cabrera and Gibson had provided Santini with a target list of a couple dozen known 20th Street members, as well as several locations where gang members were known to loiter or "post up" to control turf, including Mission Dolores and Alioto Parks. Several of the clique members were also known to troll popular tourist areas such as Golden Gate Park and Fisherman's Wharf, picking wallets from the pockets of distracted out-of-towners, or snatching valuables such as cameras, sunglasses, and laptops from unattended cars. All the locations were included in the plan to "drain the swamp" in and around the Mission.

In general, 20th Street members controlled their turf in Mission Playground by posting up a constant presence at the park. But if they wanted a quick hiatus, they would sometimes take a walk along Mission Street, or smoke some weed in one of the other nearby parks, loitering among the docile citizens enjoying the bay breezes or walking their dogs. This tendency of the clique to roam every which way through the neighborhood naturally complicated the job of netting them all in one swoop.

～

The operation commenced with a swarm of almost sixty SFPD cops, CA DOJ agents, and HSI special agents split into small teams and simultaneously hitting the streets, alleys, and parks of the Mission, scouting for 20th Street members. Dressed in jeans, sneakers, and a T-shirt, Santini joined another HSI agent, along with Cabrera, Gibson, and two plainclothes state cops, forming one of several cross-agency units participating in the sweep.

It wasn't long before Santini's squad made their first contact with a group of gangbangers sporting their trademark Sureño blue clothing accessories, loitering in front of Jocelyn's El Salvadoran Bakery at Lexington and 20th Streets. Jocelyn's catered to Central Americans in the neighborhood with the foods they liked, prepared the way it was done back home.

Owned and operated by a Salvadoran family, the bakery was a favorite hangout for the 20th Street crew. The local cops knew the gang lingered here regularly while a group of crooks often fenced stolen goods such as car stereos, ridiculously expensive, decorative wheel rims and spinners, and other accoutrements of the well-equipped homie's gangsta ride. In addition to grabbing a bite at Jocelyn's, the 20th Street clique— some of whom specialized in car theft—could turn a fast buck selling their spoils from their thefts and burglaries.

Approaching the crew from 20th Street, Santini thought they looked shifty and dangerous. None of them seemed particularly concerned about the group of cops who were heading straight their way. The mostly young homies seemed slightly amused, making wise cracks to one another in Spanish, laughing, and smiling cockily. They all sported gang colors with sports jerseys with the number 20 or 13 and blue belts, belt buckles molded in the number 20 and blue accents on everything. They even had MS-13 jewelry, such as earrings that included blue MS letters.

The elder of the group, Blackie, was a Salvadoran with a shaved head decked out in all blue, including blue laces in his Nike Air Jordans. He had a patch over his left eye, which he lost a few years ago in a knife fight, making him look like a seasoned gangster pirate. Blackie attempted to slide away inconspicuously down the street, while the others put on an ostentatious show of fearlessness, standing their ground in the face of the police heat bearing down.

"Hey!" Gibson called to Blackie, "C'mere a minute." The homie stopped and turned, disgust crossing his face. He blew out a hiss of frustration and walked back toward the front of the bakery. The rest of the gang maintained their poses of contempt for the cops, meeting their gazes and glaring back with open scorn. Santini was struck by how thuggish they were. He had encountered plenty of mean hombres during his time with the border patrol and to him these guys were obviously hardcore street criminals, especially Blackie.

"Let me see some ID," Gibson told Blackie, while keeping an eye on the others, who were boxed in by two SFPD officers as well as Santini and his HSI partner. Blackie reached into his jacket pocket and extracted a driver's license. He handed it to Gibson, who scanned it briefly and passed it over to Santini, who in turn gave the ID to his partner to run a check.

"Hold tight right there," Gibson told Blackie, as he moved down the line to the next homie.

"ID?" Gibson said.

Spanky, a portly thug with a "2" tattooed on one forearm and a "0" on the other, pulled out his wallet and removed a driver's license for Gibson, who eyeballed it closely. Something about it didn't look right. He handed it to a plainclothes California DOJ agent who was providing backup.

The homies' confidence seemed to be fading under this unfamiliar protocol. They had been shaken down by SFPD cops too many times to remember, but this was different. There were several cops they didn't recognize, and they were paying extra close attention to their IDs. "He's got a prior deport," Santini's partner told him after the check was done on Blackie's driver license. "His immigration status is illegal."

At the mention of immigration, spoken loud enough for the homies to hear, Santini watched the gangbangers' faces drop. In an instant, they went from mildly impatient and contemptuous, to clearly worried. All the homies had jobs or girlfriends or children in the States, and the possibility of being deported would seriously screw up their lives. The cops in Honduras or El Salvador might want them for felonies in their home countries. Even if they weren't arrested upon arrival and locked up for something, returning to the States to resume their lives in San Francisco could easily take several weeks but more likely months, probably meaning they'd lose their jobs. A night in the San Francisco County Jail was no problem, but a ticket home was a serious detriment.

The original intent of Mission Possible—the way it was sold by Santini to the SFPD chain of command—was an intelligence-gathering operation only. There was to be no enforcement of immigration laws. But busting these thugs was too tempting. Santini wanted them off the street, immediately.

"What do you think?" he said to Gibson. "Should I go ahead and lock them up? Their asses will be deported for sure. I promise to ask the US Attorney's Office if they would consider a reentry prosecution too, but at the minimum, they will be shipped."

Gibson exchanged looks with Cabrera. Both knew it could cause some serious problems for them if word got out that SFPD was helping ICE to round up, detain, and deport illegals. Still, the Gang Task Force officers were sick of the thugs running roughshod in the neighborhood. If HSI had a tool in their arsenal that could remove these menacing thugs from the neighborhood, both the citizens of the city and the police would benefit.

Santini suggested that Cabrera and Gibson leave the gangsters with him and his HSI partners, while the local cops continued patrolling the neighborhood. Cabrera and Gibson nodded in ascent and headed toward their patrol car. After they pulled away, it was Santini's show.

"Let's haul them in," he told his partner.

They ran immigration checks on the rest of the homies outside Jocelyn's. One turned out to be in possession of a fake green card, which was a deportable offense. Another admitted to being in the country illegally. In total, five of them were busted on illegal immigration charges and taken into custody by ICE.

After shaking down the gang at the bakery and loading the five thugs into an ICE van, Santini reconnected with Gibson and Cabrera. They proceeded to execute a probation search at the residence of another 20th Street member named Maurice Montega, aka Colmillo, Spanish for "Fang."

Colmillo was on probation for an assault charge stemming from an altercation with a rival gangster a year prior. He lived with his mother and some other family members in a two-bedroom apartment a few blocks from Mission Playground. As the task force approached the apartment building, they spotted MS-13 graffiti painted all over the sidewalk out front, on the mailboxes inside the entrance, and in the elevator on the way up to the fourth floor. Nobody answered the knock at Colmillo's apartment door, so the SFPD team contacted a building manager who arrived shortly with a master key.

Inside, the residence was clean and well kept. Everywhere were testaments to Colmillo's mother's Christian devotion, with numerous sacred icons and pictures of crucifixes. Multiple Virgin Marys decorated the living room walls and shelves.

The search team went straight to Colmillo's bedroom, which Gibson was familiar with from previous visits to the home. It was obvious as soon as they entered that "Fang" was hardcore MS-13. Gang paraphernalia was everywhere. There was a collection of blue bandannas, ball caps, belts, and sneakers, as well as letters to Colmillo from various gang members in prison. There was also an aluminum baseball bat with gang symbols scribbled in magic marker. A framed photo on the wall showed a couple dozen 20th Street members assembled in Mission Playground immediately after a murdered homie's funeral, all of them wearing gang blues. They were lined up in three rows as if in a soccer team photo, smiling and throwing devil-horn hand signs for the camera.

Santini thought: *These guys obviously feel like they own the neighborhood!*

On the nightstand was a photo of Colmillo inside a cheap frame bordered with crayon stick figures and smiley faces and an inscription that read, "Me and My Daddy." Colmillo was holding his young son, flashing a proud smile and donned in his best MS-13 ceremonial blues. He held the boy in one arm, while flashing the devil-horns salute with the other. The baby was dressed in a Sureño blue onesie. Observing the father-and-son photo, Santini was struck by how it so clearly illustrated the tragedy of generational allegiance within the gang. Little boys grew up watching their fathers, uncles, cousins, and older siblings as role models living the life of a marero. Influenced so heavily from an early age, the odds were stacked high against the boys breaking the cycle of criminality. The kids were practically set up for failure.

An SFPD cop gathered up Colmillo's gang swag and spread it out on the bed to take photos as evidence of his parole violations. Meanwhile, Gibson rummaged through the furniture . . . and bingo! In the center drawer of a battered, wooden dresser, tucked under a pile of mismatched socks, he found a loaded black, .45 caliber handgun and two boxes of ammunition.

"I'm sure this hasn't been used in any crimes," Gibson cracked, wearing surgical gloves and holding the gun up for the others to see.

They bagged and tagged the gun and gang paraphernalia, while Gibson called Colmillo's mom to ask where her son was. She indicated he was working at a construction site in Daly City and would be home by five o'clock that afternoon. Gibson asked her to have Colmillo give him a call, and told her it was likely her son would be spending the night in county jail for violating the terms of his parole.

"He'll probably be out in a day or two," Gibson told Santini, after hanging up with Colmillo's mother.

Gibson knew from years of frustrating experience with San Francisco's justice system Colmillo would be assigned a public defender and plead not guilty, claiming ignorance about the gun in his dresser drawer. Chances were high he would be granted bail and the DA would eventually drop the charges.

For Santini and his HSI partners, observing the gang's criminal culture up close and personal during the Mission Possible operation provided a unique glimpse of San Francisco's underworld. It also served to focus their list of 20th Street members to target. But the only way to truly take apart the gang was from inside the ranks, Santini knew. And for that he would need a reliable informant, a trusted marero with access to 20th Street's network of thugs.

CHAPTER 4

Turning an Informant

ICE Immigration holding facility, San Francisco

Santini looked through the two-way mirror at the Honduran whom the ICE detention officers brought in for interrogation. Diego was picked up a few days earlier by SFPD and interviewed by an ICE special agent, who determined he was in the country illegally. He admitted to being a gang member, so the SFPD dropped the bogus jaywalking charge and one count of presenting a fake ID and turned him over to the feds.

Wearing an orange jumpsuit, Diego had a cagey air about him, an alert energy. His brown eyes followed Santini into the room as he sat down across the interview table from him. Santini identified himself as a federal special agent and immediately got down to business.

"So, what do those mean?" he said, pointing at three dots tattooed in a triangle pattern on the back of Diego's left hand. Diego held up his arm so Santini could see the design closer.

"They are the three possible destinations in life for a marero," Diego said. "Jail, the hospital, or the cemetery."

Going over Diego's complex mash-up of tattoos, Santini pressed him to explain what each one signified. The Ace card on his left bicep stood for the daily gamble of a gangster's life, he said. There were two large "MS" monograms initialed on his chest, one in block font and one in gothic, as well as "Salvatrucha" written on his back. He had an *M* and an *S* on his left and right ears, respectively, and there were two pictures on his arms that depicted himself, the gangbanger known in San Pedro Sula as "Tromposo."

At Santini's request, Diego stood up and unzipped his jumpsuit, revealing more skin ink. The name of his hometown clique, "Los Limenos Locos," was permanently blazoned on the center of his chest, and "West Side" was tattooed on his lower stomach, in honor of the section of Los Angeles where MS-13 originated. Two hands clasped in prayer and grasping a rosary on his left forearm represented the pardon he sought from his mother, for making her suffer and worry about his life of crime.

Diego told Santini the face of another woman on his arm was a portrait of his sister, Lizette, who had been murdered by MS-13 gang members seeking revenge for Diego's failure to execute the prison grenade-smuggling scheme. Lizette's name was also tattooed at numerous other places on his body, in one spot with a tombstone inscribed "R.I.P."

Santini could tell with near certainty that Diego had the markings of a seasoned marero soldier, hardened in the depths of Central America's gang-infested subculture. He knew that in Diego's world you couldn't display such a body of tattoos without spending plenty of time locked up.

Here was a genuine, hardcore MS-13 marero who was subject to immediate deportation. He would obviously possess significant inside knowledge about the gang that could be useful to Santini's new investigation to take down the 20th Street clique. The question was what and whom did Diego know, exactly? And how could Santini persuade him to cooperate? The agent began interrogating Diego about his upbringing and how he became involved with MS-13.

Diego was born in 1981, he said, in San Pedro Sula. It was the same year Honduras formally ended its eleven-year conflict with El Salvador known as the Soccer War, which was named after a huge riot in 1970 that erupted during a qualifying round for the World Cup. San Pedro Sula was a large city on the north coast of the country, with a population of roughly four hundred thousand.

Diego's father was never regularly employed, but made money as a thief and burglar. When Diego was nine years old, his family—father, mother, brother, and sister—all moved from their small house built of plywood to the nearby town of La Lima. Three years later, at the age of twelve, he dropped out of school and began working as a salesman at a store that specialized in refurbished home appliances. In 1996, with the country's economic conditions looking bleak for a fifteen-year-old with limited education, Diego made his first attempt to join the wave of Hondurans sneaking into the United States in search of better lives.

When he first set out from La Lima, if Diego thought his traveling companion, his father's friend named Santo Quintana, would see him safely into America, it was a reasonable assumption. Santo had made the round trip twice before, successfully eluding border patrols both times. The typical passage for a Central American migrant to the United States entailed slipping through the Petén Jungle in northern Guatemala, which covers five million acres and is designated a national forest. The terrain offers thick cover for drug and human traffickers who trudge on foot through the dense forest and swamps under the shadow of ancient Mayan ruins. Thick stands of old-growth mahogany and tropical cedars provide habitat to jaguars and rainbow-colored scarlet macaw.

Diego told Santini that in his first attempt sneaking into the United States he was one of a small percentage of Central American migrants snagged by police during the initial jungle-crossing leg of the journey through Guatemala. He and Santo never made it across the Usumacinta River. They were picked up by Guatemalan immigration officers and with no money to bribe the cops, were locked up in jail. Released three months later, the discouraged pair headed back south, home to Honduras.

"What did you do when you got back home?" Santini asked. "How did you get mixed up with MS-13?"

"I could not get my job back at the appliance store," he said. "I began to hang out on the streets more, and I met some mareros from San Manuel Cortez."

These older males, numbering around eighty and covered in gang tattoos, were recently deported from the United States in an anti-gang operation in Los Angeles. They were well-seasoned, hardcore MS-13 members.

In La Parque Central de La Lima, a rundown, open-air public space located in the town's commercial center, in view of a cluster of small houses and a strip of ramshackle commercial buildings, Diego felt his first cruel embrace from MS-13. There on the packed dirt, beneath the gently waving fronds of palm trees, he was surrounded by a small group of mareros who punched and kicked him brutally for the prescribed thirteen seconds. Meanwhile, a gang member shouted out, slowly counting up to thirteen, starting with, "Uno!" then slowly, "Dos! . . . Tres! . . . Cuatro! . . ."

Diego grimaced in pain as the barrage of kicks and punches knocked the wind from his lungs and badly bruised his head and torso, until the countdown finally finished.

"Trece!" the clique leader shouted. "Bienvenidos a La Mara!"

Diego was accepted as a member of MS-13 and baptized with the street name Tromposo. By the summer of 1996, he told Santini, the local MS clique he belonged to had grown to around three hundred members. Their main rival, the 18th Street gang, also was enjoying a rapid surge in recruitment. Claiming the La Planeta district of San Pedro Sula as their territory, the 18th Street gang was named after the section in Los Angeles where it originated.

For a gang member like Diego, the daily threats to life and limb in San Pedro Sula were constant. If a rival gang didn't get hold of him, then the police might. Any day, his corpse might turn up in a ditch, its hands bound behind the back and a bullet in the back of the head. Then again, if a group of rival gang members or the police didn't get him, pissed-off citizen vigilantes might snuff him out "extra judicially," using the same MO as the police. A secret civilian paramilitary group of Hondurans, calling themselves Sombra Negra, or "Black Shadow," committed itself to regularly targeting and killing obvious gang members. Basically, Santini realized, Diego had been living for years with a target on his back.

When Diego was sixteen years old, a group of several rival gang members caught him alone on the street, he told Santini. They beat him almost to death, badly cutting him several times with machetes. If not for a Good Samaritan citizen wielding a shotgun who chased off his attackers, Diego's life almost certainly would have ended there in a pool of blood on the street. As it happened, he recovered from his wounds during a month-long stay at the Mario Catarino Riva Hospital.

"What did you do when you got out of the hospital?" Santini said. "Did you go right back with the gang?"

"Yes," he said. "There was nothing else to do. I had no choice. You cannot escape *La Mara*."

Released from the hospital with some serious scars from the attack to back up his credentials as a street soldier, Diego dove deeper into the life of an MS-13 thug. Armed with crude homemade guns called *chimbas*—single-shot guns with a steel pipe and makeshift firing pin, and stuffed with a slug and gunpowder—he and his MS-13 partners in crime robbed businesses and residents of San Pedro Sula. An older man whom Diego attempted to rob in the street turned out to have his own chimba, which he drew in defense. After a momentary standoff, it was Diego who fired first, shooting the man in his shoulder.

"Did you kill him?" Santini said.

"No," Diego insisted. "He did not die."

A year later, Diego rose to become the leader of Los Limenos Locos, an MS-13 clique in San Pedro Sula. The gang was engaged in a bloody street war with 18th Street, primarily turf battles entailing sporadic skirmishes that lasted for days at a time. Diego told Santini he often fired weapons at rival gang members during hasty drive-by shootings or sneak attacks, but admitted to killing no one.

He was caught by Honduran police carrying a chimba and sent to prison for a couple months, without ever appearing in court. The next year, he was arrested again for kidnapping and attempted murder, after he and a group of his homies captured and assaulted an enemy gang member. He was arrested again while riding in a carload of MS-13 members carrying guns.

"What did you do next, after you got out of prison?" Santini said.

"I tried to come to the US," he said. "I wanted to get away from all the craziness."

This indication of a previous desire by Diego to escape the insanity and brutality of gang life in his home country caused the agent to speculate a hope for redemption might still flicker within. Santini contemplated Diego's tattoo of two hands praying—an homage to his devoted mother and a symbol of regret for his criminal ways.

"And?" Santini said. "What happened when you tried to cross the border?"

"I almost made it," Diego said, "but not all the way north."

This time he made it all the way to the Rio Grande, crossing over to Laredo, Texas, where he took sanctuary in a Catholic church. Attempting to travel further north from the Rio Grande, he was nabbed by the US Border Patrol and deported back to San Pedro Sula.

Only two months passed for Diego back out on the streets of San Pedro Sula before he was picked up again by the police and charged with robbing a liquor store—a crime that Diego told Santini he did not commit. Without a trial, he was sent to a prison called La Granja or "the farm," outside the city of La Ceiba. There he spent the next three years locked up before ever appearing in front of a judge. While incarcerated in La Granja, Diego obtained many of his tattoos.

Upon his release from prison, he told Santini, he met the woman who would become his wife, Ana. They had a baby and Diego moved in with Ana's family to put distance between himself and MS-13. Gang members began threatening Diego's parents and siblings to find out where he was lying low. They confronted his father on the street and demanded he tell them where Diego was. When the old thief refused to divulge his son's whereabouts, they shot him dead with a shotgun blast to the chest. Diego moved back in with his mother to protect the family home from a gang onslaught.

One night shortly thereafter, a group of heavily armed MS-13 members disguised as police showed up. The thugs banged on the door and demanded Diego come outside. His brother opened the front door and they opened fire, killing him. A gunman stepped over the body and saw Diego's sister inside. He shot and killed her, too. The assassins quickly made their escape, leaving Diego, Ana, the baby, and Diego's mother unharmed.

As Diego and Ana were preparing for a hasty getaway from Honduras to run for their lives, Santo arranged for a smuggler to get them across the Mexico-Texas border. Santo coordinated the deal with a coyote through an MS-13 gang member named Mocho, a former soldier from the Los Limenos Locos clique who had been living in Houston ever since he left Honduras in 1996.

As arranged, after another long journey north, Mocho picked up Diego and Ana in Laredo, Texas, and transported them to Houston, where they stayed for about a month in a two-story apartment complex. It was located on a tree-lined street at the intersection of Bellfort Avenue and Bob White Drive. Diego told Santini he worked for a company installing siding on houses in Houston to earn money during their stay.

Over the next several days, Santini continued interrogating Diego about his past and his knowledge of MS-13's history and lore, which was encyclopedic. He described precise details of the gang's origins, leadership, current structure, and international criminal activities. The agent grew increasingly hopeful he had a valuable asset on his hands to deploy against the 20th Street clique.

Knowing what he had already learned, though, the agent wondered if Diego was even capable of living a "normal" life, anymore. Youths recruited by MS-13 were drilled over and over with the hard rule that a commitment to the gang was all the way to the morgue. One of the gang's mottos was, *Vivo por mi madre, muero por mi barrio!* or, "I live for my mother, I die for my barrio!" The image of a spiderweb, which many mareros had tattooed somewhere on their bodies, symbolized the unrelenting hold of MS on its members. Diego also had a spiderweb tattoo.

Santini was tactical and determined in his interviews with Diego. To keep him talking and feel out what leverage he had on him, Santini floated a suggestion that the US government might provide protection for him, as well as his wife and baby, if he cooperated fully as an informant.

"You could start a new life, with a clean slate," Santini told him. "Think about it—a good job with nobody hassling you, no concerns for another deportation, a nice car, a good future for your wife and child, free of MS-13."

The prospect of remaining in the United States legally seemed to have an almost hypnotic effect on Diego, as he daydreamed about living a new life in the States. As a legal resident, he wouldn't have to worry about the second glance of a police officer or the threat of deportation. He could have all things that most Americans took for granted, Santini told him. After so many years of the stress and brutality of gang life in Honduras, it seemed almost too much for Diego to even consider escaping.

But his options were limited. He was running for his life. The gang had already murdered his father, sister, and brother for his failures in the eyes of MS leaders. Either he took his chances with the US government and became an informant, or he was very likely dead on arrival if he was deported back home.

"Sí," Diego finally told Santini, after several days of prodding. "I will cooperate."

With a master's degree in criminal justice earned at John Jay College in New York, one of the country's premier law enforcement academies, Santini dove into the existing criminal literature about MS-13. He discovered a complicated, murky world involving international networks, prison systems, and cultish allegiance. What quickly became apparent was that inserting Diego as an undercover informant with the 20th Street clique would require overcoming a difficult set of hurdles.

Typically, police informants were groomed because they already had access to the targeted individuals or had specific knowledge of their criminal activity—or both. The challenge for Santini in this case was that, even though Diego was obviously a hardened MS-13 marero, he had no direct connection with the 20th Street clique. If he made unsolicited contact with them, the gang members were likely to be extremely wary. In the world of MS-13 it was highly unusual for an unknown marero to just show up on the street without a local sponsor. The cliques didn't take in strangers.

A call from an MS-13 sponsor in Central America usually provided notice to a clique about a member headed their way in the States. Without a sponsor, or even with one, it was normal for the gang to mandate a background investigation. The local clique where the visiting marero presented himself often initiated a check on his bona fides. This could consist of a series of phone calls to the new arrival's original MS-13 clique back home, family, and friends—or even the dispatch of gang members to investigate and conduct interviews in person. One 20th Street thug who followed up on a suspicious hunch about Diego could easily spell his speedy death.

Further complicating Santini's mission, some MS-13 cliques forced new recruits to prove themselves by committing acts of serious violence on rival gang members as a pass-or-fail test, to ensure they were committed and tough enough to hang with the homies. Underlying this test was an understanding that a rat working for the cops would be reluctant to perform a hit job. Somehow, Santini needed to safely orchestrate Diego's acceptance by the 20th Street clique without allowing him to commit any violence to prove himself worthy to the gang.

Sitting at his desk on a Friday afternoon, Santini stared at the funeral card Cabrera had given him with a portrait of the boy Brian Martinez, shot and killed as he walked down a Mission sidewalk. A completely senseless murder. Something about the child's face troubled him. It was the sheer optimism, his expression of pure wonder, eyes shining wide and bright into the camera. Santini imagined the exact moment the boy's life was taken, when a car drove past and gunshots erupted and echoed down the street. He saw the youth drop to the pavement, fatally wounded and bleeding, struggling in his last moment to grasp the evil befallen him, wishing his mother or father were there to save him . . .

On the agent's desktop, an entire series of crime scene photos was spread out. The boy's crumpled body and his spilled blood taken from every angle. Santini gathered the pictures in a stack and placed them in a case folder, along with the funeral card.

It was five o'clock on Friday, quitting time.

The crowd at Blondie's bar in the Mission would soon be packed tight. The place served massively oversized martinis of every flavor known to man, served in big mason jars. Good musicians entertained the room from a stage situated smack dab in the middle, directly across from the bar stools. Usually, the women there were exceptionally attractive and frequently willing to flirt. Just what the doctor ordered.

He only needed to wave a finger at the familiar bartender who immediately knew what to prepare, a dirty martini with extra olive juice, saltier than hell just the way Santini liked them. Taking his first sip as the band cranked too loudly for conversation, for some reason his mind turned to his father, though he rarely thought about the man anymore.

His parents' marriage had begun to crumble when he was about ten years old and his father's alcoholism became apparent. Ground down by the daily commute from Long Island into Manhattan and the stress of work as a broker on the New York Stock Exchange, he quit the job with no plan to financially support the family. Santini's mother was working part-time at the Macy's in Massapequa when his father quit. She started working full-time at the store to make ends meet.

The fights between his parents grew increasingly frequent and loud. Santini would lie in bed, listening to his father yelling at his mother. The drunken tirades were laced with profanity. He began developing a hatred for the man with whom he used to be so close. Santini's older brother, now nineteen, had been practicing taekwondo for several years. One night while their father was drunk and yelling at their mother, Santini's brother intervened, warning his father he would kick his ass if he yelled at their mother again. A few weeks later, their father moved out of the house, never to return. The divorce was finalized within a year.

As a teenager, Santini was engrossed in the heavy metal music of bands such as Metallica, Iron Maiden, and Black Sabbath. His tastes later developed into a fascination with super heavy death metal bands like Slayer, Megadeth, and Death Angel (all of which were big favorites of the founders of MS-13 in Los Angeles, too). He grew his hair long and traveled with like-minded friends to concert halls on Long Island and in New York City, including the famous CBGBs, guzzling booze and jumping into the mosh pit, often returning home battered and bruised.

Things haven't changed much, he thought. He knocked back the martini and ordered another one as the loud music pounded the troubling memories away.

--- ---

The next Monday morning, focused on writing investigation reports, Santini began receiving e-mail notices from ICE's Enforcement and Removal Operations (ERO) division, regarding the five gang members recently arrested outside Jocelyn's Bakery. According to the notices, the five homies currently held at the Yuba City detention center would be arriving at immigration court in San Francisco the next day for deportation hearings. Reading the messages from ERO, Santini had an epiphany—maybe the perfect way to introduce Diego to the 20th Street clique.

Santini devised a strategy where he would arrange to have the five MS-13 gangsters transferred from the ICE detention center in Yuba to the Sansome Street detention facility, presumably for immigration hearings. Once at the facility and locked up in a cell together, the gang members would be told the judge overseeing their cases had called in sick and the hearings were cancelled for the day. The whole thing would be a ruse by which to introduce Diego to the clique. It seemed like the perfect setup. Santini rushed to postpone the transfer of the gangsters to Sansome for a week, buying himself time to orchestrate the trap.

A week later, the five detained 20th Street clique members arrived at Sansome at the crack of dawn and were ushered into a cell rigged with hidden cameras and microphones. Diego arrived at the facility around the same time on a different bus and was locked up in a separate cell.

Around ten a.m., Santini and two other HSI agents brought Diego into an interview room to prep him for his meeting with the 20th Street crew. He was understandably nervous, having no idea if any of the MS-13 members he was about to meet had connections to his Los Limenos Locos clique back in San Pedro Sula, where he was known as the gangbanger Tromposo—now green-lighted for death by the Big Homies.

Diego knew what was at stake. If the meeting with the 20th Street homies didn't go well, the US government would have no further use for him and would probably ship him back to Honduras. Santini coached him to be calm and assertive, to engage in conversation readily and not allow for any long, awkward silences. He needed to maintain a confident presence and quickly gain respect from the 20th Street crew. If the meeting started to go badly and it looked like he was about to get jumped, Santini instructed Diego to signal distress by placing both of his hands on his head, which would bring the HSI agents running to the rescue.

Santini sat in the detention center control room, watching the security video from the cell that held the five 20th Street homies. The picture was clear, but their voices were barely audible through the hidden microphones, due to outside street traffic noise coming through an open window. If the agents were going to hear what the gang members said, the audio of their conversation would have to come later from another recorder hidden inside the ductwork.

At eleven a.m., guards led Diego to the cell door and his handcuffs were removed. He paused for a moment and took a deep breath. This was it, his big entrance. Everything was riding on it for him. The guard swung open the cell door.

"*Que andas*, homies?" Diego said, stepping into the lockup.

Inside the small cell, furnished with two benches, four of the 20th Street thugs sat, while Blackie stood in a corner, arms crossed and glaring. They all stared at Diego, sizing him up. The gangsters were still wearing the same all-blue street dress as the day they were arrested a few weeks prior.

"I'm Little Loco, from Honduras," Diego announced. "I am with La Mara."

"What clica you claim, homie?" Blackie said, after a long, uneasy silence.

This is where it got dicey for Diego. Knowing that the homies would grill him thoroughly before accepting him as one of their own, he had to give detailed answers without disclosing his real identity and getting caught up in a lie about his true gang affiliations in Honduras. He didn't know whom these mareros in the cell knew. He did, however, quickly detect that none of them were Hondurans, so he took a chance.

"I am from the Hollywood Locotes Salvatruchos clica, in San Pedro Sula," he said.

"The *vato* has the markings of the barrio!" Spanky said, pointing to Diego's tattoos that peeked over the neck of his T-shirt.

They fired questions at Diego about his past and his home clique. In his usual monotone voice, he gave them a careful mixture of truth and lies about his affiliations in Honduras, his leadership roles, and his criminal exploits there. He cleverly told them he had recently helped mastermind the Christmas Eve bus massacre outside San Pedro Sula, a widely publicized incident that was already achieving legendary status within MS-13's transnational grapevine.

When Spanky asked him details about his tattoos, Diego took off his shirt, exposing his shoulders and torso covered in Mara Salvatrucha ink. The five gang members rose in wonder to look closer at his tats, as he stood like a golem in the center of the cell, turning and posing, an object of intense curiosity. Diego had more tattoos than all five mareros put together. They were mesmerized.

After interrogating Diego about his trip from Honduras to Houston, and from there to San Francisco, the crew seemed satisfied that the new MS-13 marero in town was the real deal. Blackie told Cyper to give Diego his phone number so he could contact him when they were released from jail, adding that Cyper would be free within a matter of days because he had a good immigration lawyer. Blackie himself and the other three homies in detention would probably be deported to El Salvador, he said. Nevertheless, they would all sneak back into the States soon, Blackie promised. And they would see "Little Loco" on the streets when they returned.

After leaving Diego in the cell to hang out for a few more hours to get better acquainted with the 20th Street homies, Santini had him removed by the guards. The agent's new informant had obtained a phone number and an invitation to meet additional members of the clique in the Mission.

From now on, as far as Santini was concerned, Diego would be a tool to pry open the 20th Street clique and take them apart. What Diego did on his own time, as long as it was legal, was his own business. But Santini would decide what was Diego's own time and what was the US government's. And it wasn't going to be normal business hours. Not by a long shot.

Santini reiterated to Diego what was expected of him and what he would receive from the government in return. If he did his job and helped bring down 20th Street, he could start a new life in the States, with financial support and protection from the gang. HSI would have his back on the street to the greatest extent possible, but the work would still be dangerous.

Diego already knew the risk he was taking. He knew the type of thugs he'd be dealing with. He had been one of them since age fifteen.

Santini wrapped up the briefing with Diego and had him sign a litany of documents making him an official government informant. He told Diego that he could not make him any promises. The government was careful not to commit anything to informants. Diego knew he would have to work hard to take down the gang . . . his gang. He was assigned a source number and a fake name.

Santini watched from the lobby of the federal building on Sansome Street, as Diego exited onto the sidewalk and blended back into the city. His name moving forward was no longer Diego. He was now federal criminal informant Number 1301, aka Little Loco.

CHAPTER 5

Clueless in San Francisco

GAVIN NEWSOM, A PHOTOGENIC FORMER HIGH SCHOOL BASKETBALL star and San Francisco's recently elected mayor, was spinning a soccer ball on one finger, showing off for the news cameras lined up in Mission Playground. Standing right next to the mayor were Luis Fuentes, aka Memo, leader of MS-13's 20th Street clique, and Ivan Cerna, aka Tigre, the gang's second in command.

Clueless about the criminal background of his present company, Newsom's handlers had called a press conference to announce that Luis, Ivan, and their *futbol* teammates deserved a better field than the rundown one in Mission Playground where they currently played. The new mayor was committed to seeing they get it.

What the mayor did not understand was that Memo and his MS-13 gang claimed Mission Playground as their own turf. Anyone entering the playground wearing something red—anything, a jacket, cap, shoelaces— was asking for serious trouble. Red was the color of MS-13's enemies, the Norteños. If a 20th Street member walked up to you in the park and asked what you "claimed," meaning what was your gang affiliation, chances were good you'd be beaten, stabbed, or shot before you had a chance to answer. The question contained an accusation and a sentence, all wrapped up in swift MS-13 justice.

Memo, 20th Street's leader, was the father of a six-year-old boy. He worked by day as a car mechanic, as well as serving as a community liaison for the Neighborhood Safety Partnership, an anticrime program funded by the mayor's office. Twice a week, Memo practiced corner kicks and headers with the Guanacos, a club soccer team that scrimmaged at Mission Playground.[1]

Five years prior, Earl Sanders, then SFPD's assistant chief of police, had stood on the very same spot in the playground and declared to the media gathered, that he was absolutely committed to clearing out gang members who were terrorizing residents. A gangbanger had recently tried to stab a city recreation director with a screwdriver in the park. Vietnamese kids who tried to play soccer on the field had been completely scared away by the gang.

"We're coordinating a plan to protect that park. I guarantee this will be handled," Sanders proclaimed.[2] The assistant police chief said his strategy included more frequent patrols and more investigations into who was causing all the violence. Despite Sanders's pledge, conditions at Mission Playground had only worsened.

Soon before Newsom took office as mayor, Sanders, who had risen to chief of police, was forced to resign over a scandal dubbed Fajita-gate. The incident at the center of the affair involved some drunk off-duty city cops, including the son of then SFPD assistant chief Alex Fagan. The cops beat up a citizen badly outside a bar in the Marina District after he refused to share his takeout Mexican meal with them. The attempted cover-up ran all the way to the top of the department, dragging SFPD through mud for two years.

With the SFPD seriously demoralized on many levels by the time Newsom took office, San Francisco was experiencing an epidemic of bloody crime. The city had an annual murder rate of ten per one hundred thousand in 2003, compared to six per one hundred thousand for the entire state of California. On top of that, SFPD's homicide-case solution rate was the worst of any large metro police department in the United States—28 percent compared to the national average of 42 percent. A *San Francisco Chronicle* article at the time revealed that the city's "once vaunted Bureau of Inspectors" didn't even attempt to investigate nearly 70 percent of reported robberies and serious assaults. SFPD detectives often investigated crimes "from their desks," the newspaper reported.[3] The police department had devolved into a generally apathetic, over-politicized, and demoralized force.

In the Mission District, almost no one felt very safe, especially not young Latinos who attended the local public schools and were ripe for recruitment by the gang. Beatings and verbal abuse were the order of the day for youths in the community, thanks to the veteran thugs who were now enjoying a warm, public embrace by the new mayor of San Francisco. In front of the cameras, the mayor assured the homies standing beside him they would get a nice, new soccer field, paid for by the city's taxpayers.

It was eight o'clock on a Saturday night, not long after his public appearance with the mayor, and Memo was walking along the sidewalk on 24th Street in the Mission with his young son, Miguel. They walked hand in hand, out for a little fresh air before it was the little boy's bedtime. The two stopped and waited for a streetlight to change at the crosswalk in front of the China Express Food & Donuts shop.

"Mira para los dos lados!" Memo told his little boy when the light turned green.

He wanted to make sure his son learned that just because the sign said go, it didn't mean some fool couldn't run you over anyway. The streets were a jungle just beneath the surface and the sooner a person started to understand it, the better his chances of survival were.

"Okay, vamos," he said.

They stepped onto the crosswalk holding hands and made their way toward the BART subway station pavilion on the opposite corner. It was party night in the barrio. The Mission streets were busy with people shopping and enjoying themselves all around.

Memo knew the 20th Street homies were circulating throughout the neighborhood and earning cash by selling dime bags of weed and coke. They were also collecting their usual *renta* from the Miceros, who had begun reconstituting their fake ID business, despite the setbacks from Santini's recent takedown of the network. It appeared to Memo all was as it should be in the barrio.

A veteran of many battles, he was usually extremely alert to his surroundings on the street, always on the lookout for enemies on the horizon. But the weather was fine and the barrio was in a festive mood. The old soldier failed to notice a man wearing a black hoodie tailing him.

Just as Memo and Miguel reached the middle of the crowded subway pavilion, the stalker made his move and broke into a sprint. He came right up behind Memo and stopped short, then pulled out a revolver from his waistband. "Hey, buster!" he shouted, aiming the gun at the back of Memo's head.

"Fuck La Mara!" the man yelled.

When Memo turned, he fired point-blank into his face. The bullet penetrated the front of Memo's skull, causing an eruption of blood that splattered all around and over the little boy's clothes and shoes. The father's grip let loose of his son's hand.

The boy froze in shock and fear as Memo fell to the bricks and the assassin stepped closer, his gun pointed downward at his prostrate back. Horrified pedestrians fled in all directions as the killer fired again and again into the back of Memo's head, causing it to bounce off the ground each time.

After killing Memo, the eighteen-year-old Norteño gang member from Daly City took off running, but two witnesses to the incident had the guts to follow him and watched as he dumped the smoking gun into some flowerpots. He ducked into a laundromat to hide, but was arrested almost immediately by SFPD officers.

———

Twenty-six years old and handsome, with dark, curly hair, 20th Street member Edwin Zavala, aka Casper, a native of El Salvador, was giving a ride through the Mission to a fellow MS-13 gangbanger named Criminal. Casper's cell phone rang and he answered. A neighborhood girl named Nubia on the other end told him that Memo had just been shot dead on the sidewalk.

The news dropped on Casper like a bombshell. He couldn't believe it at first, so he told Nubia to double check her sources. Five minutes later, she called back and confirmed that Memo had been shot.

Casper passed on the bad news to Criminal, who said they should head directly to 20th Street to see what the other homies knew about what happened. When they arrived, a war party of the clique was already gathered. They all knew that Memo was hit by the Norteños and were planning to strike back, immediately. From Casper's car, Criminal yelled at the other gang members to relocate over to Mission Playground.

Spanky, Diablito, and Happy jumped into one car and pulled behind Casper's vehicle, as he drove away toward Portrero Avenue. Casper wanted to see for himself that Memo was dead, so at 24th Street he peeled off to the right. And there on an ambulance gurney he saw his gang leader's bullet-ridden and bloody body being covered with a white sheet by emergency medical personnel.

Casper took an immediate right turn and was stopped by some SFPD cops blocking off the street around the murder scene. The cops told Casper he couldn't pass, but when he responded that he lived on the block they let him through, along with the three other gang members following in the car right behind.

Before the two cars reached the corner at 23rd Street, Casper spotted three 22B (22nd and Bryant Street) Norteños in bright red attire, traveling on foot and flashing their gang salute for the world to see—one finger on the left hand and four on the right, representing the fourteenth letter of the alphabet, *N*. They were jumping up and down and dancing, celebrating Memo's death.

At an unexpected eruption of gunfire just behind him, Casper flinched and spun around in the driver's seat to see Happy was hanging out of the passenger side window of Spanky's car and blasting a handgun at the Norteños, who scrambled for cover on the sidewalk. Terrified bystanders ducked and fled all around. Casper and Spanky sped away in opposite directions, taking alternate routes back to the playground.

The gang members gathered at the park were all stunned that Memo, being such a savvy gang leader, could have let his guard down and gotten dropped the way he did—right on their home turf. They were especially outraged the Norteño had shot Memo in front of his little boy. Even for the two sworn enemy gangs, who had been at bloody war with one another for several years, this was taking the rules of engagement to a new level. It was a major, unexpected blow for 20th Street, leaving a leadership vacuum that would have to be filled quickly to hold them together.

CHAPTER 6

Informant 1301 Dives In

AS PLANNED DURING HIS INTRODUCTION TO 20TH STREET AT THE immigration hold, Diego met Cyper a few days later at the corner of 19th and Valencia Streets, and the two of them walked to the Mission Playground together. Cyper was wearing all blue, including an L.A. Dodgers T-shirt, baggy pants, and Nike Cortez sneakers. Cyper told Diego he had only recently been jumped in by 20th Street and that he was still sore from the beating. He also said he planned on getting a large "Mara Salvatrucha" tattoo on his back.

Diego understood that Cyper, being a rookie marero, was especially dangerous to him because he still had something to prove to the gang. Killing a rat like Diego, if he was ferreted out, would be a big feather in a new member's cap. Walking toward Mission Playground, Cyper bragged on and on about *pegados*, or hits, on rival gang members whom MS-13 members called *chavalas* or *chapetes*, as well as hits on suspected rats inside 20th Street.

On the way to the park, the two were joined by another 20th Street member named Vaselina. He was a slender twenty years old, with long, greased-back hair. As the three walked along, they discussed the possibility that there was a *ratta* named Dreamer currently in the clique. Dreamer was now in the gang's crosshairs for talking to SFPD cops about other gang members, and senior members of 20th Street had ordered him to get his forearms tattooed with 'M' and 'S' to confirm his allegiance to the gang.

At Mission Playground, the three homies watched two local soccer teams compete. The gangsters bullshitted and felt one another out for a while, before parting ways for the night. The next day, Diego met Cyper and Colmillo (whose bedroom Santini had stood in during Operation Mission Possible), a more seasoned 20th Street gangster with a shaved head and a gold earring that read "MS." Colmillo wore baggy blue pants and Nike brand Cortez sneakers. He was older than Diego, who sensed that his interactions with Colmillo were an important test. Colmillo was obviously street hard and Diego was certain that Cyper had purposely set up this meeting so Colmillo could check him out.

While eating tacos at the Casa Sanchez Taqueria, Colmillo bragged that some 20th Street clique members had committed four killings in just that month alone. He also indicated that all the homicides involved the use of a "community" gun, a forty-five-caliber pistol that Colmillo kept in his possession.

When they finished eating, the three homies walked to Mission Playground. Diego sensed another important test for him was about to occur. Numerous mareros from the 20th Street clique were present. He took a deep breath and strolled into the park alongside Cyper and Colmillo. There he met some other 20th Street members for the first time, including Dreamer (the suspected rat) and Tigre, the gang leader.

Tigre didn't wear gang colors or look like a gangster at first glance. He looked like a typical blue-collar Latino man. What Diego noticed about him was that he was obviously hardened from the barrio, but also had a smooth confidence. Tigre wasn't trying to act tough like most of the younger gangsters did. He just was, and he was taking a liking to Diego as the group discussed numerous gang-related issues, most importantly the current lack of organization within 20th Street.

"The clica needs more direction," Tigre told Diego. "I am glad you are here. You know how things should run. You could help with the new homies who need to learn La Mara's reglos—the right way."

"Sí," Diego said. "I can help. I am very familiar with the rules of La Mara."

Thirty-four years old, married, and the father of two young daughters, Tigre was one of the founding members of 20th Street in the mid-1990s along with his best friend Memo. Five-foot-nine, a hundred seventy pounds, with a square head, broad shoulders, and short-cropped black beard, he was regularly employed as a union carpenter. He had emigrated from El Salvador as a teenager and was now living in the country legally.

Despite the city's sanctuary policy, which officially forbade SFPD from working with HSI, with the help of Gibson, Santini accessed the SFPD's criminal records on Tigre and learned he had a history of serious violence. "Tigre may look unassuming but he has had his hands in a lot of dirt over the years," Gibson relayed during a recent meet with Santini. "He's been loyal to the gang from the start and although he stays out of the mainstream, not hanging out with the homies in the park, he is in it for the long haul. Tigre doesn't have to commit crime anymore, he just orders it."

One evening four years earlier, during the start of Christmas season, a fifteen-year-old girl hurried down the stairs to greet her mother in the garage of their modest, single-family home in the Ingleside Heights neighborhood. She was on her way to help her mother with a bunch of bags from a long day of holiday shopping. The excited teenager paused for a moment in the front hallway, admiring a big wreath her father had just hung on the front door.

Making her way to the garage, she heard her mother's voice, full of distress. "Please, someone help me!" her mother called.

"I'm coming, Mom," the girl replied, imagining her mother was struggling with an armful of shopping bags. The girl pushed open the door to the garage and saw two men—Tigre and another MS-13 gangster named Oscar Gonzalez, aka Nino Manioso—wearing black ski masks and dark clothing, holding guns.

"Call the police!" her mother yelled.

"Don't move!" Tigre shouted, causing the girl to scream in fear.

At that, Tigre smashed the mother in the face and head repeatedly with his pistol. The terrified girl saw blood poor from her mother's nose. She ran screaming through the first floor of the house, back toward the staircase leading to the second floor, with the second gunman chasing close behind.

In the garage, the mother was half-conscious from the vicious pistol whipping, as Tigre screamed at her in a thick Spanish accent, "Give me the money!"

The stunned woman fumbled through her purse, handing him a bundle of $725 in cash. He counted it quickly, then shouted, "Fuck! All of the money, lady! I know there's more than this. We've been following you for a long time!"

Tigre grabbed her and pulled her inside the house. He yanked three rings from her fingers—one with a diamond, and two with sapphires.

"We are Arabian," he offered, lamely. "We are part of a terrorist group."

Meanwhile, the terrified daughter had stopped running halfway up the stairs to the second floor, where she met her father and a male cousin who heard her screams and came running to her aid. Nino Manioso confronted all three family members on the staircase and ordered the two males to come down to the living room and lie facedown on the floor, while the girl sat at the kitchen table, shaking in terror.

"Where is the money?! I know you collected it!" Tigre screamed at the father. The thug was after rent from the family's Excelsior District investment property, which the sole tenants paid every month in cash.

"I don't know what you're talking about!" the man pleaded.

Manioso positioned the crying and bloody mother next to her husband on the floor.

"We've been following you for two months!" Tigre demanded. "Give us the fucking rent money now!"

"I didn't collect the rent. I swear! I came straight home!" the father said.

The gunmen were incensed now and screaming at the man, pointing their guns. Tigre took his watch and wallet, and began scavenging the room for valuables while Manioso covered the family with his gun.

Upstairs, unnoticed by the thugs, a teenage male member of the family had heard the screaming and quietly slipped into a bathroom with a phone. He dialed 9-1-1. While on the phone with the police dispatcher, he heard a knock on the bathroom door.

"Is anybody in there?!" Manioso called.

The frightened teenager laid the phone on the floor, still connected with the dispatcher.

"I called the police!" he shouted through the door.

Manioso attempted unsuccessfully to force it open.

"They called the cops!" He yelled downstairs to Tigre. "Let's get the fuck out of here!"

Tigre and Manioso ran together from the home through the garage door, where they were met by a police car that had raced to the scene. Caught in the headlights, they both raised their hands as the cops approached them with firearms raised. The police screamed at the two thugs to get down on the ground. Instead, they ran back into the garage, smashed out a rear window, and jumped over the backyard fence.

Both the Ingleside and Taraval police stations called out to responding units that the suspects were running southbound on the train tracks toward the Daly City BART station. A unit responded on the radio just moments later that a possible suspect was in custody at the Rite Aid pharmacy on Alemany Boulevard. Manioso was arrested in possession of $2,700 in cash and a Rolex watch from the home invasion. Tigre, on the other hand, escaped.

———

Several months later, at around two o'clock in the morning, at 22nd and Bryant Streets in the Mission District, a Norteño member named Dexter and four of his friends were sitting on the front steps of his home, drinking beer and chatting about hip-hop music. The group heard car tires screeching toward them on Florida Street and saw a small red Honda Civic stop abruptly in front of the house. From the passenger side of the car, Tigre leaned out the passenger window.

"Fuck Norte!" he shouted, before firing a gun several times at them, then speeding away. As the group of Norteños began to register what had just occurred, they realized Dexter was moaning in pain and holding the side of his face.

He had been shot in his right cheek and couldn't speak. Dexter's friend, Brandy, took off her sweatshirt and pressed it against his wound to stem the bleeding, while a male in the group called for an ambulance. Two SFPD officers arrived moments later, as did paramedics who tended

Dexter's wounds. They discovered a bullet lodged in his cheek, which would require surgery to remove.

Brandy told the cops she recognized the shooter, Tigre, because she previously dated his younger brother. She also told the cops Tigre was an MS-13 gang member. The cops were notified by radio that the red Honda had been located, abandoned just six blocks away on the 400 block of Shotwell Street. It was double parked with the engine running and the ignition "punched," a common technique used by car thieves.

A subsequent investigation by the SFPD Gang Task Force revealed that besides Tigre the passengers in the Honda included the gang leader Memo, and two females named Mafalda and Gorda. Photo spreads were given to all the witnesses at the scene of the crime, including Dexter. Three of the witnesses identified Tigre as the shooter.

SFPD visited Tigre's residence that same morning and arrested him without incident. He was wearing a baseball cap with a patch on it that read "San Francisco Conservation Corps," a jobs program for at-risk youth funded by private and public funds, including the city's Office of Economic and Workforce Development, as well as the Juvenile Probation Department–Log Cabin Ranch. The cap also had "MS" written in block letters on the bill, as well as Tigre's name.

The police seized a .38 caliber handgun, .25 caliber ammunition, as well as a safe they opened after the boyfriend of Tigre's mother agreed to provide the lock combination. Inside, detectives discovered more ammunition including .38 special, .38 short, .25 and .22 caliber. It also contained a diamond ring and two sapphire rings.

Neither the Excelsior family home invasion nor the attack where an eyewitness identified Tigre as the shooter was ever prosecuted by the city's district attorney. As Santini was discovering, Tigre's ability to escape punishment was consistent with a common pattern in San Francisco of gang members getting away with serious violent crimes. Even after all the mayhem and terror Tigre had instigated, he had remained free to stand next to Mayor Newsom at a press conference, representing the city's community of innocent Latinos just looking for a safe place to encourage youths to participate in healthy and productive activities.

A few days after their initial meeting in the park, Tigre called Diego and arranged to pick him up at 20th and Van Ness in the Mission in a beat-up gray Toyota for a ride south to Santa Cruz. Tigre asked Diego to ride along with him to meet some MS-13 members who were trying to stand up a new clique.

The ninety-minute drive from San Francisco to Santa Cruz seemed cathartic to Tigre. He hadn't bonded with a senior fellow gang member like Diego that he respected from outside the bay area in a long time. He was upbeat and excited, leaning his head out the window as they drove south on Freeway 101, the wind blowing back his hair.

"Ever since Memo got dropped, I have been trying to keep these youngsters in line," Tigre said. "But I didn't ask for this position."

He said he never wanted to become the clique leader, but was told by the Big Homies that was how things were going to be for the time being. Tigre's childhood friendship with Camaron, one of the gang's top thirteen "Ranfleros" (Capo) in El Salvador, was the reason he had been thrust into leadership of 20th Street, he said.

It was obvious to Diego that Tigre was committed to the clique, but overwhelmed and confused about how to manage it in accordance with the established rules of La Mara. Discipline among younger members of 20th Street was increasingly lacking. They were frequently failing to show up for meetings and pay dues. When they did show up, many of them were high or drunk—or both. None of this behavior was permitted in the better-run cliques in Los Angeles and Central America, where failure to abide by gang regulations was met with far swifter and more severe punishment. Under effective clique leaders, the ranks were kept in check through fear and brutal intimidation.

If Tigre were honest with himself at this point, he would have recognized his best days as an MS-13 gangbanger were probably past. Old dogs like him with a steady job, a wife, and growing children, tended to "age out" of the gang. This didn't mean quitting, which was never an acceptable option, but rather a tacit consent to ease out of daily participation in the gang's business. In MS-13 culture, it was possible for aged-out veterans to retain positions as respected elders who mainly looked out for the welfare of younger homies that didn't have families nearby and required some supervision and protection.

Driving to Santa Cruz, Diego and Tigre discussed the need for the formation of an advisory board or congress comprised of five or six, senior 20th Street members. Diego told Tigre that such a board, or *consejeria*, was typical of MS-13 cliques in many places, including the barrios of Central America. Diego agreed to serve on a new consejeria for 20th Street.

After an hour and a half on the road, the two men arrived at a quiet block near an amusement park in Santa Cruz. Diego could see the top of the red-and-white Giant Dipper roller coaster in the distance, and the beachfront miniature golf course called Neptune's Kingdom. They pulled over at a corner where three young Latino males lingered. The trio didn't look like gangsters. They simply looked like three laborers after a long day of landscaping rich folks' manicured lawns in the neighborhoods of Half Moon Bay.

In a brief conversation, the three Santa Cruz homies sought permission from Tigre to establish an MS-13 clique in Santa Cruz, to be known as the "Beach Flats Locotes Salvatruchos." Tigre told them he was amenable to the plan, but he also had to consult with senior gang leaders "down below."

"How many you have?" Tigre asked an MS-13 member named Spider who was proclaiming to be a leader.

"Fifteen right now, but we have many prospects that we are working on. We expect we can have thirty in a few months." Spider replied.

"Okay," Tigre said. "Keep working on the numbers and I'll reach out to the elders this week. I don't anticipate any push back, but you'll have to pay allegiance to 20th Street if you want support."

The gang members shook hands good-bye and Tigre shouted "Trucha homies!" as he started the car for the trek back to the city.

By bringing Diego along for the ride to meet with the crew in Santa Cruz, Tigre was demonstrating to Little Loco that he was currently the top MS-13 boss in all Northern California. No gang members in the region could stand up a new clique without his approval, although he would only grant it after consulting with the Big Homies. Tigre's display of authority indicated he was connected with the very top echelon of MS-13. Making Little Loco privy to these key organizational connections meant Tigre was quickly accepting Diego as a trusted confidant.

Diego was hanging on the street with some 20th Street homies in the little park, when Spanky and his cousin pulled up next to him in a gray Toyota.

"Yo, Loco," he said. "We headed to Richmond to check out the PLS homies. You wanna ride with us, dog?"

"Sí, homie," Diego said with a shrug. "Let's go."

The Pasadena Locos Sureños, or PLS, clique in Richmond had been sent to the bay area by senior MS leaders in Los Angeles and El Salvador in part to keep an eye 20th Street following Memo's assassination. The PLS clique was meaner, more aggressive, and quicker to pick up a gun than the 20th Street homies, especially since 20th had come under Tigre's more moderate influence. Although they still remained "officially" in the Mission District–based clique, several malcontents from 20th Street were spending more time in Richmond with the PLS now.

Diego, Spanky, and his cousin drove from the Mission and across the Bay Bridge toward Richmond, listening to hip-hop on the radio and bantering about family members and girlfriends in the States and back home. Below the bridge on the sparkling bay, sailboats rode the steady ocean breeze blowing along the coastline of Oakland and Berkeley.

Across the bridge, they headed north to Richmond. A city of one hundred thousand people, Richmond had a murder rate ten times the national average. While most of the violence was being committed between black gangs, the Latino gang population in the city was gaining force.

Diego, Spanky, and his cousin arrived at a small, well-kept house in a dilapidated neighborhood on 7th Street. It was surrounded by a white picket fence with a slipshod iron security gate across the front walkway, and a yard full of flowers. Spanky told Diego the place was rented by a woman named Gata, the PLS clique's "mama." As many as twenty-five MS-13 gang members resided there, crammed together into the eleven-hundred-square-foot, two-bedroom home.

They were greeted at the front door by a group of six gang members and two women. Diego was introduced to Gata and her younger sister, Diablita, a thin, quiet Salvadoran who looked to be in her mid-twenties, dressed in tight jeans and a sheer top fitted snugly over her small breasts. She emitted a cool air of danger and self-reliance.

Gata's age appeared indeterminate—still young enough to attract lonely, horny young bachelors far from home, but old enough to be their mother, too. She smiled quickly and laughed heartily like a man, her large mouth opening cavernously to reveal a formidable set of strangely glinting teeth. She wore a white tank top, with her cleavage generously exposed, a pair of baby blue soccer shorts, and flip-flops showing off her blue-polished toenails. Her coal-black hair was tied in a horsetail that hung all the way down her back to her buttocks.

The PLS homies gathered in the living room sized up Diego, the unfamiliar marero in town from San Pedro Sula, as Gata returned to the kitchen and a huge batch of *pupusas* in progress—enough to feed a platoon. From the stove, she could still observe Diego, in between flipping corn tortillas and stirring the ground pork and refried beans. Diablita sat sideways in a worn-out Barcalounger, her legs dangling over one armrest, looking bored and disinterested, buffing her fingernails with a file.

Four more PLS homies arrived in time for dinner. Among them was Wilfredo Reyes, aka Flaco, a twenty-four-year-old with a sloping forehead, short haircut, and thick lips that seemed permanently pursed to cover an exaggerated overbite. He had a slight dimple in his chin. Immediately, the new arrivals to the party began bragging about having just attacked some Norteños a few blocks away with machetes.

"We fucked those chapetes up good, man!" Flaco said.

"They gonna start calling us 'The Macheteros' around here!" said another one of the PLS homies, laughing. The PLS gangbangers described how they trapped their victims in a surprise attack and went at them with machetes, slashing and chopping as the unprepared Norteños scattered.

The group passed a joint of weed around the room.

"Listen, homies," Flaco said. He drew a deep breath of pot smoke into his lungs and held it for a moment, then blew out an acrid cloud. "I know where to get some Uzis if any homies want one," he said. This was a point of excitement for the gang members who all agreed they could do some hardcore work with a compact, automatic weapon like an Uzi.

Gata announced the pupusas were ready. The gang jumped up to fill their paper plates and dug in, relishing the familiar home cooking. Gata brought a plate for Diego and handed it to him, flashing her most winning smile—something between a maternal expression of love and a hooker's come-on. Her servile gesture was a sign of respect for an obviously hardened marero.

"Gracias," Diego said. He nodded appreciation and went to work on the food with a plastic fork. "Ah, muy bueno!"

She watched him closely while he ate and the gang continued bragging about their feats in the turf battle. When they had all finished eating and the plates were tossed in the garbage, Diego, Spanky, and his cousin, now joined by Flaco, got back into the car and drove back to the Mission.

Once back at Sutro Park, they met up with other gang members and walked together to the Cancun Taqueria on Mission Street. Inside the taqueria, seated with the homies around a picnic-style wooden bench, Diego learned they were about to place a phone call to a Big Homie named Santos, who was locked up in a Salvadoran prison. The purpose of the call was to get instructions concerning the removal of Tigre as leader of 20th Street. The group huddled around a cell phone set to speaker mode as the call went through.

"Sí!" Santos answered.

Even though he was in prison, Santos sounded in a hurry. Diego knew from experience this was probably because he wanted to conserve his phone battery, because chargers were hard to come by in Central American prisons.

"We want to know what we should do about the problem with 20th Street," Flaco said.

"I'm still checking with the others on how to deal with it," Santos said. "I'll contact you soon."

That was it. Santos hung up.

When Diego told Santini about the phone conversation with Santos, the agent realized he was dealing with a morphing target. The 20th Street gang was in a state of organizational flux. In essence, it was a large, dynamic group rife with internal conflict, treachery, and deceit. If Santini was going to make any progress, his assessment of the hierarchy and his tactical approaches needed to remain flexible. His investigation needed to expand now—geographically and in terms of MS-13 cliques—to include the PLS in Richmond.

CHAPTER 7

Meet-up at Tommy's Joynt

A FEW DAYS LATER, SANTINI GOT THE CALL FROM DIEGO. HE WAS IN Mission Playground with some senior 20th Street homies and about to accompany them to an important gang meeting. This was going to be the informant's first interaction with all the clique's senior leadership together, and Santini was excited. He saw a real opportunity to start gathering intelligence and quite possibly evidence of crimes committed by the gang.

Santini and a colleague at HSI had discussed with Diego the option of wearing a concealed audio recording device to capture the meeting about to occur. Although he was nervous, Diego agreed to do it. The recorder was the size of a pack of gum, and could easily be concealed in his jacket pocket.

A few hours earlier, Diego snuck away from the gang briefly and met with the HSI agents to be fitted with the body wire. In only a few moments, the agents were able to set him up to record the meeting. Because the wire offered a live feed, Santini and his team would be able to listen in on the conversation and ensure Diego's safety.

Now, talking rapidly and in hushed tones into the wire, Diego told Santini he hadn't been able to learn the name of the restaurant where the gang was headed for the meet-up. All he knew was the place was located on the other side of town and that the homies would be driving in a white van and a dark-colored Acura.

The agents' surveillance was initiated at around 9 p.m. at Mission and 20th Streets, with the HSI team picking up a tail on the gang's van heading through the SOMA neighborhood. They continued to Civic Center and the intersection of Geary and Franklin Streets, where Santini's task force partners from the California Department of Justice observed a small group of Latino males standing on the street corner. As the vehicle carrying Diego parked at the club, the agents observed a separate pair of Latino males walking together toward the entrance of Tommy's Joynt, located at the intersection of Van Ness and Geary.

Tommy's seemed to Santini like an odd location for a meeting of MS-13 gang members. He often ate there himself. The place was an institution in the city, having been in business since 1947. It was especially famous for its beef brisket. A bright neon sign outside advertised SANDWICHES, and COCKTAILS, and an inscription on the front door proclaimed, WHERE TURKEY IS KING.

The assembled group of gang members entered a side door to the building and climbed some stairs to the second-floor dining room, where they took an out-of-the-way table. All eight of the 20th Street clique members crammed together in a booth, where they wouldn't be overheard or interrupted by the tourists and locals who filled the busy eatery. At the bar, an undercover HSI agent blending in with the clientele texted outside to Santini that the meeting of 20th Street shot callers had begun.

"We're all here now, right?" Tigre said. "I couldn't grab all the people that would normally have to be here so that more of us are present, but anyway you all are the ones that are more alert to what this thing of the two letters [MS] is about," he said.

Outside in an unmarked van, Santini grew excited, listening to Diego's wire and what Tigre was saying. The sound quality was good and Tigre was openly discussing gang-related issues. The operation was going off perfectly, so far.

"The way the new kids are behaving lately is not good," Tigre continued. "It looks bad for us old-timers when these kids come to meetings and raise their voices louder than ours. That's no good."

Tigre was obviously conflicted. His new status as leader of 20th Street was an ego boost, but he also knew that the interest of federal law enforcement in MS-13 had increased significantly. The younger members of the 20th Street clique were showing a wild, reckless streak in the way they were working the streets, a situation that Tigre feared could end up biting him in the ass. He wanted to see his two daughters grow up—and not from behind bars.

"As for me, I've always told you that I can't be responsible for you all," he continued. "The rules are the rules, and they have to be followed. But the younger homies are constantly arguing with us. So this is why I've called us all together, so you can help me with this thing."

This was what Santini hoped for—good audio quality and the gang leader discussing key issues related to managing the clique. *Hello RICO*, Santini thought.

"Word, homie," Diego said. "Uh, pardon me, homies."

He continued, "I'm Little Loco. Most of you don't know me yet, because I'm new here. I recently got busted and locked up with some of the 20th. So far, I've only been to one meeting, the last one held at the park. The truth of the matter is it didn't exactly look like a meeting, you know what I mean? I used to be in the Mara Salvatrucha meetings in Honduras, and the truth is that meetings are supposed to bring up serious issues for the clique, homies."

Diego scanned the group to gauge their reaction to his speech so far, and judged it wise to keep talking.

"Tigre has to have a work program here on the streets, you know what I mean? A leader is the one who carries the entire responsibility over the clique. Some day in the future, the one who will be held accountable by the Big Homies will be that man," he said, pointing to Tigre. "And if he hasn't run everything straight, like it should be, he knows about the consequences of the clique," Diego said.

"We have a rule book in the clique, homies," he added. "And the majority of the rules carry a death penalty."

Diego's gambit at playing a veteran, savvy shot caller from Honduras, who deserved to be heard and heeded, seemed to be going over well with the gang. They all understood their clique suffered from a severe lack of discipline, with many gang members even failing to wear their blue colors on the street. Some were performing drive-by hits, instead of confronting the enemy up close before shooting him in the face, as dictated by MS-13 rules. Too many 20th Street members were spending most of their time hanging out in bars and doing drugs, and not enough were getting their hands dirty killing Norteños and earning money for the gang.

"Simone," Tigre said. "It's about time this thing gets fixed."

"We're brothers in the fight," Casper said.

"The clique is first before all things," another homie added.

As the meeting progressed, Tigre and the rest talked about the need to establish several funds to finance various criminal activities of the gang. They agreed a mandatory collection of cash from every member at all future meetings of the clique would be taken up. The money would be pooled and multiplied through a variety of criminal endeavors. An initial fund would be designated for drug deals. Another would be established for buying and selling guns, and another one for bailing out 20th Street members who were arrested. Tigre said the consejeria would be responsible for organizing and managing the funds and certain gang members would be assigned to specific roles, such as money collection and bookkeeping.

For Santini, whose overriding mission was to nail the gang on federal RICO charges, requiring hard evidence of a conspiracy, all this recorded discussion between 20th Street members about committing crimes together and sharing funds was potentially pure gold.

The gang's attention next turned to the problem of certain cops in the Mission District.

"What about Ricardo (Cabrera)?" Diego said.

Santini had instructed him to bring up the topic when he heard it was rumored that the gang wanted Cabrera dead.

"He's the one in charge," Casper said.

"He's the one who has sworn to get rid of us," Tigre said.

Tigre said he intended to appoint a gang member to conduct surveillance on Cabrera. The gang discussed forming a *gatillero*, or trigger squad, composed of younger clique members to carry out future hits as ordered by the clique's shot callers. This line of discussion about killing a cop—while alarming on one level—was more potentially powerful evidence for the RICO case that Santini hoped to build.

At the end of the meeting, the gang at the table agreed they should keep the evening's discussion confidential for the time being among only the members present. Tigre said he would call a clique-wide meeting in the next few days to educate the newer gang members about the reforms they discussed.

"From here on out everything is going to be serious," Tigre said. "And when I say serious, I mean, like, 100 percent serious."

CHAPTER 8

Peloncito Threatens Tigre

ALTHOUGH TIGRE INSISTED ON SECRECY BETWEEN THE SENIOR GANG leaders about their discussion at Tommy's Joynt, word soon leaked out to the younger 20th Street members—very likely through Indio, who was present at the meeting. Indio's allegiance to the older homies in the gang had diminished lately due to the influence of his brother and fellow gang member, Cyco, a violent hothead with his own aspirations for clique leadership.

In fact, word of the meeting spread all the way through the gang's international grapevine to the Ciudad Barrios Prison in the municipality of San Miguel, El Salvador, to two Big Homies named Snoopy and Meow. Meow took exception to the fact that Tigre was restructuring the clique in San Francisco with himself as leader. He knew that Tigre had a skeleton in his closet that would be of serious concern for any MS-13 member who learned of it. Determined that Tigre's secret come to light in advance of any reorganization of 20th Street, Meow sent word to a uniquely ruthless gang member residing in San Francisco named Peloncito, to press the issue.

Angel Guevara, aka Peloncito, Spanish for "handsome bald man," was a husky twenty-six-year-old with menacing eyes and a grimace that made most people in his company uncomfortable. According to word on the street, Peloncito was cofounder and leader of the Candelaria clique of MS-13 in Custcatlán, El Salvador. He was dispatched to San Francisco by the Big Homies to investigate the legitimacy of Tigre's new role as leader of 20th Street.

Rumor among the gang, Diego told Santini, was that Peloncito was a devoted devil worshipper and a stone-cold killer. He was also highly street savvy, having sold crack in the Tenderloin and Mission as far back as 1995, at the age of fifteen. After spending four years in a California Youth Authority facility for shooting at some pedestrians in the Mission, Peloncito was deported to El Salvador, where he earned his stripes as leader of la Candelaria.

Killing and maiming seemed to be what Peloncito lived for. That, and the fear he instilled in others—even other gang members—whom he enjoyed regaling with detailed accounts of his bloody exploits on the street. He wanted them all to know he was a true killer among killers, most of whom didn't have the seemingly bottomless bloodlust Peloncito did. His girlfriend, a minor by the street name of Flaca, was also Peloncito's occasional partner in vicious attacks against rival gang enemies and strangers alike.

At Tigre's request, Diego met Peloncito for the first time at a row of wooden benches in Mission Playground just after dusk on a chilly, August night. The two exchanged small talk about gang life in their home countries, walking together to Jocelyn's Bakery, where they were picked up in a car by Tigre.

Sitting in the front passenger seat, Peloncito immediately confronted Tigre about his presumed leadership position in the gang.

"You ain't never been jumped in, homie," he accused. "Have you?!"

It was Tigre's dirty little secret. "There weren't enough homies in San Francisco to jump me in when Memo and me stood up 20th Street!" he insisted.

"How can you be leader when you ain't even been jumped in?" Peloncito shouted. "All the youngsters—they all got jumped in. How they supposed to see you as leader of the clica?!"

Hearing the heated exchange from the backseat of the car, Diego thought he understood now why Tigre wanted him along for the meeting with Peloncito. He appeared to fear Peloncito, and having Little Loco by his side—a hardened gangster from Honduras—might offer Tigre some reinforcement.

"These dumb-ass kids don't listen to me!" Tigre shouted. "Not since Memo got dropped! They think they know everything already!"

He complained he wasn't receiving enough guidance from senior gang members in Los Angeles and El Salvador. Peloncito accused Tigre of claiming he had support from the top gang leaders in El Salvador he didn't really have. He challenged Tigre to provide him names and phone numbers of Big Homies in El Salvador with whom he claimed to be in regular contact. Tigre refused.

When the argument finally ran out of steam, Tigre drove Peloncito and Diego back to Jocelyn's Bakery and dropped them out front. Peloncito was still furious. It was clear to Diego he needed to be extremely wary of his murderous rage. If it ever got out Diego was a rat, there was no doubt in his mind Peloncito would relish the opportunity to whack him.

Diego's main hope for continuing to escape detection as a rat stemmed from a lack of Hondurans in 20th Street who could easily check his credentials. Without good connections in his home country, any investigation of his cover story was likely to hit a dead end. This was especially true since he was using an alias gang name, Little Loco, instead of Tromposo. Nevertheless, the possibility of Diego being found out was very real, and he knew Peloncito would be his likely executioner if his identity were ever revealed.

Situated atop a hill at the westernmost point of Lands End, Sutro Park offered spectacular views of the Pacific Ocean. On the leeward side of the park, well-manicured, multimillion-dollar homes formed a quiet, prosperous neighborhood. When the waves of the Pacific were breaking the right way, visitors standing on the park's high bluff overlooking the sea could watch the wetsuit-wearing surfers catching rides far down below.

Santini and his partner John got to the park early, before the 20th Street members started arriving. As cover, the two HSI agents brought a cooler full of beers and sat with them on a small merry-go-round, blending in with park visitors who were taking strolls and enjoying the panoramic views.

As the sun set over the ocean, the flow of 20th Street members into the park accelerated. It suddenly dawned on Santini that he and his partner were badly outnumbered. There were well over thirty gang members present now. Who knew what kind of craziness they might get into, or what kind of firepower they might have brought with them? With darkness descending, the two agents repositioned to a small, white pagoda from which they could observe the meeting through a high-powered night vision scope.

They watched as the gang huddled together in a big circle at the edge of a bluff overlooking Ocean Beach, with Diego in their midst. In the center stood Tigre, who appeared to have shaken off the jitters from his encounter earlier in the day with Peloncito.

"Well, let's take roll call first," Tigre said. "And call your names out slowly, so I can write them down."

The gang members called out:

"Catracho!"

"Droopy!"

"Fantasma!"

One by one, they called out their street names for the official record of attendance.

"Okay, you have to consider one thing," Tigre said, once the sound-off was completed. "If you want me to continue doing this thing, well then you have to pay attention."

He paused and told the gang members to gather in a tighter circle, so he could talk softer and not be overheard by anyone.

"If I'm going to be at the front of this clique, then I need all of you to back me up. If someone doesn't want me to, now is the time to speak out. Because if not, then how am I going to read you some rules that we're going to follow?"

He stopped and looked around the group intensely. No one said anything.

"Because from here on out, as far as the meetings go and what the rules are, we're going to have to respect them."

He looked down at the sheet of paper in his hand and started reading: "Rule number one: La Mara has no boss. La Mara, what it is, the entire name of La Mara, there is no one person in particular that runs this show.

"Number two: Zero rock and crystal, or heavy drugs, aside from weed or small things like that. You know these things are not tolerated.

"Rule number three: No rapes, or gang rapes. We have to respect women.

"Number four: No rats. Whoever rats us out, the consequence to him is death. None of that can exist here with us. One person talking about some small things here and there—that has a big effect on all of us. And our lives are in danger in all this. So that doesn't go.

"Number five: No talking to the cops. Remember that the cops are two-faced. If they catch someone and want to talk to them, then of course they're going to try to make him their friend.

"Number six: Respect among all the homeboys. All of us have to respect. Remember that if you have your family, your mother, your father, your siblings—you respect them. The same goes for La Mara. We have to respect each other. We have to love each other like a family. Because if we don't have a family at home, La Mara is who guides us.

"Number seven: Respect the lives of the civilians. The majority of us want to mess with anybody when we're a little messed up with drugs or alcohol. La Mara has to respect the people that are not involved in any of our thing.

"Number eight: Respect the neighborhood leaders. We need to respect the men that run their own deals. Let's respect everybody, not just from La Mara here, but any other cliques that are affiliated with La Mara. Especially here in San Francisco, since we have two more, which are the 19s and the 11s. They both are Sureños. And yeah, they're fine with us. We need to respect each other."

Tigre was finished reading the rules, and Marvin Carcomo, aka Cyco, was the first to chime in.

"All this shit is cool, man," Cyco said. "The only thing is that we are all here, but it's not only about being at the meetings and that's all. You have to put in work." Cyco reminded his homies that "work" for the gang essentially meant attacking rivals, preferably killing them. Their primary mission, always, was to claim and protect their territory.

"Okay, you're right," Tigre said. "It's not just about coming and showing your face here and that's it, like, 'I've done my duty.' As for me, you won't hear me telling you right now, 'Hey, you have to do this and that.' It can't be. It's voluntary. But each of us knows what he needs to do. Remember, the enemy is abundant. And one way or another, we have to reduce it."

Diego sensed that Tigre's momentum with the homies was flagging.

"Word, homie," Diego said. "I agree with the word you just laid down. I think the best thing for us is to stick close to the rules. That is very useful to everyone here, so we can have a better understanding of how things in the 'hood are. As far as the rules go, well, it's right there. It's clear. If we break a rule, we'll have to face the consequences. If we break a death rule, then it's death."

Concealed behind the pagoda, Santini and his partner took turns with the night vision gear, hoping the wire Diego was wearing picked up the gang's conversation.

"All of us here are burned with the two letters," Tigre picked back up. "We can't be changing flags, or nothing like that. We've been unorganized for a long time, and it has to stop now.

"Trucha, homies!" he called out.

His speech was done. The meeting broke up and gang members began forming into smaller groups, drinking, smoking weed, bantering, and juggling soccer balls in the air with their feet.

To avoid bumping into any of the homies exiting the park, Santini and his partner quickly packed their gear and hurried away to their car. The agents were excited. There was an entire roll call of the gang, and the leader discussed organizational rules and discipline. If the listening device worked, they had recorded an entire meeting of around thirty members of 20th Street discussing issues that met several criteria of a racketeering case. Santini suggested to his partner John that they call it a night and go drink the beers that had been chilling in the cooler.

CHAPTER 9

Hell in Honduras

THE RUNWAY AT TONCONTÍN AIRPORT IN TEGUCIGALPA, HONDURAS, basically amounted to an oversized driveway crammed into the middle of a narrow valley, surrounded closely on all sides by jagged mountain outcrops. During final approach, pilots had to carefully thread their planes through the rocky mountain peaks before executing an abrupt, hairpin turn just prior to touching down.

With a death grip on his seat's armrest, Santini peeked nervously out the window and watched as the airliner's wings seemed to soar just inches over the rooftops and TV antennas atop ragged houses along the hillsides surrounding the city. His stomach churned and he worried he might vomit.

After what felt like an eternity, the plane finally kissed the ground and rolled to a stop at the terminal. Santini grabbed his bag and headed through the concourse, straight for the Honduran immigration office. There he spotted a short, heavyset man accompanied by another, thinner man.

Although the huskier one looked slightly disheveled, with a scruffy beard and messy hair, Santini guessed they were both law enforcement officers from the way they dressed—Merrell shoes and 511 brand cargo pants—standard street apparel for plainclothes cops across much of the globe. The two in fact were Honduras-based HSI special agents Oscar Tapia and Alvin Ortega, who were waiting to greet him. HSI had agents posted worldwide in sixty-seven countries to facilitate international investigations for the agency.

"You guys fly out of here often?" Santini asked, after the three men shook hands. "Seems like a suicide mission just getting on and off the ground."

"You get used to it," Tapia said, grinning.

From the airport, the three agents sped off together in an unmarked car through the streets of Tegucigalpa.

Watching the city roll by, Santini was struck by the fact that almost every small retail business seemed to have security guards posted out front, armed with shotguns. It was evident that street crime was pervasive in Honduras, known unofficially as The Murder Capital of the World. The business owners here were taking lots of precautions to protect their properties.

The brutal civil war just across the border in El Salvador had ended more than ten years ago in 1992, with an estimated seventy-five thousand people killed, prompting a pullout by the US military from Honduras. But living conditions in the region still had not improved. Over a million people were displaced by the conflict, and many of them headed north across Mexico and into the United States to escape. In both El Salvador and Honduras, the governments were both still controlled by repressive militaries, and the lines between military and police—and between police and criminals—were blurry at best.

In addition to conducting a due diligence investigation on Diego, the purpose of Santini's trip and his meeting with the special prosecutor and head of Honduran National Police was largely diplomatic. Since Honduran law enforcement personnel seemed to like to rub shoulders with their American counterparts, Santini's higher-ups hoped his schmoozing would pay off with full cooperation from the HNP gang unit. HSI wanted a workable ongoing relationship, not just for his investigation of 20th Street in San Francisco, but also for future cases involving other Central American gangs operating throughout the United States.

After a brief courtesy visit with HNP's special prosecutor of the Organized Crime Prosecutions Unit, as well as with the head of the HNP's National Criminal Investigation Directorate (DNIC), Santini and his two escorts headed for DNIC's main precinct in Tegucigalpa. Here they met with Inspector Diego Mendoza, a nationally recognized expert on street gangs in Honduras. If anyone could shed light on the background and criminal history of Santini's informant Diego, it would be Mendoza and his team of gang officers.

Mendoza was young and personable. However, Santini knew that despite his age, he was a seasoned officer. He spoke of gangs and gang violence in almost scientific terms, with a solid background in criminal justice theory. After a brief history of gang proliferation in Honduras, as well as the current state of affairs, Mendoza introduced Santini to about eight other detectives who worked in the gang-infested barrios of Tegucigalpa.

All of them were in their early to mid twenties. They looked to Santini like a bunch of ragtag cops wearing old, unholstered handguns tucked into their waistbands, extra ammo magazines stuffed into their back pockets, and handcuffs hanging from their belts. Despite their hand-me-down gear, they looked to be genuinely hardened by the real dangers that they faced on the streets every day.

With long hair tied in a ponytail and just a few whiskers on his face that made him look like he just reached puberty, Inspector Mateo Salcedo was a twenty-seven-year-old officer with about five years of police experience. He invited Santini to sit with him at a table in the station room, where he shared a file on Diego prepared in the weeks prior to Santini's visit.

The report contained just a few pages of basic bio information, none of it revealing anything Santini didn't already know. It did at least confirm what Diego had told Santini about his past. Many of the important details Diego had relayed were verified, including where he lived and grew up, his family lineage, as well as the tragic deaths of his father, brother, and sister. This was a relief to Santini, since it gave Diego more credibility as a potential informant and future prosecution witness.

"How well are you able to develop good sources of intel on the gangs here in Honduras?" Santini asked Salcedo.

"It is very difficult," the local cop said, "because of the risks involved, for both our officers and the informants."

The most valuable tools for gang cops in Honduras, he told Santini with a bitter laugh, were their balaclavas, or concealment masks, which were used to cover their faces during field operations. The gang cops often lived near the same neighborhoods they policed and deadly retribution was almost certain if they were identified. Even worse, the level of police corruption here was such that police officers had to be just as wary of their fellow cops as they were of the thugs. One could never be certain about who within their ranks might be taking bribes and passing intelligence to the gangs.

"One good thing," Salcedo confided. "We do have a new informant."

He told Santini that his unit had begun grooming a promising young source just in the past week. The girlfriend of a gang leader in the Colonia 3 de Mayo neighborhood of Tegucigalpa, she had agreed to cooperate with HNP after seeing one of her friends murdered by the gang. The experience had scared her straight and she wanted out of the life.

"She's nineteen years old, and muy bonita," Castro Ramos said.

In 2000, MS-13 began solidifying its hierarchy in Honduran prisons as a result of the efforts of high-ranking gang members in its US-based cliques. According to Diego, while he was in prison at La Granja (The Farm) a gang member named Power visited senior MS-13 members behind bars on four separate occasions to disseminate forty new rules for the gang, almost all of which carried a death penalty for disobedience.

MS-13 was becoming increasingly violent toward even its own members during this time, and many individuals were green-lighted for murder by the Big Homies. In La Granja, Diego witnessed numerous killings, including the decapitation and mutilation of an MS-13 member during a gang meeting. He was next on deck to be killed that day in similar fashion, but was saved at the last minute by a high-ranking gang member who stepped in and declared him to be "clean."

In May 2003, toward the end of Diego's incarceration at La Granja, after a weapons search of the facility conducted by police with the help of inmate trustees turned up various makeshift killing devices, the gang members were confined to their cells as punishment. Two days later, a leader of the gang and some of his homies confronted a nongang-member inmate whom they blamed for tipping off guards about their hidden weapons. A fight broke out and a trustee was killed.[1]

That's where the official story diverged dramatically from what some of the gang members who survived the ensuing massacre reported happening. According to statements made to a local newspaper by an 18th Street gang member who was present for the battle, he was standing on the prison's basketball court when the fight broke out. He heard gunshots coming from a nearby cell used by the trustees as an unofficial office. The police stormed in with automatic weapons, and the gang members retreated to their cells, leaving the dead prisoner's body and another badly injured inmate lying on the prison yard. It was then, the 18th Street member said, that police began to shoot at gang members who were holed up in their cells, hitting him with a bullet that broke his arm. With the help of some trustees, the police then started a raging fire, trapping forty prisoners in a cell and engulfing them in flames.

When it was all over, sixty-nine gang members lay dead and another thirty-nine were seriously injured. Burnt corpses and legs, arms, and teeth of dismembered bodies were strewn across the prison grounds. One police officer was injured.

Within hours of the massacre, Ricardo Maduro, then president of Honduras, arrived at the prison to survey the ghastly scene. Maduro's own son had been kidnapped and murdered by MS-13 members four years earlier, giving him a plausible motive for revenge. Standing among the dead and wounded, the president promised there would be a full investigation of what happened at the prison that day. Families of the dead prisoners who thought they might get some honest, official accounting of what occurred during the prison slaughter were still waiting for it fifteen years later.

It was this horrendous environment that piqued Santini's interest in taking a prison tour while setting up his itinerary for the trip. The day after his meeting with the DNIC, Santini was met by Anthony Breslin, the State Department's International Narcotics Affairs and Law Enforcement (INL) program liaison. INL funneled money into policing projects in countries suffering from rampant corruption. Breslin had been a great resource for Santini by telephone leading up to his trip, assisting HSI to grease the skids with Honduran officials prior to the agent's arrival.

It was a thirty-four-mile drive north up the Carretera del Norte freeway through the mountains to the National Penitentiary located in Tamara, Honduras. They drove through La Colonia Maria Jose, alleged to be one of the most crime-ridden areas outside the capital. Along the way, they passed the Santa Cruz memorial, a roadside cemetery centered around a large sandstone statue of the savior bearing his cross.

From a distance, the prison appeared as a campus of administrative buildings surrounded by a white stone wall. Santini was led by prison officials through a twenty-foot-high iron gate into the yard at the Marco Soto ward. The wall's interior was painted with three large skulls. The one on the left had two skeleton hands covering its ears, the middle one covering its eyes, and the third covering its mouth. Underneath the skulls, an inscription read, "*No oigo, no miro, no hablo,*" or "I do not hear, I do not see, I do not speak," an apparent warning to all who entered the yard that gang rules applied here. It was the mantra of the Mara 18 gang housed at the Marco Soto cell block.

There was no place in the yard for a rat.

Mara 18 or "18th Street" was the arch-nemesis of MS-13 in Honduras and all Central America. Although Santini had spent the morning driving with his hosts from INL with the intent of touring the MS-13 wing of the prison, the warden had a different plan. He considered the current state of the MS-13 housing section too decrepit and dangerous for an American visitor to walk through. Instead, they were given a bird's-eye view of 18th Street's section in a newer, safer wing of the prison.

In sharp contrast to US prisons, which were generally painted in amateurish graffiti, the Marco Soto facility was covered wall-to-wall with gang murals that looked as if they were painted by a team of accomplished artists. As the American visitors worked their way through the yard and into the depths of the holding cells, it seemed every wall in the facility had been touched by the gang's brushes. Every corner and crevice seemed to have graffiti with every letter style, marking, and symbol.

Santini stood in front of the tractor-trailer-sized painting of a graveyard depicting seven tombstones with the inscription, "For My Homies," written above in cursive. Each tombstone was covered with a long list of dead gang members' names. It became blatantly obvious to Santini that the mareros ran the Tamara prison. If the graffiti didn't tell the story, the slipshod security—even the timid looks on the guards' faces—said it all. This was a prison run by gangs, with a corrections force of puppets who did what they were told.

———

When Mendoza picked up Santini the next day to take him to the airport for his return flight to San Francisco, he handed the HSI agent the morning edition of the local *El Diario* newspaper.

Santini glanced at a photo on the front page that showed a large cardboard box deposited the night before in the plaza of La Esperanza. This was the same neighborhood where Salcedo's new informant lived, the beautiful young gang member he mentioned to Santini during his visit a couple days before at the HNP office.

As Santini struggled to read the *El Diario* article with his limited knowledge of Spanish, Mendoza explained the cardboard box was discovered to contain the mutilated body of a young woman who had been brutally tortured. Salcedo's pretty new informant, the one who wanted out of gang life, had been ratted out—likely by an insider at DNIC—and murdered by gang thugs. Her breasts and nose were cut off and numerous gang insignia had been carved into her flesh.

A note scribbled in black marker and taped to the top of the box, read, "*No oigo, no miro, no hablo.*"

Chapter 10

Casper Turns Ratta

"ARE YOU FUCKING KIDDING ME?" SANTINI, BACK IN SAN FRANCISCO, yelled at his supervisor. "The leader of the gang? Really? I have to tell him he's in danger?! How the fuck are we supposed to investigate these knuckleheads if we have to notify them every time they are in danger? They are always in fucking danger! They're gang members, for Christ's sake!"

Santini had received word from Diego that Tigre might be greenlighted for murder by the gang's leaders in El Salvador. The revelation triggered a newly issued agency requirement to notify the alleged target that he was in potential danger. Of course, doing so would alert Tigre that the police were privy to inside gang secrets, which could spook him and undermine Santini's investigation. Despite the agent's misgivings, however, he needed to comply with the policy and get word to Tigre that law enforcement considered him the possible target of a hit.

Santini reached out to SFPD Lieutenant Jim Sawyer, who suggested that the local police leave a note on Tigre's car windshield warning him. But Santini's supervisor demanded there be documented verification the message was received. Sawyer sent an SFPD patrol officer to locate the gang leader and give him the message in person. The patrolman could only find Tigre's wife, so he asked her to tell Tigre to contact Sawyer about a matter of life and death as soon as he got home.

Late in the evening, Sawyer received a call from Tigre, who was obviously perplexed by the tip and suspicious where it had come from. Sawyer told him that "word on the street" was he had been green-lighted for death by the gang. Sawyer invited Tigre to meet with him at the

SFPD's Mission District station to discuss the situation, but Tigre predictably declined.

The bad news, Santini thought, was that Tigre would certainly be suspicious about how the information had been discovered by SFPD. The good news was he probably had no idea where the tip came from.

Driving an unmarked car, Santini spotted Diego standing on a corner in the Castro District. It was a safe place for the two to connect without being spotted by any gang members, who strictly avoided setting foot in the predominately gay neighborhood. The agent pulled the car next to Diego, who quickly hopped into the backseat and leaned way down so no one could see his face through the car windows.

Santini drove away and headed toward the upscale neighborhood of Telegraph Hill, where he could debrief his informant. Driving up Stockton Street through Chinatown, Santini checked Diego in the rearview mirror. He looked more tired and sullen than usual. The agent had been running him hard, pushing him to spend long hours working the street digging for as much dirt as possible from as many gang sources as possible.

They drove up Castle Street, turned down a quiet side road, and parked next to the curb a block away from Coit Tower, overlooking the mouth of the bay.

"So," Santini said, turning around and leaning over the front seat, "que pasa?"

"There have been two clica meetings," Diego said. "At one, they jumped on Tigre."

"Who did?" Santini said.

"Peloncito and a few others," Diego said. "Twenty seconds. They kicked the shit out of him."

"Okay," Santini said. "What else you got for me, homie?"

"Spanky says he and Droops made some hits on Norteños, with guns and clubs."

"Where?" Santini said.

"One on Geneva Street," Diego said.

"Okay," Santini said. "Where else?"

"I don't remember any other names," Diego said.

"You don't remember? C'mon, man!" Santini said. "Think!"

Diego struggled for a moment to remember the other street names where Spanky had mentioned making hits on Norteños, but it was no use. He shook his head. He was new to San Francisco himself, and still learning the lay of the land. Keeping track of all the place names was still an extra challenge for the Honduran, who spoke only rudimentary English.

"Okay, what else?" Santini said.

"Casper led the last meeting. The homies were asking him where Tigre was and if the Big Homies put a green light on him."

"And?" Santini said.

"Casper said he didn't know about it," Diego said.

"What else?" Santini said.

"Popeye said he knows about twenty guys in South San Francisco who want to jump into 20th. Casper said they would jump in some of them soon."

Diego gazed out the window at the bay and Santini observed his tired profile. He was a tough dude, but the grind and tension of his rat role inside the gang, while holding down a job as a dishwasher, was definitely wearing him down. His shoulders were slumped and fatigue lines creased around the corner of his eyes. He looked as if he could fall asleep any minute right there in the backseat of the car.

"You okay, man?" Santini said.

Diego turned to face him. "Everything costs so much here," he said.

"Whadya mean?" Santini said. "What does?"

"Everything," Diego said, his voice rising in pitch. "Diapers, food, clothes . . . all the things for a baby. I cannot afford to pay for it all."

This was not a condition that Santini liked to see his informant in. He needed Diego thinking clearly, with his mental faculties sharp. The work was too dangerous if he was emotionally frayed.

The two men were about the same age, but their lives were very different. When they went separate ways after their regular clandestine meetings, one went to a nice office or furnished apartment, maybe a good meal with a date or some friends at one of the city's innumerable fine eateries. The other man went to work in a kitchen, scraping plates, loading dishwasher racks, and scrubbing pans, then home to a young wife and an infant who relied on him to put food on the table. Then back out to hang with the homies late into the night, playing the chess game of survival on the streets, while gathering and recording useful information that would keep his control agent, Santini, satisfied.

"The other homies have nice cars, nice clothes," Diego said. "They are making good money with the drugs and stealing cars. I have this!" He pinched the front of his shirt, a stained and threadbare polo his wife bought at Goodwill, and looked away in disgust.

Santini thought about his own dresser and closet at home full of practically brand-new clothes, things he'd worn only once or twice. The two men were, coincidentally, about the same size. He resolved to throw some clothes in a bag and give them to Diego the next time they met.

"Listen, man," Santini said. "Hang in there. We'll get you taken care of. Just be cool, okay? I know things will get easier for you."

Diego looked skeptical.

"You alright?" Santini said. "You with me?"

"Sí," Diego said.

But the agent wasn't convinced. "I'll call you tomorrow," he said. "I need you to stick with it."

"Sí," Diego repeated in the same detached voice.

They drove back to the Castro District with the informant slumped down in the backseat, just the top of his head visible at street level through the side window.

Santini pulled over near the BART station at Mission and 16th, and Diego hopped out. On the sidewalk, he instinctively darted glances over both shoulders, before blending back into the crowd and heading for the escalator down to the subway.

With an uneasy feeling, the agent watched his informant 1301 vanish into the hustle and bustle of San Francisco. He wondered how long Diego, now several months into his undercover role, would be able to effectively maintain his balance. Signs he was starting to crack had begun to emerge, but for the sake of his investigation Santini was unwilling to accept Diego had reached anywhere near the end of his usefulness. Too much was riding on the Honduran's ability to continue acting as a rat burrowed deep inside 20th Street.

—⁓—

While questions remained for Santini about Diego's ability to continue enduring the stress of life as an MS-13 rat, the informant continued proving himself a valuable tool for his controller. When Santini called, Diego answered. He showed up for regular clandestine meetings where Santini could grill him about the latest developments within 20th Street. As long as Diego produced, Santini was content to keep pushing him as hard as he could.

The general pace of violence for 20th Street was continuing unabated when Diego received a panicky call from Spanky, obviously in a major rush. He told Diego he needed a place immediately for "Flaco's nine-year-old girl to stay for a few days."

Diego knew right away that Spanky wasn't talking about a young girl needing refuge. He was referring to a nine-millimeter handgun belonging to Flaco, which had probably just been used in a shooting. It was another opportunity for Diego to snag a gang gun off the streets, which he knew would please Santini. Besides, it wouldn't look good for Diego with the gang members if he denied a favor to a homie in an emergency.

Diego agreed on the phone to help Spanky take care of the problem. A half hour later, Spanky knocked on his door. "Here, homie," he said, and tossed Diego a small bag. "I'll pick this up in a few days."

Diego understood what was going down. Spanky was rushing home to shower and clean any gun-shot residue or tiny unseen blood splatters containing DNA evidence off his body and clothes. If he had to guess, Diego figured that Spanky—or maybe Flaco—had just blasted somebody up close with the gun.

As soon as Spanky hurried away, Diego called one of Santini's partners to tell him about the situation and the agent immediately called Santini to pass the word. Santini wanted the gun, which might prove to be conviction-worthy evidence of one or more serious crimes committed by the gang. The problem was how to get custody of it without blowing Diego's cover.

Santini turned to Cabrera for ideas. Together they devised a ruse to take possession of the gun while providing a plausible excuse for Diego. They agreed to stage a fake fire alarm in the apartment next door to where Diego lived with his wife and baby. This would give SFPD justification to enter their unit and search the home, ostensibly to check if the fire was spreading through the building's walls. In the process, the cops would "discover" Flaco's gun.

The next morning, right before the fake fire alarm was triggered, Diego met with a few of the younger homies at the park. When Santini sent him the signal in a text message, Diego invited the homies to tag along with him on foot back to his apartment. A fire truck and three SFPD patrol cars were already parked outside with their lights flashing. For the benefit of the young homies accompanying him, Diego acted shocked and panicky to see the police cars. He led them at a fast pace back to Mission Street, where he pretended to call his wife, Ana, speaking in a voice loud enough for the homies to hear.

"Que paso, amore?! A fire?!" he said. "Are they inside our unit? Si? Oh, fuck. . . ."

He ended the bogus call and told the homies about the fire. Diego told them the cops had entered his apartment to check for signs that the fire might be spreading, and that they had discovered Flaco's gun.

"God, I hope Ana isn't arrested with the baby!" Diego told the homies.

For the rest of the day, he delivered a sustained, Oscar-winning performance, playing the freaked-out husband, father, and gang member who just had a hot gun seized from his apartment by the cops. The young homies bought his act, and Diego knew they would relay his concocted cover story back to the rest of the clique. Essentially, they would serve as alibi witnesses for him with anyone who might question how the gang's gun had been seized.

Earlier that same morning, before the staged scene played out, Santini and his partner took custody of the gun from Diego. It was a black, nine-millimeter semiautomatic pistol with a clip containing four rounds. The barrel was dirty, indicating it had been fired recently.

A day after seizing the gun, Santini received a phone call from a rookie FBI agent in San Francisco who was working on the Bureau's team focusing on gangs in the city. To Santini's amazement, the new FBI agent began yelling at him over the phone for not informing the Bureau ahead of time about the operation to seize Flaco's gun.

"We are to be included in any such future enforcement actions on the street!" the FBI agent yelled through the phone. "You got that?!"

Santini was dumbstruck by the young agent's gall. He knew the guy only had a few months' experience on the job. Yet, here he had the temerity to take a condescending, authoritative tone with Santini about an operation involving Diego, his informant, to get a gang gun off the streets.

"If you ever talk to me like that again . . ." Santini started to yell back. Then he checked himself. "This is an HSI led investigation!" he said. "The Bureau has to play by our rules! You got that?!" With that, he slammed down the phone, thoroughly pissed.

In a weird way, it felt encouraging to Santini that the FBI was so keenly interested in every step of his investigation's progress. They were obviously falling over themselves and tapping their connections with SFPD to keep extremely close track of his investigation—eager to horn in on his work and grab any glory, he suspected.

In any case, with his primary informant showing signs of mission fatigue, Santini knew his investigation was in danger of a potentially game-killing setback. The agent knew there was no guarantee Diego would continue coming through for him. He needed new sources inside the gang, but who?

—◦—

Seated at an interview table in jail, Edwin Zavala, aka Casper, appeared anxious to Santini, like a man who might be ready to crack. He rambled disconnectedly through his life story, as if he were high on weed, which Santini suspected he actually was.

He said he came to the United States when he was fourteen years old. Upon arrival, he scored too well on an English test to go to "newcomers" school for recently arrived immigrants in San Francisco. Instead, he went straight to Mission High, where he immediately encountered Norteños, who quickly categorized him as MS-13 because he had an El Salvador flag patch on his backpack.

Casper's brother Freddy Zavala, aka Snoopy, now a Big Homie, joined the clique first. Casper and Snoopy passed the Mission Playground daily on the way home from school, and Snoopy was impressed by the crew. He said the homies looked tough and that no one would fuck with him if he had that group on his side. Casper attempted to steer clear of the gang until about four months after Snoopy joined. With regular contact with MS-13 members playing soccer at the little park, it was a foregone conclusion that he would soon be jumped in.

Casper told Santini he began running with the crew and doing work with them. He remembered slamming a boombox into the heads of some *paisas* drinking in the area of the Cinco de Mayo parade in the city. He maintained a relatively low profile in the gang until his brother Snoopy was deported and put in prison in El Salvador. Then Snoopy pushed the gang to respect Casper as his representative and a senior member.

Now, busted for illegal possession of a 9 mm,[1] Casper knew he was up against the wall, facing deportation back to El Salvador. He didn't want to go. He had spent his entire adolescence in San Francisco and become well Americanized. He liked the quality of life here and had started a family, even though it had broken up. If Casper was sent back to a ghetto in El Salvador, he feared he might never see his young daughter again.

"Look, you have a real opportunity here to get out of the life," Santini told Casper.

Here came the pitch. Santini had made it numerous times by now.

In one hand, he held ICE's big hammer—the threat of deportation. In the other hand, he held out the carrots of government money and protection from gang retribution, including the possibility of entering the witness protection program and creating an entirely new identity and life in America.

"Hey, you said yourself that you want a better life for your baby, right?" Santini said.

"You don't know La Mara," Casper said. "They can find you anytime, anywhere. They are that strong."

"Look, homie, there's always risk," Santini said. "But with risk comes reward. I can't sit here and promise this will end well, but I can tell you that the government will do its best to protect you. It might be a long, hard road, but imagine when it's all over, years from now. You're alive, you're free of the life, and you're protected."

The pitch seemed to be working its magic. Casper seemed enchanted by the idea of a future life free from the gang and constantly looking over his shoulder. But deciding to cooperate also meant betraying the gang that had been like a family to him since he was practically a kid. It included his own brother and Tigre, who had taken Casper under his wing after Snoopy left San Francisco.

"One day, you and me will sit and have a plate of carne asada together," Santini said, laying it on thick. "We'll sit and think back on this day. It will be in the past. And once you've paid your dues for the bad that you've done, you'll be free, homie. Free of the life and free to be a normal dad and husband. You can do this, homie. I can see it in you!"

Casper thought about it.

"Okay, let's give it a shot," he said.

Santini could barely believe what he was hearing, that Casper was flipping so easily. It seemed that the threat of deportation was a heavier hammer than the threat of time in the state can. A homie would rather marinate in a local jail for several months than be shipped back to El Salvador to face the police, vigilante militias, or rival gangs.

If Casper stuck to his decision to sign on with Santini's investigation—one that he had arrived at in a matter of just half an hour or so—the undercover operation would now have its existing, productive informant in the middle rungs of the gang, Diego, and another one in a more senior position. Developing Casper as a quality source could go a long way in nailing Tigre, as well as maybe even some of the Big Homies in El Salvador, Santini hoped. This was potentially a big breakthrough for the Devil Horns investigation.

Within days of Casper agreeing to cooperate, the local FBI team investigating MS-13 learned about it. They immediately approached Santini and requested HSI turn Casper over to them to control as an informant. At first, Santini thought he should comply with the FBI's request as a token of professional cooperation. But his supervisor at HSI quickly quashed that idea.

"Hell no!" was his supervisor's response.

Santini was relieved. Finally, someone in HSI management was pushing back against the Bureau's poaching of pre-vetted informants, all wrapped up with a bow and ready to sing. SFPD had turned over Dreamer to the FBI, but Casper, a far-better-positioned member of 20th Street, with direct ties to the Big Homies, would remain under Santini's control. He knew this particular interagency battle was won, but the constant war to claim glory for Operation Devil Horns was far from over.

CHAPTER 11

Making the Case in D.C.

BY THE MIDDLE OF 2006, NEARLY TWO YEARS AFTER SANTINI STARTED his investigation of MS-13's 20th Street clique, the violent crime situation in San Francisco had reached a crisis point. The murder and assault rates in the city had only worsened since Newsom took the reins as mayor in 2004. His administration was hard put to maintain the fiction that SFPD, under the command of Police Chief Heather Fong, was doing an effective job keeping the city streets safe.

While the city's homicide rate was climbing, the number of murder arrests in San Francisco was steadily dropping, according to statistics compiled by the mayor's own Office of Criminal Justice. In 2004, there were forty-three arrests made in homicide cases, and in 2005, there were thirty-four. Kamala Harris, then the city's district attorney, was openly accused by some law enforcement veterans of cherry-picking cases for prosecution. In this way, she could boast a higher conviction rate and beef up her résumé as she prepared to seek higher office, they claimed.[1]

A special hearing to address the dysfunctional situation at SFPD was convened that summer by the International Institute of Criminal Justice (ISCJ), an affiliate of University of San Francisco. The conference brought together a star-studded panel of law enforcement experts including former US attorney for Northern California Joe Russoniello, two former SFPD police captains, and a former head of the local FBI office for Northern California, among others. The public testimony of expert witnesses at the hearing included accusations that "clear-cut police leadership no longer exists in San Francisco. . . . Those who shape the San

Francisco Police Department stalemate each other with open contempt, or wait for consensus from those who don't find it."[2]

Newsom's track record as the police chief's boss came under direct fire during the hearing. "The mayor fails leadership by announcing consensus efforts that don't coalesce, the Police Commission is driven by politics, the Office of Citizens Complaints (OCC) solicits complaints outside its authority, and the Police Department stymies the investigation of police officers. . . . Meanwhile, homicide rates continue to climb as . . . officers cut proactive arrests by 30% for fear of their own prosecution, and 40% of San Franciscans are afraid of the streets."[3]

Amid all the public turmoil surrounding the SFPD, one member of the police commission named Theresa Sparks chose to resign her position, citing the city government's overall ineffective management of the police department as the cause of her departure. Sparks, who served as CEO of a Mission District–based, sex-toy manufacturer called Good Vibrations, was appointed to the commission in 2004 by board of supervisor member Tom Ammiano, a political nemesis of Newsom. Sparks publicly described the SFPD as beset by "leadership failure, communication breakdown, low morale, politics, and mistrust." She told a reporter with the *San Francisco Chronicle* that the absence of leadership at SFPD was occurring when "homicides have continued to reach new highs, staffing levels have plummeted and morale is approaching a new low in the department."[4]

Meanwhile, Fong, the chief of SFPD, a Chinese American who wore big round, wire-rim glasses, continued to keep her public profile low—nearly invisible—in the midst of all the controversy. Known as "Feather" to her critics inside SFPD, Fong was arguably completely lacking in command presence to be the police chief of a major city. She was also unusually bad at public relations on the rare occasions she tried her hand at it. The police department was clearly lacking charisma at the top, not to mention an allegedly egregious lack of effective political leadership that ran all the way up the city government's chain of command to the mayor's office.

Such was the political situation at SFPD and City Hall when Santini boarded a plane at San Francisco International Airport, bound for

Washington to request additional funds for the Devil Horns investigation from HSI headquarters. His goal was to set up an undercover stolen car–fencing operation to nail members of 20th Street who specialized in auto theft.

The bosses at HSI headquarters agreed to pay for Santini to fly to D.C. to make his pitch for funds. To succeed, he needed to persuade about twenty senior managers at the agency, as well as a group of attorneys from DOJ headquarters. The special agent had tried for many months to raise interest with the local US Attorney's Office for an officially recognized RICO case against 20th Street, which would provide him more resources. But they had continually stonewalled him.

During his presentation to HSI's Special Operations Division, Santini painted a picture of relentless violence perpetrated by 20th Street gangbangers in San Francisco. He described their leadership structure and the gang's penchant for stealing cars and using them to commit assaults and murders. He gave a rundown of the unsolved homicides and aggravated assaults in and around the Mission. He showed them photos of the sullen mugs of 20th Street members, their torsos stripped to reveal gaudy, satanic tattoos. And that was all it took. Operation Devil Horns was approved as the first HQ-funded gang-related operation in agency history.

Santini had effectively proven that HSI's unique enforcement capability, with a blend of immigration and federal criminal authorities, was the perfect set of tools to confront street gangs from south of the border. The coffers were now open and Santini would potentially have access to hundreds of thousands of dollars of HQ funds to work the 20th Street investigation.

The following day, Santini and a few of the HSI HQ managers hiked the long walk across the mall to DOJ headquarters to tackle the second task of the D.C. trip. The agent would now have to meet with the chief of the Criminal Division and the lead prosecutor for gang RICO cases at DOJ. Since Santini wasn't getting any traction from the local US Attorney's Office, HSI HQ leadership decided he should skip a rung on the ladder and talk to the DOJ bosses. It was risky in that if DOJ declined to assist at the HQ level, any federal prosecutions related to the Devil Horns investigation would be effectively blacklisted back in San Francisco. Santini had to take the chance to reach his goal for a RICO case.

Wearing the same new suit as the day before, he delivered a mirror-image presentation of the one he did the day prior with HSI HQ. He made a pitch to the DOJ folks that HSI was an agency that could handle a RICO case. DOJ seemed reluctant and immediately began to question why the FBI was not more involved in the case. They rightfully indicated that the FBI had a long, proven history of pursuing successful RICO cases, whereas HSI had none. Although impressed with the evidence gathered to date by Santini and his team, they weren't convinced that the agent and his counterparts at HSI could succeed without the behemoth of resources and personnel the FBI could easily bring to bear. Santini and his HQ counterparts respectfully disagreed and left the meeting without a definitive answer. DOJ indicated they would need a week or so to mull over the case's potential before making a final decision.

Less than a week later, while Santini was prepping an operation plan for some surveillance on an upcoming gang meeting, he received the call from DOJ. It was done. DOJ agreed to prosecute 20th Street for RICO with HSI as the lead agency. They would immediately assign a full-time prosecutor from D.C. to travel biweekly to San Francisco to oversee the case.

Santini's initial goal was now a distinctively real possibility. This was the kind of investigation that could make a special agent's career. He had effectively gone over the heads of the US Attorney's Office in San Francisco. But screw it, he thought. He had beaten his head against the wall for months trying to get them on board. If they didn't have the balls to go after the gang, that was their problem. The political chips would fall where they may. The local federal prosecutors in San Francisco would have to play nice with his RICO investigation now, even if they hated his guts for going straight to their top management. Now it was up to Santini and his HSI colleagues to get enough evidence to make charges stick against 20th Street in federal court.

CHAPTER 12

Cyco and Peloncito on the Rise

To MAINTAIN AUTHORITY OVER THE CLIQUE, IT WAS IMPORTANT FOR ITS leader to show up on the street on a regular basis. But after a couple years in charge, Tigre was increasingly living his version of the American Dream. A legal resident, he had a growing family and a steady job. Meanwhile, most of the 20th Street homies were posting up in the Mission and maintaining the clique's claim on their turf, getting their hands dirty with "work."

When Tigre made his first attempts to herd the clique back into line at the meeting in Sutro Park, immediately after Memo's murder, his list of rules for the gang demanded nonaggression toward other Sureño gangs in the city, including the 11th Street Sureños. These gangs had a natural right to earn a living in the "barrio" the same as the 20th Street clique did, Tigre insisted, and they should be left alone to do it.

In Tigre's increasing absence on the street, Cyco and Peloncito assumed more control over the clique, especially the newer, younger recruits. The "new booties" in the gang did not maintain much allegiance to Tigre. Cyco and Peloncito meanwhile were grabbing the reins of power and launching a violent campaign to assert the gang's dominance over its rivals, including the other Sureño gangs that Tigre insisted should be left alone.

When a junior member of 20th Street informed Cyco that a friend of his, a member of the 11th Street Sureños, was bragging about how much money they were making from selling crack in the Tenderloin District, Cyco was enraged. The fact they weren't paying 20th Street a cut was a serious case of disrespect, as far as he was concerned. The only way to remedy the situation for Cyco and his favorite henchman, Peloncito, was the MS-13 way—to send a message sealed in blood.

Late one evening a crew of around ten 20th Street soldiers led by Peloncito attacked three 11th Street Sureños outside the Civic Center BART station. Peloncito brandished a large kitchen knife during the brawl but kept himself composed enough not to cut up any of the Sureños, while his crew brutally battered the three 11th Street members into half consciousness.

"Pay the fucking tax, *chingado!*" Peloncito shouted.

He leaned over one of the badly beaten Sureños and grabbed his collar, pulling his face within an inch of his own. He spit and heaved a heavy breath into the teenager's face, brandishing the knife near his throat.

"The next time, someone gets chopped up!" Peloncito said.

The 20th Street soldiers ripped through the Sureños' pockets, taking their drugs and cash, leaving them dazed and bleeding.

The following day, as some of the 20th Street clique were playing soccer in Mission Playground, two leaders of the 11th Street Sureños marched into the park. They confronted Cyco and demanded to speak with Tigre. Knowing they were there to complain about the attack on their homies the night before, Cyco told them that Tigre never came to the hood anymore. The pair of Sureños left the park, rebuffed.

Cyco and Peloncito now expected some retaliation from 11th Street. They were intentionally opening 20th Street's war on multiple fronts. After an extended period of truce under Tigre's more moderate leadership, it wasn't just the Norteños that the clique was attacking. With a force of around one hundred thirty members by now, 20th Street was moving against the 11th Street Sureños, as well as setting their sights on the Miceros. The Miceros were also making bank with their reestablished fake ID business and selling drugs in the Mission. Now they were on Cyco's and Peloncito's list of rivals to be terrorized into compliance.

The deep fissure dividing the 20th Street clique between its old guard and new booties became apparent to Santini when he learned that Cyco and Peloncito called a gang meeting and invited only those newer members who were loyal to their emergent leadership. The "unsanctioned" meeting was held in Dolores Park a few blocks away from Mission Playground. Cyco and Peloncito jumped in a few new booties, and punished a few others with check-down beatings for minor indiscretions. Regular 20th Street business was conducted—an entire gang meeting from start to finish—with Cyco running the whole show.

After the meeting, the crew moved to the playground and were surprised to find Tigre there in the company of his wife and two daughters. Although Cyco, Peloncito, and Tigre spoke to one another, the vibe between them was tense. There was no mention of the meeting that just occurred. Cyco knew that the cagey older homie must have shown up just at that moment for a reason, and not just for a day in the park with his family. Someone must have tipped off Tigre.

Tigre now planned to call a meeting of the old homies to gauge how much support there was for him as the clique's leader. He was going to make it an all-hands gathering with both opposing factions of the gang to resolidify his leadership, or go down fighting. Tigre was determined to emerge from the big meet-up as the top dog, even though he was on the cusp of aging out. Letting go completely of an active role in the clique did not come easily after so many years. The old dog still had one last fight left in him.

It was an overcast but warm afternoon at the Polo Fields in Golden Gate Park. Despite its name, the big field was rarely, if ever, used for polo anymore. The manicured expanse of grass was split into six regulation-size soccer fields, each surrounded by a running track.

Tigre was anxious.

He wasn't sure if Cyco and his crew would show up strapping guns, but he knew a few of the old dogs present always packed heat in their waistbands for such occasions. These were the veteran homies who had been doing work on the streets of the Mission since before Peloncito and Cyco arrived in the States and earned their MS-13 stripes. They had mostly aged out of the gang by now, and it took Tigre some serious lobbying to convince them to show up.

"Cyco, Peloncito, and the youngsters are like the *marabunta*!" Tigre told the group of old dogs gathered on the benches as they waited together for the new booties to show up. "Predatory ants that are going in droves and migrating, devouring everything in their path. Like ants! You feel me? They don't respect their environment and they destroy everything with no regard for others. It has to stop now!"

After an hour and a half of waiting with no word from Cyco and his crew, Tigre was ready to postpone the meeting and let the senior mareros go home to enjoy Sunday evening with their families. He called the group together to discuss rescheduling. Just then, Cyco and Indio arrived in the parking lot, followed by a dozen young 20th Street members.

Tigre saw right away this would be the big showdown. He stood up near the bleachers with the crew of old dogs backing him up. Cyco strode right up in front of him and stood face-to-face with Tigre, with his contingent of new booties gathering around.

"So who's managing all these youngsters, Cyco?" Tigre demanded.

"Me and Peloncito are both leaders now," Cyco said.

The two stepped up closer to one another and raised their voices, started poking one another in the chest.

"Casper could be a boss, too, if he posted more on the street," Cyco said, pointing at Casper, who was standing right behind Tigre.

"I just had a new niño!" Casper yelled back.[1]

"Peloncito is selfish," Tigre yelled back at Cyco. "He uses membership dues to benefit himself, instead of the clica!"

Cyco insisted that one of the new booties was doing a good job acting as treasurer and that the gang dues were being used to purchase coke, which was sold on the streets to increase their treasury. He indicated they had recently used $250 extorted from the Miceros and leveraged the money to purchase cocaine for resale. Cyco insisted it was a good business strategy.

Tigre responded by criticizing Cyco for not using the clique's money to benefit fellow gang members' basic needs. He ridiculed Cyco as an amateur and declared that some of the clique's members were practically starving on the street, thanks to his incompetence and lack of wise leadership.

"This is bullshit!" Peloncito shouted. He announced to the group that he was officially stepping down as Cyco's co-leader.

"Who will be leader with me, then?" Cyco said. "Casper has thrown in the towel and barely represents the clique anymore!"

"We will decide who can comanage with Cyco before the next meeting!" Tigre shouted back. The heated confrontation continued. It was decided that no members would be excluded from doing "work" on the street anymore. Tigre demanded all the homies would be required to play spin-the-bottle to determine who would be assigned to do specific jobs.

At the conclusion of the meeting, it was clear the old dogs had emerged victorious. Cyco and his crew didn't have the requisite muscle or will to overcome Tigre and his crew of veteran mareros. Tigre had displayed a passion for MS-13 that most in the gang didn't realize he still possessed. Cyco knew he could not garner enough support as clique leader from the Big Homies—not yet, while Tigre stood in his way.

Pondering the fundamental conflict within the gang, Santini realized if the younger clique members eventually succeeded in grabbing power, it could mean a heightened level of violence on the city's streets. The old guard was bad enough, but Cyco and Peloncito represented a different breed that committed violence more randomly, sometimes seemingly for its own sake. Not only was the dangerous gang Santini began targeting a couple years earlier still functioning, it threatened to morph into something worse.

Before his initial release as an undercover informant, Casper was housed with other MS-13 members held in jail. He had briefed Santini that they told him 20th Street was forming into three groups, each with separate objectives. The three teams included the New Booties, who consisted of newly jumped-in recruits that were required to constantly post up the clique's turf at 20th and Mission Streets; the *gatilleros*, or gunslingers, who were charged with attacking rival gang members; and the Party Group, which concentrated on selling cocaine in the Mission District.

The New Booties didn't offer much opportunity for meaningful case building. Cyco and Peloncito were rising gatilleros, but it wasn't yet clear to Santini how to tactically gather what was needed to collect good case evidence around this group. Where he did see opportunity initially was in the Party Group.

From Casper, he learned through the gang's jailhouse grapevine that tensions over turf were flaring hotter between 20th Street and a sub-set of the Miceros gang known as the Distrito Federal (DF) gang, which was named after the capital city of Mexico where most of the Miceros originated. Now led by a Mexican version of a Big Homie named Patas, the DF controlled the fake ID business in the Mission and had started selling drugs on the street, too. That meant they were competing directly with 20th Street homies who were selling drugs on the same turf. With potential intergang conflict brewing, Santini figured it was time to focus some attention on the drug trade.

CHAPTER 13

The Cagey Coke King

IN THE LATE 1990S, THE MISSION HAD EXPERIENCED A WAVE OF URBAN pioneers flush with new money from the Nasdaq Index surge from around 1,000 points, up to nearly 5,000 by the time 2001 rolled around. Tech IPO deals were virtually spewing out of nearby Silicon Valley, and among the beneficiaries of the irrational exuberance were some of the more bohemian techies with lucrative stock options. The newly moneyed techies and weekend hipsters provided a good source of revenue for drug dealers, who offered just about any type of high that the partiers wanted—cocaine, ecstasy, meth—it was all on sale in the Mission.

On Valentine's Day, 2006, his first weekend on the street as official informant number 1312, Casper walked down Valencia Street, observing the couples all around him who were out on dates, holding hands and making out on the sidewalk. This quaint picture disappeared when he arrived in front of the Ritmo Latino record store, where Peloncito quickly brought him up to speed about the clique's new direction, to push hard on the Miceros and the 16th Street Sureños for more taxes.

He told Casper the rival gangs had begun relocating their drug-dealing operations to the Tenderloin, to keep out of the 20th Street gang's way. Peloncito also told him how he was ensuring that a healthy percentage of the clique's profits were being sent to the Big Homies in El Salvador and how it was done. First wiring the funds to the Banco El Salvador in the Mission, from there the money was withdrawn in El Salvador by a runner—a homie named Flash—and carried to the Quezalte Prison, where it was turned over to the Big Homies.[1]

Casper and Peloncito continued walking together to the Skylark Bar on 16th Street, where they met a group of 20th Street thugs, including Chachi. Compared to almost all his MS-13 homies, Chachi came from a relatively wealthy family. His mother had been married to the financially successful owner of a chain of self-serve laundries in the city. While previously a member of the 19th Street Sureños, he adopted the street name Mudo shortly before joining MS-13 when it was beginning to gain wide public notoriety as "the most dangerous gang in America."

Chachi was all about image and flash. He wore nice clothes and drove a sporty white Cadillac Escalade. His tattoos were the expensive type, not the do-it-yourself crude art most of the homies had inked onto their skin. And the other MS-13 homies mostly liked Chachi—not least of all because he regularly supplied them with free coke and weed.

Inside the long, narrow, dimly lit barroom of the Skylark, Casper watched Chachi handing off small bags of coke to paying customers in the dark corners of the club. It was as if Chachi owned the place. Whenever he and his sidekick Puppet wanted to snort a few lines themselves, they would take over the bathroom, assigning two or three gang members to stand guard outside the door while a line of drunk white kids waited to relieve their beer-filled bladders.

Fights involving gang members frequently erupted on the street outside the Skylark. Chachi and Cyco both had been arrested there—Chachi for stabbing a person on the premises and Cyco for hitting a female bystander in the head with a bottle. Outside the street entrance to the bar, several 20th Street members were constantly posted in case the Norteños attempted a surprise attack. If anybody—even a white kid who was obviously not a member of a rival gang—strolled into the bar wearing a red ball cap or shirt, he would be immediately "escorted" outside.

The Skylark wasn't the drug crew's only hangout, however. On Wednesday nights, Chachi, Puppet, and the rest of them frequented another nightclub in San Bruno called El Toro, where the air was filled with Latin hip-hop music and the smell of carne asada tacos. The club had a large disco ball in the center of the dance floor and separate bars on opposite sides of the room—one painted blue and the other red, as if they catered to both Norteño and Sureño customers.

In Casper's first few days on the street, he was providing solid eyewitness accounts of drug trafficking, but Santini had started to wonder if Casper was being too cooperative to be legit. After all, the informant had flipped with surprising ease—maybe he was actually playing Santini, somehow. Then Casper pulled off a very risky good deed, which eased the agent's concerns about his commitment to go straight.

A few days after observing Chachi's retail drug trade at the Skylark, Casper hitched a ride from the Mission to El Toro at around 11 p.m. and soon discovered that Peloncito had hatched a plan to kill Dreamer in the parking lot. Peloncito correctly believed that Dreamer was a rat, and he had convinced the other homies of it, too. They planned to tail Dreamer when he left the bar and shoot him in the back as he unlocked his car door.

While inside the bar, Casper watched Dreamer from across the room. The marked man was being shunned by the rest of the homies. He looked to Casper as if he was trying to play it cool, but he was scared. He clearly sensed something seriously bad was in the cards for him. With music blaring and club lights flashing on the dance floor, Casper asked Peloncito for a quick, one-on-one sidebar meeting to discuss the planned hit on Dreamer.

"What evidence do you have he's a ratta, homie?" Casper demanded.

"We don't need hard evidence!" Peloncito said. "Everyone knows he's a snitch!"

Peloncito's argument actually contradicted a generally accepted tenet of MS-13, which required there to be documented evidence of betrayal before a gang member could be "legally" green-lighted for death.

"That's not how La Mara works!" Casper said. "You must have hard evidence!"

"Many of the homies have seen him talking to Cabrera!" Peloncito said. "It's obvious he's a ratta!"

"Hey, Cabrera talks to all of us!" Casper said. "You can't get away from that motherfucker! He's everywhere! Are all of us rattas?! That ain't enough to green-light, homie! You better call off the hit for now, or there's going to be a price!"

Peloncito was livid, but he knew Casper was right. Some of the Big Homies down south would probably have serious issues with the execution of a gang member without hard evidence. He knew he had better wait to kill Dreamer. Peloncito agreed to back down and Casper felt an unusual sense of redemption stirring inside. If he had been just an hour later getting to El Toro, Dreamer could easily have been lying dead in the parking lot in a pool of his own blood.

As informant 1312, with a conceivable path out of gang life, Casper proved he could leverage his respected position in the clique to prevent a cold-blooded murder—at least for the time being.

Chachi was very careful about where and when he was holding any sizable amounts of drugs, so he often used Puppet as his main runner to keep any stash as distant from himself as possible. Charged with zipping around town, moving ounces of coke or baggies full of ecstasy pills, Puppet represented the key link between Chachi and a wide network of players that potentially could be leaned on to provide intel. Confident now with Casper's ability to collect useful evidence, Santini assigned him to target Puppet.

Casper began hanging out with Puppet, observing phone calls from small buyers—mostly tech hippies looking for a weekend head rush—his drop points, and how he concealed his stash. Using a water bottle with a secret compartment under the label, Puppet could be holding a half-ounce of cocaine, while at first glance the bottle looked full of water. Upon discovering how Puppet used another 20th Street homie to cut ounces into smaller, gram-size bags and sell them on the street in Daly City and the Tenderloin, Santini contacted a San Francisco–based DEA squad to implement a series of controlled purchases from Puppet. Early on, Casper reported that Puppet's girlfriend, named Judy, was also a dealer, specializing in crystal methamphetamine. Illicit meth sales warranted a steep federal penalty and Santini thought that if he could get Judy on the hook, he could leverage her to lean on Puppet. So he had

Casper arrange a buy one night in the parking lot of the Fiesta Laundry in the Mission.

Judy arrived in a red Toyota sedan driven by a young man. While they did the deal, undercover DEA agents recorded the transaction and the car's license plate, and after the Toyota drove off, the agents tailed the car back to a Daly City residence. When Santini ran the house and the Toyota, the driver had a criminal history involving narcotics.

Santini's next move was to have Casper complain about the poor quality of the meth supplied by Judy, hoping to track down additional sources. The ploy worked like a charm. Over the next few weeks, Puppet arranged two more large-scale purchases of crystal meth from different individuals.

With all these deals tightly monitored and recorded by HSI and DEA agents, convictions for Puppet and Judy on federal drug charges with minimum penalties of fifteen years were all but ensured. However, Santini still didn't have any direct evidence linking Chachi to the cocaine network, and he badly wanted to take the gang's top drug dealer down. So he started conducting covert "trash runs" at Chachi's residence in the hills overlooking South San Francisco.

It wasn't a job agents loved, but quite often trash runs could yield valuable intelligence and sometimes even evidence of criminal activity. *At least it wasn't a human trafficking case*, Santini thought to himself as he drove to meet his partner in the McDonald's parking lot up the road from the residence. When Santini was a new agent, he often worked cases where he was required to do trash runs at local brothels. He hated the memories of pulling hundreds of used condoms out of the trash to document as evidence with photos. The smell alone could kill a man.

Dressed in dark clothing at two o'clock in the morning, Santini and an HSI colleague snatched Chachi's trash cans from the street in front of his house. In a nearby alley, they poked around with rubber gloves and shovels, looking for evidence, such as used ziplock bags of different sizes or cutting agents like baking soda or corn starch, which would indicate that Chachi was breaking large quantities of coke into street-sized portions.

The agents didn't discover any hard evidence or drug paraphernalia in the trash, but did find indications that Chachi had begun to fortify his residence with security features, a common tactic for drug dealers moving large quantities of drugs. They found empty boxes for dome-style surveillance cameras as well as a receipt for a reinforced-steel door. They also found dental-clinic receipts indicating Chachi recently had several eighteen-carat gold teeth implanted. The bling-conscious homie was now rolling with a "full-gangsta" grill.

A few nights later, Casper was hanging out with Chachi, Puppet, and other clique members at the Skylark. After last call, they all went back to Chachi's place to party into the early morning hours. While gathered around a big pile of coke, Chachi pulled out a loaded M-16 rifle to show off for the homies. Santini couldn't stop thinking about Casper's description of Chachi posing with an M-16, ensconced in a multimillion-dollar home, with a front grill of gold teeth and an expensive car parked in the driveway. He was a walking recruitment poster for younger, more impressionable recruits to the gang with his flash and bling. Additionally, based on further intel from Casper, Santini now believed the 20th Street clique was dealing in much larger quantities than he originally suspected. Chachi needed to go down.

Santini's ambitions for taking down Chachi and his drug network were encouraged when he got word that Jose Alvarado, aka Joker, an older 20th Street homie, was scheduled for release from state lockup, after three years served on two felony convictions. Joker was known by Cabrera and Gibson to have a well-established relationship with Chachi, and at the time Santini thought Joker was subject to deportation, which often made it easier to flip informants. In reality, Joker actually met the standards to qualify as a "derivative citizen" of the United States, resulting from his parents' divorce and some other arcane immigration rules. Consequently, it was an empty threat of deportation that Santini wielded against Joker, though neither one of them knew it at the time.

Nonetheless, the empty threat worked, and upon his release from prison Joker began documenting meetings and drug-related conversations between Puppet and Chachi. He observed their interactions with each other, their dealer network, and their customers, and over the course of his initial reports, Joker confirmed that the clique's Party Group, headed by Chachi, was distributing whole ounces of cocaine.

Try as he might, though, Santini continued hitting dead ends in his attempt to set up Chachi. Whether or not Joker was doing his best to help nail the homie remained uncertain. Joker was a savvy, seasoned gangster, difficult to read, and his reliability as an effective informant was too much in doubt. It was time to focus on another of the gang's major means of death and destruction as well as a primary source of their revenue—guns.

Chapter 14

Tracking Guns in Reno

Reno, Nevada

INDIO'S BLACK LINCOLN NAVIGATOR ROUNDED THE CORNER OF VIR-
ginia and 4th Streets in front of the Silver Legacy hotel and casino, with
its white, half-globe roof and gilded, neo-Imperial entryway. The six
homies riding in the vehicle—Cyco, Indio, Fantasma, Cholito, Pelon (not
Peloncito) and Casper—wanted to roll in high style. It was two thirty in
the morning, but they had made no room reservations.

The purpose of their trip was to meet a Reno-based MS-13 clique
leader supplying guns to gang members up and down the West Coast.
Casper was along for the ride to scope out the Reno network for Santini,
who intended to shut it down. When they showed up at the Silver Legacy's front desk, the clerk took one look at the thugs and excused himself.
He returned from the back office a moment later, typed on his keyboard
as if he were double-checking and doing everything he could to accommodate the unexpected group.

"I'm sorry," he said. "We're completely booked."

The homies stood there for a moment. Were they getting the brush-
off because of the way they looked? They shrugged it off and walked away,
heading back to the Navigator—except for Cyco, who stared at the clerk
with seething malice. The man glanced at the switch under the counter
that alerted security personnel in case of an emergency.

"C'mon, dog!" Indio said to Cyco. He was holding the lobby door to the street open, urging his brother, whose temper and proclivity for violence he knew very well.

"Vamos, homie!"

Satisfied he had intimidated the clerk well enough for disrespecting him and his posse of senior mareros from San Francisco, Cyco finally turned and walked away. In the cool nighttime desert air, the homies huddled around the SUV.

"What the fuck we gonna do now?" Cholito said.

"I'll call Negro," Pelon said.

While he made the call, the other homies stood on the sidewalk in front of the Wicked Ink Tattoo parlor. Fantasma scoffed at the traditional tattoos displayed in the window.

"That ink needs to spell '*M S*', homies," he said.

"Fuck yeah, homie," Cyco said. "Mark of the Beast!"

"Hola," Pelon said into his phone. "Sí, we are in Reno, downtown."

The other homies quieted down to hear Pelon's conversation.

"Sí," Pelon said. "No, they ain't got no rooms, homie. . . . Sí? . . . Es no problema? . . . Sí. . . . Okay." Pelon hung up the phone. "Negro says we can stay at his mother's house tonight," he said. "But we need to keep it quiet. She's asleep."

Any change in plans like this, to stay at Negro's place now instead of the Silver Legacy fed into Casper's natural paranoia. If the gang already discovered he was a rat, this whole trip to Nevada could be a setup to whack him in the desert and leave his body for the buzzards and coyotes. Negro greeted Casper and the other homies at the front door and showed them into the living room, signaling them to be quiet so they didn't wake up his mother.

A twenty-seven-year-old native of El Salvador, Negro managed to function as a significant illegal gun dealer. Exploiting the relatively lax laws of Nevada and the state's frequent large gun shows to obtain his supply, he sold mostly to his MS-13 cohorts in California, Arizona, and Washington State.

Negro rented a garage in Sparks, Nevada, to store most of his guns, but he still had some nice pieces in the house to show off to the homies from San Francisco. He enticed them with a .357 magnum and a .22 caliber pistol that he passed around. He also brought out a shotgun and a 30-06 Springfield deer rifle. The homies were duly impressed, whispering their appreciation for the quality of guns, and bragging about future damage to be done with the weapons against their rival *chapetes*.

Negro assured them what they were looking at was just a small taste of what he had to offer. Through a network of straw purchasers, he acquired large quantities at legally sanctioned gun shows in Nevada. Straw purchasers were easy to find in the state and Negro, leader of the MS-13's Reno Locotes Sureños (RLS) clique, had several on his payroll. He told the homies that a big gun show called Crossroads of the West was coming to town the next month and several of his buyers would be in attendance. Crowds stretching a quarter-mile long around the convention center—just a few miles from the border with California—would be lining up to shop for guns and purchase them with no background checks required.

Early after sunrise the next morning, Casper and the other homies scarfed a buffet breakfast at one of Reno's second-tier casinos. They then proceeded to follow Negro to a residence in the West University section of the city that served as headquarters for the RLS clique. Here they met three additional gang members. During the homies' conversation about the situation with the local MS clique, Casper learned they consisted of only about a dozen members total, but were actively recruiting more.

A surprise honored guest was also present. Casper was stunned when he met the woman whom he had thought was a fictional character in the world of MS-13, a middle-age female Salvadoran known as La Negra, who had close ties to the Big Homies. Casper had heard of her many times, typically described as a messenger for the gang's top bosses in Central America. She traveled around the United States visiting cliques and performing "inventories," then reporting back to the Big Homies about clique-member head counts, revenues they generated, and any strategic conflicts with other gangs.

Still paranoid, Casper worried La Negra's presence in Reno might signal that a planned assassination of him was in the works. Meanwhile, the other San Francisco homies considered it an honor and privilege to spend the whole day with La Negra. They partied the afternoon and evening away, barbecuing and telling war stories about gangbanging in the States and Central America.

During the festivities, one of the RLS homies pulled out an M-16 rifle and boasted he could obtain many more of them if any 20th Street homies were interested. Cyco paid $150 for the .22 caliber handgun Negro showed off the previous night. Pelon took a shotgun on credit, since he didn't have the $200 in cash on hand to pay for it. He said the rifle would be a community gun for 20th Street's use, and that he'd collect the funds at the clique's next meeting. Both guns came fully loaded with rounds to spare.

Shortly after Casper returned to San Francisco, relieved he had not been whacked, Santini directed him to make a monitored phone call to Negro. As a senior member of 20th Street, Casper inquired about purchasing additional firearms from Negro, who said he would be happy to oblige.

Santini went to work with a plan to dismantle MS-13's Reno-San Francisco gun supply chain. He would start by targeting homies in the bay area who were on the trip with Casper to Reno. As for Negro himself, setting up the leader of the gang's multistate gun-trading operation would take a little more time and finesse.

CHAPTER 15

Success

IT WAS 6 A.M., JUST MOMENTS BEFORE "GO" TIME.

On the way to the raid, Santini loaded up the CD player with one of the thrash metal disks that he always kept stashed in his government car. Listening to some amped-up music before an operation—cranked up *loud*—had become a ritual for him. It helped get him into the right frame of mind. Today, he opted for Megadeth.

Days like this were why Santini had gotten into law enforcement in the first place—to avoid a desk job and pursue something that involved some adrenaline. He and his team of around ten HSI agents, along with their partners from the Richmond Police Department Swat Team, were prepared to raid a small, two-story, wood frame house painted yellow, with a peaked roof and small portico at the front.

Although the sun had just begun its ascent over the low hills to the east, the blue-collar neighborhood had not yet stirred awake. The target property was on a residential road that ran through a quarter-mile-wide strip of land between Interstate 80 to the east and Interstate 580 to the west, with the waters of the Richmond Inner Harbor just beyond.

A six-foot-high, solid-picket fence surrounded the yard and a busted-up, concrete driveway led from the paved street to the front of the house, with three disabled cars parked to one side. Opposite the driveway from the junk cars sat an obviously lived-in camping trailer.

Inside the residence, based on information provided by Casper, Santini expected to find the 12-guage, pump-action shotgun that Pelon had purchased from Negro a few weeks prior in Reno. According to

Casper, the clique intended to use the shotgun against the Norteños in the Mission.

A federal warrant was issued to search for Pelon on the property, based on violations of Re-entry after Deportation and Alien in Possession of a Firearm statutes. Both Pelon and another homie named Cholito who lived in the trailer were already on ICE's "fugitive alien" list, even prior to the revelation about their recent illegal gun purchases from Negro.

With a little digging, Santini discovered that after trying for a short time the previous year to obtain legal residency status in the United States, Pelon had just given up on the whole process and failed to appear for hearings. That led to a judge ordering Pelon's deportation. Cholito, for his part, had been deported three times already and was a convicted aggravated felon. He faced a minimum five years in federal lockup.

In drawing up plans for the raid, Santini, who was still a little pissed about what he considered the FBI's condescending attitude toward his investigation, purposely positioned an accompanying pair of Bureau agents at the far outside perimeter. There they would basically be relegated to the position of observers, just watching the real action unfold. In the world of macho cops, it was akin to sitting on the bench for the Bureau boys, while the "first-stringers" hogged all the glory. Santini had only invited the two FBI agents to appease his upper management, anyway.

"Breach!" came the order over the radio.

One of the biggest and strongest HSI agents led the charge into the gate of the wooden fence surrounding the house, but it didn't want to open. He struggled for a moment with the gate's mechanism, unable to spring it free. In a fit of adrenaline, the beefy agent began to kick and punch at the wooden gate like a crazy man, quickly reducing it to a splintered mess and making a hole big enough for the entry team to squeeze through in a mad rush. The RPD SWAT team sprinted to the main house on the property and quickly smashed down its front door.

Inside the home's kitchen, an enraged pit bull let out a vicious stream of growling and barking, as a woman attempted to restrain the dog on its leash. Seeing the SWAT team invading the home, the dog backed up and shook its body violently, slipping the collar, prompting one of the cops to shoot it in the head with a single round from his AR-15 assault rifle.

The terrified woman holding a now-empty collar reached her hands to her ears at the sound of the gun blast and turned away from the animal, whose rib cage rose and fell with its last, reflexive breath, blood oozing from its head wound onto the checkered linoleum floor.

Upstairs, surrounded by the heavily armed team, Pelon raised his hands in surrender and was taken into custody without incident. In a bedroom the search team found a shotgun that matched the description Casper had provided of the weapon Pelon purchased from Negro, along with a couple boxes of 12-gauge ammo. The gun had a pistol grip and sawed-off stock, and its serial number had been ground away with a metal file—a federal crime, carrying a significant penalty.

In the trailer outside, the HSI team found a loaded, .38 caliber pistol concealed in a sock and stored inside a closet. They also discovered a variety of gang indicia including MS-13 drawings, photos, jail letters, and a list of phone numbers with associated gang-member names.

On the street outside the property, alarmed and curious neighbors watched as Santini walked across the yard and into the house. He entered the hallway to the kitchen where the dead pit bull lay, its tongue hanging out sideways in a congealing pool of blood.

The media arrived moments later and were just in time to observe the tactical unit drag the dog's carcass out to the driveway and wrap it in some sheets. Film of the raid made the local TV news by midmorning, causing Santini concern that 20th Street would either disperse or transition to an inactive state while the "heat" dissipated. Negro and the others might suspect Pelon and Cholito showed up on HSI's radar as a result of their recent gun purchases. More likely, however, they assumed the raid was due to their previously outstanding warrants.

There was no reason for Santini not to continue working the gun-seizing operation up the chain of the gang's trafficking network all the way to Negro, and he intended to keep pressing. He was also planning a different line of attack on another important source of cash for the gang—stolen cars. All his preparations for a complex new sting had taken months, and now the trap was ready to set.

20th Street MS graffiti in Mission playground. SOURCE: H.S.I.

Goofy's MS graffiti. SOURCE: H.S.I.

The gang posing for group photo on Mission Street. SOURCE: GANG MEMBER

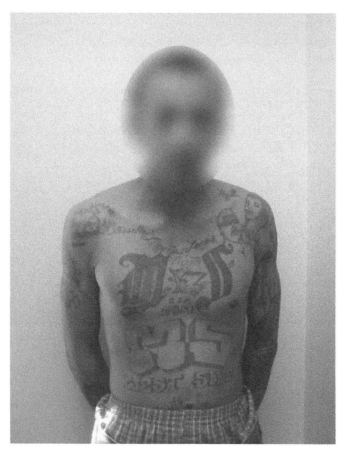

Diego, aka Little Loco. SOURCE: H.S.I.

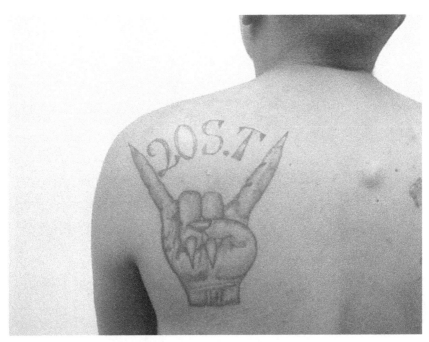

20th Street tattoo. SOURCE: H.S.I.

Front of the undercover warehouse. SOURCE: H.S.I.

Fake office in warehouse. SOURCE: H.S.I.

Undercover agent buying gun from Negro. SOURCE: H.S.I.

Undercover agent discussing stolen car purchase with Payaso. SOURCE: H.S.I.

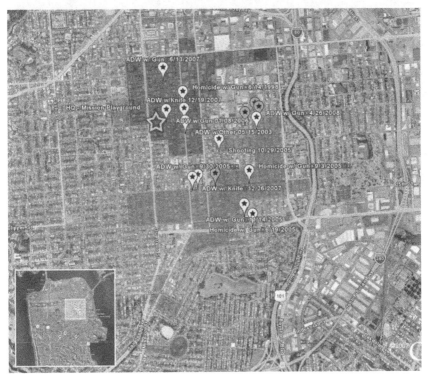

Map of violence in MS13 and Norteño turf in Mission District. SOURCE: H.S.I.

Seized shotgun with high capacity drum magazine. SOURCE: H.S.I.

Seized Tec 9 machine pistol. SOURCE: H.S.I.

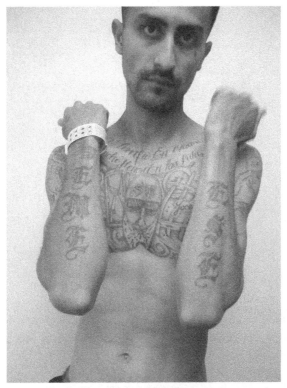

Jose Alvarado, aka Joker, during arrest. SOURCE: H.S.I.

Posting gang members including Slow Pain and Spooky (Center Top).
SOURCE: GANG MEMBER

Posting gang members including Slow Pain and Spooky (Center Bottom).
SOURCE: GANG MEMBER

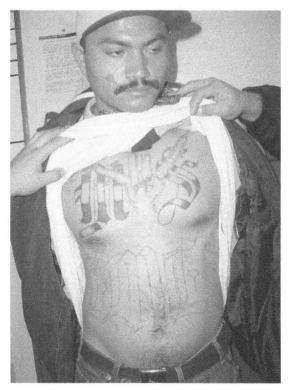

Angel Guevara, aka Peloncito, during arrest. SOURCE: H.S.I.

Gang members during field interview, including Cyco and Peloncito (Left).
SOURCE: H.S.I.

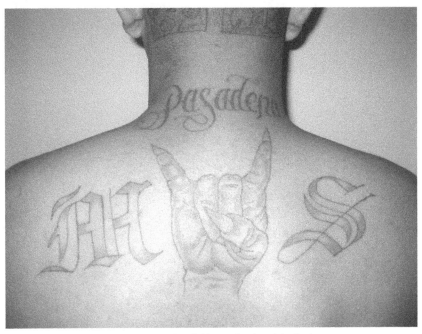
PLS gang member tattoo with the Devil Horns (la Gara) insignia. SOURCE: H.S.I.

Gang members pose for group photo at Memo's funeral. SOURCE: GANG MEMBER

CHAPTER 16

Foiled Sting

LIKE A PROUD NEW BUSINESS OWNER, SANTINI STOOD BACK AND ADMIRED the sign he had just hung on the face of the warehouse that read INTERNATIONAL EXPORTS. The three-by-four-foot metal placard was a hand-me-down prop from a previous undercover operation conducted by the California Highway Patrol, which Santini recruited to assist with his new ruse.

Four months had passed since the desk rats at HSI headquarters approved funding for the costly undercover operation. It had taken three months to locate and rent the building, install surveillance equipment, and furnish the garage and office to make it look like an authentic auto-repair business. To outfit the building, Santini started at the recycling heaps of a junkyard called Sunset Scavengers. With items supplied by the helpful salvage man, Santini's team furnished the warehouse office and stocked the garage with scrapped car hoods, bumpers, seats, rims, mechanic's tools, repair manuals, and office furniture. For an extra degree of authenticity, the agents strewed fast-food wrappers throughout the garage.

Like theatrical stage designers, they sprayed machine grease and antifreeze stains on a pair of new coveralls that they hung from a hook in the office. They sprinkled cigarette butts in various spots that made it feel like the workspace of a messy, nicotine-hooked grease monkey. For a final touch of cultural authenticity, they bought some Catholic holy candles at a Latino grocery store, bearing decals of the Virgin Mary, which they prominently displayed in the front office.

With everything in place, at Santini's direction Casper began spreading word within the gang about his "cousin" who managed a garage in Richmond and moonlighted as a stolen-car fence. Casper told the homies his cousin usually paid around five hundred dollars for stolen cars and that he was looking for more supply to move through buyers who shipped them overseas.

A contingent of the gang members were glad to hear about the new sales channel to add to the ones they already had, including A&C Auto Wreckers and ABC Auto Parts in the Bay View/Hunters Point section of the city. They had been fencing stolen cars and parts at these corrupt local businesses for years.

Santini soon received a late-night call from Casper saying that Payaso and Dog had stolen a Honda Civic that they wanted to unload. An hour earlier, Casper said, the pair of thieves departed their Mission residence on 20th Street, intending to steal a good car. They soon returned with the jacked Honda, its steering column slightly mangled from where they tore it apart to get it started. Santini put out the call to the undercover team at the warehouse to get ready for a visit from the homies, and to his state police partners to put a tail on the thieves en route.

Having successfully stolen the Honda, Dog claimed he was too drunk now to drive it all the way to the warehouse in Richmond. Payaso didn't know how to drive a stick shift, so another homie present named Marlon offered to drive it instead. Casper and Marlon left in the stolen Honda and headed for the warehouse, with Payaso following close behind in Marlon's own vehicle.

A little after midnight, on the Richmond Parkway near Gertrude Street, a Contra Costa County sheriff's deputy—clueless about the police sting operation under way—pulled Payaso over in the Acura. A surveillance team of undercover California Highway Patrol officers tailing the gang members hastily placed a call to the Contra Costa County dispatcher, requesting that the officer on the scene allow Payaso to continue on his way unimpeded. To their relief, the officer received the message in time before busting Payaso. He let the homie go on his way, despite the fact he was driving without a license and had an outstanding warrant related to a drug bust in San Francisco.

Moments after Payaso was pulled over by the sheriff's deputy, Casper and Marlon arrived at the warehouse. Casper phoned the two undercover agents manning the warehouse and they opened the gate to let the homies drive through, directing them to park the stolen car in front of an open shipping container. Payaso arrived in the Acura moments later and the undercover agents led the three homies into the warehouse office.

"Shit, homie, I thought that fucking cop was going to bust my ass for sure!" Payaso said.

"You're a lucky, dog!" Marlon said. "What the fuck did you tell the cop, homie?"

"I told him I was coming home from work and going to my mother's house," Payaso said. "He tells me 'be careful' and he just lets me go down the road."

The two undercover agents laughed along at the homies' stroke of good luck.

"So, listen, we'll give you four hundred for the car," one of the agents said.

"Four hundred?" Payaso said. "That shit worth more than four hundred. Dat bitch worth seven hundred at least!"

"Tell you what, man," the agent said. "I'll give you five."

Payaso stared the agent in the eye.

"Five?" he said.

The agent nodded.

"That's all I can go, dog," he said.

Payaso turned to Marlon, who nodded.

"Okay, five," Payaso said.

"Cool," the agent said.

He pulled out an envelope of cash from a drawer and counted out the bills. Five hundred. Payaso stuck the money inside his jacket and grinned like a fool. Casper clasped fists with his "cousin," and the 20th Street homies got up to leave.

"Next time, you guys need to be more careful, homies," the agent said. "Be better if you make any deliveries earlier at night than this, when the fucking cops are between shifts."

"Okay," Casper said. "These homies are cool, man. Next time at ten o'clock, okay homies?"

"Yeah, man," Payaso said. "Next time, we'll hit you up at ten. No problem."

For several weeks, all was well with the sting operation. Santini's team had purchased an impressive sixteen cars from various 20th Street clique members as well as some other criminal associates who were not in the gang. Then an unfortunate thing occurred for the operation.

Following the success of NBC's popular show *To Catch a Predator*, which baited and trapped predators prowling online for underage sex partners, the network spun off a new show called, *To Catch a Car Thief.* The program showed video-surveillance footage with undercover cops posing as stolen-car fences, meeting with unsuspecting thieves at a warehouse secretly wired for sound and video. Some of the 20th Street homies happened to tune into the show and it got them thinking: The warehouse setup on TV looked a whole lot like the one run by Casper's cousin in Richmond.

As a matter of fact, Indio, who was Cyco's brother, had been a little suspicious of Casper and the warehouse deal from the start. He thought he might have recognized an undercover cop there from the California Highway Patrol. When the TV show aired, Casper warned Santini that the chatter among the 20th Street clique was that his shop looked like a setup and to stay away. Just like that, after pleading with HSI management for funds to lease the warehouse, furnishing it to look legit, wiring it for sound and video, the operation fizzled. But not until after they had made buys of more than twenty stolen vehicles and at least eight gangbangers were on the hook for federal charges including the exportation of stolen vehicles.

Casper, on the other hand, now had a problem. He was the one who had set the whole thing up with the homies, introducing them to his cousin. Casper had some serious suspicions among the 20th Street homies to contend with now. A good fast talker, he assured them his cousin could be trusted. If the guys at the warehouse were really cops, then they would all have been busted already, he argued. No arrests stemming from the warehouse operation had occurred. His logic seemed to quell their suspicions.

Still, a hoodlum named Daniel Gonzales who was not in MS-13, but who associated with some of the 20th Street homies, had brought a stolen car to sell to the warehouse. Gonzales was not so easily convinced that Casper wasn't involved in a setup with the cops. When Gonzales's brother heard about the situation, he went looking for Casper and found him walking down the sidewalk in the Mission.

"You set up my brother, motherfucker," he said.

With that, he proceeded to kick Casper's ass, punching him and throwing him through a storefront window, the broken glass gashing his face. A few days later, Casper showed up for a clandestine meeting with Santini, his face a mess of cuts and bruises.

"What happened to you, man?" Santini said.

Casper told him about the attack by Gonzales, which raised serious alarms. One of his two main informants was beat up as a result of his undercover role. As his handler, it was the agent's responsibility to ensure Casper's safety to the greatest extent possible.

"So, what do you think, man?" Santini said. "Can you still work without getting hurt? You want out?"

Casper shook his head and touched the bandage on his jaw.

"No, I'm alright," he said.

"If you want out, you need to tell me," Santini said.

Casper shook his head again.

Santini couldn't help but admire Casper's guts. He was walking a very tricky tightrope with the gang and somehow seemed to be keeping his cool in extremely dangerous circumstances. He was able to maintain a smooth swagger that took in the other homies, who were constantly sniffing around for rats in their camp as a matter of routine. Casper either had steel balls, or he wasn't particularly bright, Santini thought. Either way, it was the agent's job to keep him safe, which was looking increasingly difficult.

—◦—

In the parking lot of the Scandia Family Fun Center just off Interstate 80 near Sacramento, Santini watched as his HSI colleague wired Casper up for sound. Soon they expected a call from Negro, whom

Casper was scheduled to meet at a Holiday Inn parking lot a couple miles away, where they would conduct the controlled purchase of a high-powered rifle.

Under Santini's direction, Casper had been talking over the phone off and on for a few weeks with Negro in a series of recorded phone calls to set up the deal. He convinced Negro to meet him in Sacramento for the handoff, halfway between San Francisco and Reno. This meant Negro would be crossing state lines to sell the gun, making for an additional federal offense.

At around 6:30 p.m., Casper, wearing a wire, got the call from Negro.

"I'm on the way, homie," Negro said. "Me and two other homies."

"Okay, cool," Casper said. "Where you at?"

"On Route 80, homie. Near Exit 22," Negro said.

"Okay, just keep on coming down Eighty, dog. You'll see a big sign for the Holiday Inn. Just take that exit and swing around into the parking lot behind the hotel. What you driving, homie?"

"A red Chevy Blazer," Negro said. "We should be there in, like, an hour and a half."

"Cool," Casper said. "I'm in a green truck, homie. I'll meet you there at eight o'clock. I got another homie with me, too."

"Yeah?" Negro said. "Cuantos? Uno?"

"Sí, solamente uno," Casper said.

"Okay, cool," Negro said.

At around 7:55 p.m., a surveillance agent positioned at the outer perimeter of the Holiday Inn observed a red Chevy Blazer with Nevada license plates entering the hotel parking lot. Negro contacted Casper on his cell phone. The informant guided Negro to the spot where he was waiting in the truck with an undercover HSI special agent, a native Spanish speaker.

Negro's red Blazer pulled into the spot right next to the green pickup.

"So, we got your SKS, homie," Negro said.

"Nice, homie," Casper said.

Negro scanned the parking lot for anyone watching. He moved to the back of the Blazer and pulled out a rifle wrapped in an extra-large T-shirt and put it in the back of Casper's truck.

"Let me know if your 20th homies want any Uzis," Negro said. "I just sold one to some homies in Texas and they tore up some chavalas with that shit, I'm telling you, dog!"

"Simone!" Casper said.

The men shook hands and Negro turned toward the Blazer to head back to Reno.

"Mara Salvatrucha forever!" Negro called over his shoulder.

"Mara siempre!" Casper called back.

Afterward, Santini and the rest of the surveillance team met at a parking lot several miles away for a debriefing with Casper. The agents cleared and packaged the Russian made SKS-7 assault rifle, six hundred forty rounds of ammo, and a thirty-round ammo clip. They also processed a Remington shotgun that Negro supplied as a gesture of good will from the RLS clique to 20th Street.

Subsequent computer checks revealed no hits on the assault rifle but the shotgun came up positive. Records indicated it was stolen in Reno the previous August. A license-plate check on the red Chevy Blazer carrying Negro and his crew showed the vehicle was registered to a native Salvadoran who currently resided in Sparks, Nevada. He had a lightweight criminal history, including two misdemeanor convictions for driving under the influence.

The focus of Santini's investigation continued to be 20th Street and their closely allied clique in Richmond, the PLS. But it also now most definitely included the RLS clique headed by Negro. The owner of the Blazer and all the individuals Casper met on his earlier gun-shopping trip to Reno with the San Francisco homies were added to Santini's multiplying target list. All of them were on the hook for criminal conspiracy.

CHAPTER 17

Growing Pressure

SANTINI LAY IN BED AT NIGHT IN HIS MISSION DISTRICT APARTMENT, worrying. How would HSI headquarters react to the premature shutdown of the auto-theft sting? The operation had now succeeded in seizing more than twenty vehicles, but he had hoped for more. His team had taken numerous guns from the gang, but he also knew they could likely get new ones.

He had two main informants to manage now and Casper was likely suspected as a rat by the gang. The FBI was *constantly* breathing down his neck. The murder rate in the city was on the rise, while arrests for homicides were down. Had he bitten off more than he could chew? The old fear of failure, to follow in his father's footsteps that way, churned his gut.

Unable to fall asleep, he listened to the wind and rain pelting the apartment's windowpanes. El Niño, the periodic Pacific weather machine, was deluging the California coast again, as it did every few years. In the city, water overflowed every pothole and planter. It gushed down storm drains in torrents, flushing away the stench from vagrants who pissed and defecated openly in San Francisco's parks and alleys. He drifted into half-sleep, the sound of downpouring rain infiltrating his dreams with shards of memory from his time as a Border Patrol agent.

It was six years ago—another El Niño Year. The heavy rains hit Southern California hard. . . .

More than once, he gave high-speed pursuit to coyote vehicles laden with human cargo and watched them crash to a stop, the passengers scrambling out and sprinting away into the darkened landscape in every direction. The sheer desperation of the border jumpers to get into the States was palpable. If they could just get past the border zone, their chances of finding safe haven with family members or fellow countrymen in some town or city in America, where a person could find work that paid decently in US dollars, would dramatically improve.

The sprint across the border was a make-it-or-break-it moment for them and the high stakes seemed to add an extra gear to their foot speed, as they beat it toward freedom. The speediest among them often got away. All Santini saw of them was their backsides as they vanished into the nighttime landscape, leaving him and his partners to corral the ones they could snag and hold in place until backup arrived. The detainees were loaded into vans and taken to newly formed immigration courts, where they were scanned biometrically and checked for criminal records or outstanding warrants.

One night alone on patrol, driving in a Ford Bronco in a remote area of the hills across the border from Tijuana, Santini received a call over the radio from patrol spotters equipped with night vision goggles. They reported a group of five people sneaking across the line in Santini's vicinity and directed him to pursue on foot. He parked the truck and made his way toward the suspects in the dark. When he got close enough, he flipped on his spotlight.

This was the moment of truth that he'd been through dozens of times before—when the light came on and the faces of the hunted were revealed, their eyes lit up by the flashlight's beam. Was it a family? A father and mother, with six kids in tow? A pack of armed drug smugglers with a load of coke? These were questions that needed to be answered in an instant.

This time it was five adult or adolescent males and Santini ordered them to raise their hands. At first, they complied and marched ahead of him back to the truck. Then the situation began to unravel. The five men moved around to the opposite side of the truck from Santini, who ordered them to stand still. Every time he moved toward their side of the truck to get them corralled, they would circle back around to the opposite side.

The men started taunting Santini, laughing and calling him a fucking *migra* (roughly equivalent to "pig" for a cop in English). One of the suspects decided to come around to Santini's side of the truck and face him up. At the same time, the other four males began to inch around from the other side of the Bronco, behind him. Santini reached for his collapsible steel baton and smashed the guy confronting him on the outside of his knee as he'd been trained to do—at the point of the peroneal nerve—dropping him. In the moment it took for him to reach for his baton and swing it, three of the others took off running in the dark. With the one guy down on the ground, cursing in pain and holding his leg, Santini drew his firearm and ordered the remaining one who had not run away with the others to get down on the ground.

Two out of five in custody, three on the lam, and backup on the way. With the situation somewhat under control, Santini could get a closer look at the face of the guy who had decided to test him. He had tattoos all over his neck and hands. Both his eyelids were tattooed. The left one said, "FUCK," and the right one said, "POLICE."

On the ground where Santini had dropped the thug, he spotted a five-inch butterfly knife, its blade in the open position and ready for use—to gash him. It could have easily happened. He imagined the steel blade ripping his guts, bleeding him out in the dark terrain. . . .

It was no use trying to sleep anymore. He got out of bed and headed to the kitchen for a cup of coffee.

—◦—

Folsom Prison, California

Santini pulled into the visitor's parking lot and sat for a minute gazing at the prison's stone arch entranceway. The place looked like a medieval castle erected alongside the banks of the American River, about twenty-five miles east of Sacramento.

Built a hundred and forty years ago, Folsom was the second-oldest prison in California, occupying the former site of a mining camp. After it opened in 1880 in the wake of the Gold Rush, with a designed capacity of eighteen hundred inmates, the prison quickly became legendary for its harsh conditions. Inmates occupied stone cells that measured just four feet by eight feet, with solid steel doors and just an eye-slot to peek through.

Santini had come to Folsom to talk with Diablito, one of the 20th Street homies who had been riding in the car with Happy on the day that Memo was murdered three years before, when Happy opened fire on the busy Mission street at the Norteños. Diablito was now doing time for an assault with a deadly weapon and was scheduled for release and deportation in six months.

Recruiting and retaining MS-13 informants typically presented a maddening challenge, Santini had learned by now. Even gang members who wanted to get out of the life were constantly pulled back in by the gravitational force of group loyalty. As a result, their behavior often seemed fickle and unpredictable, but it did make more sense when viewed through their eyes. To break free of the gang, an individual needed to abandon personal connections and deep loyalties that defined his self-image, leaving an uncertain psychological void in its place.

Diego had recently and unexpectedly flaked out on Santini after having provided so much valuable intel, at considerable risk to his own life. He stopped answering all calls from Santini. When the agent went looking for him at the Crab Shack restaurant on Pier 26, where Diego was employed as a dishwasher, he discovered the informant had quit the job. He and his wife had moved out of their apartment, with no forwarding address. Unable to track him down, HSI now officially labeled Diego a fugitive. It had been a difficult decision. The downside for Santini was that he was losing what had been an extremely valuable informant. However, HSI would be eliminating a public safety liability they had with Diego loose on the streets. Santini didn't think Diego would start back up gangbanging in the States, but there was always that chance. He had certainly proven he was capable of it previously in Honduras.

Whatever the story with Diego, Santini wanted more intelligence on 20th Street's ongoing violent crimes, and to get it he needed new sources inside the gang. Based on what the agent learned through his two main informants and SFPD Gang Task Force partners, Cabrera and Gibson, he thought he might be able to flip Diablito.

Waiting in the prison's main visiting room, Santini considered the vagaries of working potential informants. He could spend hours and hours, drive hundreds of miles back and forth from San Francisco to

Folsom to try flipping Diablito, just to hit a dead end. On the other hand, if he just happened to get hold of a criminal at the right moment for whatever reason—like with Casper—a half hour of prodding and cajoling might be enough to turn him.

Santini was informed by prison administrators that Diablito seemed to be steering clear of other MS-13 gang members while behind bars. Unlike many prisons, it was possible for an acknowledged gang member to be housed away from his homies in Folsom, if that's what he wanted. Diablito was working a job in the prison kitchen and had avoided getting into any trouble.

The agent watched as the guards checked Diablito through the metal gates that led from the cell blocks into a separate wing where families, friends, and lawyers came to visit. The guards patted him down all over his denim prison uniform, then led him into the big visiting room with thirty-foot-high vaulted ceilings, the floor filled with folding chairs all lined up in rows as if ready for a high school pep rally.

"You would like to stay in the US with your woman and baby when you get out of here, right?" Santini said.

"Yeah, sure," Diablito said. "So, what you want from me?"

"Look," Santini said, "I know you know who dropped the dude at the liquor store," referring to the murder of a member of 20th Street's rival Army Street Gang suspected to be committed by Cyco.

"I'm just asking you to tell me what you know, and I can see about getting a good deal for you," the agent said. "Make it so you can stay in the country and get a good job and start a new life for your family?"

"What I gotta do for that?" Diablito said.

"You need to tell me everything you know about the shooting at the liquor store, for starters," Santini said.

He could see that Diablito was maybe open to a deal, but he didn't want to push him too hard, too fast.

"Hey, take a few days to think about it and I'll come back next week, alright?" Santini said.

"Yeah, I'll think about it," Diablito said.

A week later Santini returned and Diablito told him he might be open to negotiate. On the other hand, Diablito said, he was just as likely to keep his mouth shut and accept deportation when he was released in a matter of months. He hadn't visited his mother in a long time and he was eager to see the old country again.

Over the next several weeks, Santini was accompanied by Cabrera and Gibson on visits to Folsom. Based on their extensive knowledge of past crimes on the city's streets, the SFPD gang cops peppered Diablito with questions about what he knew about specific violent incidents.

One piece of information provided by Diablito led Santini to immediately put another gang member named Cobra on his front burner. According to Diablito, Cobra had shot and killed a young Samoan man named Manolo Muna in the Sunnydale Projects section of San Francisco. Muna was standing on the street with some friends at the time and wearing a red 49ers team jacket, drinking a beer, when he was shot down. SFPD homicide detectives had assumed at the time that a black gang was responsible for the killing, not MS-13. What made Santini and his partners especially anxious to bust Cobra was that he recently enlisted in the US Marines. His induction into the Corps was imminent.

Soon, Santini worried, a murderous thug would be wearing the uniform of America's vaunted fighting force. He'd be trained up in the use of a high-powered rifle and possibly stationed overseas, maybe even guarding an embassy. His fellow marines would rely on him to cover their backs in a fight. Maybe he'd be put on patrol in the neighborhoods of an occupied country like Iraq or Afghanistan. And God help the locals there if Cobra's beast within found release on their streets. The thought of it had Santini and his partners scrambling to prevent Cobra's enlistment.

"We know you capped Muna," Santini said.

He had called up Cobra and requested a meeting at a Starbucks in South San Francisco.

"No, man," Cobra said. "I didn't shoot nobody. That's bullshit. Who told you that?"

"Never mind," Santini said. "We know you did it. You can forget about being a marine. That ain't going to happen."

"You can't stop me," Cobra said. "I didn't do nothin'."

"Just admit what you did and they'll go easy on you. You'll be out in, maybe, five years and it'll be behind you. You can start fresh."

"I ain't admittin' nothin'," Cobra said. "I didn't do it."

On a few more occasions, Santini tried to break Cobra, calling him up and requesting face-to-face meetings. Each time Cobra showed up, probably just trying to find out what exactly Santini knew, and how he knew it. But each time the interviews were stalemates. Cobra admitted to nothing and Santini couldn't crack him.

Cobra was right. Without admissible evidence that he had committed the Muna murder—not just the unsworn statement of Diablito, an MS-13 jailbird—there was nothing Santini could do to stop his induction into the marines. Soon, Cobra raised his right hand in the recruiter's office and swore his allegiance to the red, white, and blue, to defend the Constitution against all enemies foreign and domestic. He shipped off for basic and three months later emerged as a full-fledged private in the US Marines.

Diablito eventually stopped talking. He decided he wanted to go back home to see his mother in El Salvador. The agent's inability to flip another 20th Street member was aggravated by his larger frustration with Diego, who had gone to ground and stopped communicating with his government controllers. Every attempt by Santini to contact him failed. He still had no idea where Diego was or what he was doing.

─ ─

On her way to the office, an HSI agent who had worked extensively with Santini and Diego happened to drive right by the fugitive walking along Davis Street and recognized him. She immediately pulled her car over and grabbed her cell phone to call Santini.

"Hey, Michael," she said. "I have Diego in my sights."

"Where?!" Santini said.

"I'm near the corner of Davis and Sacramento," she said. "He's just walking down the sidewalk with what looks like some grocery bags."

"Keep your eye on him," Santini said. "I'm on my way!"

He leapt from his seat and ran down the hall to his partner's office. "1301 is at Embarcadero 3!" Santini called.

Without a word, his partner set down his coffee mug and raced to follow Santini who was already at the elevator, pushing compulsively on the DOWN button, pacing back and forth. The elevator doors slid open and a group of passengers, sensing the agents' urgency, quickly made space for them. At ground level they ran across the lobby and through the revolving doors to the street.

They broke into a sprint, rounding the corner at Battery Street. And there was Diego, walking with his back to them and carrying several grocery bags. Santini rushed up quietly behind him and grabbed him by the shoulder, spinning him around. When Diego saw who it was he dropped his arms to the side, deflated. Santini reached for his handcuffs and spun him back around, snapping them on his wrists. The Honduran seemed to wither under Santini's furious stares. He knew he was screwed.

"I am sorry, Michael," he said.

"Ain't no 'sorry,' brother," Santini said. "We had a deal. And you broke it."

The agents called for a vehicle and the ride back to the office with Diego was intensely silent. There was nothing to be said. The informant had taken his chances and decided to put the demands of his family and a new day job ahead of what Santini and his partners were requiring from him.

Unfortunately for Diego, he had decided to take employment at a restaurant literally only three blocks from the HSI SAC Office, a move that had severely degraded his odds of evading capture. The big wheels of justice had spun and landed on "DEPORT" for Diego. He was headed back home to Honduras. Santini was losing one of his two main informants and a potentially critical witness for any future prosecutions. But HSI could not afford the risk of allowing him to remain in the country, now that he had proved unreliable.

Franklin Square Park

Sitting in an unmarked car with Casper, Santini pulled out a compact digital recorder and switched it on. "This is Special Agent Michael

Santini. The date is April 21, 2007. The time is thirteen hundred hours. HSI source 1312 will meet with gang leader Ivan Cerna to discuss gang-related activity."

He hit the stop button and handed the recorder to Casper, who was sitting in the backseat, waiting to do his thing. He looked nervous, wiping sweat from his brow. Casper was on edge because Tigre was one of his oldest friends. Through the years, Tigre had always treated him like a younger brother. Casper was conflicted about stabbing Tigre in the back, but he was also determined to do what it took to escape the gang life.

Santini was nervous, too. He had concluded that Casper was fast approaching his expiration date—the point at which the risk of the gang discovering he was an informant outweighed the value of whatever further intelligence he might be able to produce. Ever since the fiasco of the auto warehouse sting, it seemed that Casper had been skating on thin ice. He was brave, the agent had to give him that. But he wasn't sure if Casper's courage had to do with his Big Homie brother, Snoopy, or simply because he was too dumb to be scared.

"Game time, perro!" Santini told Casper. "Let's go fight some crime!"

"Yes, homie," Casper said. "Let's see what the boss has to say today."

Santini reminded Casper of what to coax Tigre into discussing. He specifically wanted recordings of Tigre talking about gang leadership, taxing the Miceros, evidence of the Big Homies calling shots for 20th Street, and details on gang members committing specific crimes. Casper said he understood what Santini wanted him to do and the agent started the car.

He dropped Casper on the corner at a bus stop just a few blocks away from Franklin Square Park, where Casper had arranged to meet Tigre. For Santini, this was a crucial operation. Tigre had been a no-show on the streets for months and this was going to be a unique opportunity for the agent to get a recorded conversation between the clique leader and another senior gang member. It could provide the type of evidence the US Attorney's Office salivated over.

Santini watched from a distance as Tigre's tan pickup truck rolled slowly into view in the lot adjacent to Franklin Square Park. He could see Casper and Tigre sitting together in the truck's cab. They parked at the entrance to the soccer field and the two homies strolled onto the grass where they could observe three youngsters kicking a ball around.

"Have you talked lately with the ones down below?" Casper said

"No, not lately," Tigre said. "But I am worried about Peloncito. He is doing work on his own, without checking for approval."

"Yes," Casper said. "He does not seem to understand the rules of La Mara."

"He is pushing too hard on Patas and the Miceros," Tigre said. "It is causing trouble. The 20th Street is not strong enough to push it. Besides, there is plenty to go around for everyone. Peloncito should not be so greedy."

Tigre stretched out on the grass, his body tired and aching from a long day on the construction site. "The three-letter suit-and-tie guys [FBI agents] came to talk with me again," he said. "Those fuckers are snooping around for something. I think maybe I should contact them and tell them I'm definitely not the one they want."

"I don't know," Casper said. "I wouldn't trust those sons of bitches for anything. I wouldn't do it."

"Sí," Tigre said. "You're probably right."

Tigre stood up straight and jingled his truck keys, signaling he was ready to head out. His family was waiting for him to eat dinner. The kids would want to play some *futbol* before homework and bedtime. He held out his hand for Casper to shake.

"A La Mara," he said.

"Mara Salvatrucha forever," Casper said.

When Santini and his partner debriefed Casper immediately after the meeting, Casper told them the FBI had been attempting to flip Tigre as an informant. Tigre told Casper the Bureau agents actually came to his house and questioned him about his gang involvement.

Santini could hardly fathom that the FBI would jeopardize his investigation by making direct contact with his number-one target. He immediately complained to his counterparts at the Bureau, who admitted they had gone to Tigre's residence in an attempt to turn him as an informant.

The fallout from the incident was exceptional, with reports sent from HSI in San Francisco to agency headquarters in D.C. In turn, top brass at

HSI and FBI headquarters had several heated exchanges. In the end, the Bureau made the rookie agent who facilitated the "knock and talk" with Tigre—the same one who had screamed at Santini on the phone earlier in the investigation—seem to vanish from the face of the earth, probably relegated to a dead-end desk job.

Interagency law enforcement politics and rivalries aside, 20th Street was taking a more violent and ruthless turn. Violent attacks on Mission streets were escalating. No amount of talking the problem down in the media by city government officials or newly announced plans to tackle the gang crime situation were having the desired effects, actual or perceived.

Santini felt the growing pressure. Three years of hard work had produced a significant amount of evidence, but no improvement in terms of public safety. If anything, conditions on the street for Mission residents were worse than ever. The clock inside Santini's head was ticking all the time. Every new violent crime that occurred in the neighborhood was a stark reminder for him of what he still had not accomplished. There was no guarantee he could succeed in dismantling 20th Street.

PART II

CHAPTER 18

A Proven Prosecutor

LAURA GWINN, A FIFTY-ONE-YEAR-OLD FEDERAL PROSECUTOR WITH red hair and piercing blue eyes, arrived at the San Francisco Airport, exhausted. Not just tired from the cross-country flight, she was worn out from all the recent weeks of preparing a prosecution of two MS-13 thugs in Maryland. Then there was the thirteen-day trial, not to mention five days of waiting while the jury deliberated over the charges of "racketeering and conspiracy to commit murder to further the racketeering enterprise."

The jury had convicted both defendants, but victory in the courtroom did not equal a badly needed rest for Gwinn.

She had been going after MS-13 gang members in the Washington, D.C., area for several years now and was considered a leading expert in the field. As an assistant state's attorney in Prince Georges County, Maryland, she was assigned in 2003 to prosecute two suspects in the nonfatal shooting of a student near High Point High School. In a subsequent case, she persuaded a county jury in 2005 to convict an MS-13 member named Mario Ayala of first-degree murder in the beating death of a man in a Maryland cemetery. After that, the US Attorney's Office invited Gwinn to join their team, which was dealing with an expanding presence of MS-13 cliques throughout the D.C. region.

For months now, Gwinn had been splitting her time between the office of the state's attorney in Upper Marlboro, Maryland, and the federal courthouse in Greenbelt, Maryland, effectively working two jobs. It was taking a toll on her. Even as she stepped off the plane in San Francisco, there was another pending murder trial back home that required her attention—the double murder of a married couple, both veterinarians, whose throats were slit during a robbery at their clinic.

Although fatigued, when Gwinn was presented with the case file on Operation Devil Horns in San Francisco, it stirred the natural-born fighter in her. She was keenly aware of MS-13 gang members' violent nature and their threat to public safety, and she knew from experience how to put together a successful RICO prosecution. It was too tempting for Gwinn, a divorced mother of two grown children, not to pick up the case. It's what she knew how to do best.

Tired to the bone, she wheeled her luggage through the airport and headed for the street to hail a cab. Well, she thought, here we go again.

Santini hurried through the lobby of the federal building on Golden Gate Avenue to meet with the new prosecutor assigned by Main Justice to his case for the first time. He was excited. Gwinn's reputation of success against MS-13 on the East Coast preceded her. Santini hoped she could build solid RICO convictions and prison sentences from the untold hours he and his fellow agents had spent over nearly three years of cajoling informants, hidden-surveillance operations, and controlled purchases of drugs, guns, and stolen cars.

At the receptionist's desk, he asked where he could find Gwinn, who was expecting him. Santini was not a particularly popular person in these offices. He was the guy who had gone over the local DOJ office's heads. Gwinn was the visible embodiment of that effort now, a big gun sent from headquarters to handle his case. Any powwow between Santini and Gwinn in clear view of everyone was a reminder of the major case that the local US Attorney's Office had stonewalled, repeatedly. Now they were forced to share it with Main Justice in Washington.

Gwinn was received professionally and cordially by local DOJ staff and provided an office to occupy in their headquarters. She soon concluded, however, there was scant enthusiasm to support a RICO case against 20th Street. Before long she would elect to decamp to a desk at the HSI office in the Financial District, where Santini was based, for the duration of the investigation.

Santini poked his head into Gwinn's office doorway. She was hard at work on some documents, a determined-looking professional. He rapped his knuckles softly on the doorjamb.

"Laura?" he said, "Michael Santini."

He stuck out his hand to shake. She sized him up with a quick, keen glance. After the standard polite introductions and questions about travel and lodging accommodations, she got right down to business.

"I've reviewed the reports of investigation and you have obviously done a lot of great work, Michael," she said.

He liked what he was hearing so far.

She pointed at the stack of reports on the desk in front her. "You've worked the guns, the dope, and the cars," she said.

"We worked every angle we could think of," he said.

She nodded. "I think we have to work the violence angle harder," she said. "These thugs are regularly committing acts of violence which are predicate offenses for RICO. Some of the evidence is already here."

"Yes, it is," Santini agreed.

"If we can nail them for murder in the aid of racketeering, we can put them away longer," she said.

In her steady gaze, Santini read a woman on a mission. Just like he was. He sensed a new confidence about the likelihood that his investigation was going to amount to something big.

Santini lacked experience in investigating murders, however. The feds usually left those cases to state and local police, as they had teams of detectives with specialized training. Gwinn was inferring that Santini and his team would need to investigate homicides. He was nervous, but excited.

───

Over the course of his investigation, Santini had come to realize just how deep the gang's psychological inculcation ran for its members. Standing in the rooms where some of them lived and slept, he saw how they surrounded themselves with gang icons and insignia—the Satanic symbols, the baseball bats inscribed with MS-13 mottos, and photos of fellow gang members flashing devil-horn salutes. Their deepest identities in life came from the gang. The gang was who these guys were.

Joker, the government informant now assigned by Tigre as the clique's new treasurer, was signed on with the government on a probationary basis, only. Santini had serious reservations about whether Joker had any genuine desire to escape the world of MS-13 and start building a "legit" life.

Joker was smart, but he had been deeply steeped in the ways of La Mara. He had done hard time cooped up with the homies in jail. What it took for a hardened marero to break free psychologically from the cult-like grip of MS-13 was not to be underestimated, Santini had learned by now.

One night, not long after the Polo Grounds confrontation between the old dogs and new booties and his appointment as clique treasurer, Joker hitched a ride with Kapone and his girlfriend from Daly City to the Mission District. They all planned to hook up and party at Blondies, along with Puppet and another gang member named Menace.

Located near 16th and Valencia Streets, Blondies was a small club with an open sidewalk façade that exposed a long wooden bar, usually tended by scantily clad women sporting full-sleeve tats and face piercings. One of the place's main claims to fame was a humongous, eleven-dollar martini that drew in people elbow-to-elbow on weekend nights.

Santini occasionally patronized the place himself, prior to the start of his 20th Street investigation, when he came to realize it was a regular hangout for the gang. The bar was frequented by all types, including Mission District gangbangers who cruised the diverse clientele for white chicks and customers for their dime bags of weed and coke.

When Joker arrived at Blondies, sporting a blue ball cap and T-shirt, someone in the back of the crowded barroom stood up and yelled, "Scraps not welcome here!"

It was a Norteño, using his gang's derogatory term for Sureños, which included MS-13. Enraged, Joker began weaving his way through the crowd toward the Norteño, but Kapone and Puppet grabbed him and held him back, distracting him by pointing out the bartender's large breasts and offering to buy him a drink. While the MS-13 trio were being served their beverages, they scowled darkly at the offending Norteño and his sidekick, as the two walked past them and exited the bar.

What Joker and his crew didn't realize was that a half dozen more Norteños were keeping a low profile in the rear of the club. When Kapone and his girlfriend walked across the street to grab a quick slice of pizza, Joker was caught alone smoking a cigarette on the sidewalk out front by the Norteño crew, who attacked him and stabbed him several times with knives. Joker stumbled and fell on the sidewalk with wounds to his neck, arms, and back. He was transported by emergency medical personnel in critical condition to San Francisco General Hospital.

Joker was lucky enough to survive the vicious attack, which was all caught on surveillance cameras and turned over to SFPD officers Gibson and Cabrera. Though he lived, he permanently lost the use of his left arm as a result of wounds to his neck, which severed the spinal region that controls movement from the shoulder down.

Joker's days as an informant were done, but not because of his paralyzed arm. It had become clear to Santini his would-be informant was too tied up in the whole MS-13 gangster lifestyle. He couldn't play it cool when necessary, to stay out of a fight.

Playing the part of an informant wasn't for everyone. It took the right blend of street smarts and strategic calculation, in addition to a true desire to eventually get out of the gang life. Joker obviously did not possess the needed combination of character traits to make him useful, Santini realized.

Joker was done as an informant, as far as Santini was concerned. Unfortunately, it meant the agent's plan to use Joker as a tool for getting at Chachi, the clique's main drug dealer, wouldn't pan out as he had hoped.

For 20th Street, the Norteños' attack on Joker prompted a wave of retaliation over the next two days. Casper reported to Santini that Chachi offered to Cyco and the rest of the new booties access to his firearms arsenal to use in revenge attacks, including two .38 caliber handguns and an M4 machine gun.

According to what Peloncito told Casper, one 20th Street member named Sapo didn't need any of Chachi's guns to exact his revenge. An ice pick was good enough for Sapo, who claimed he stalked a lone Norteño walking down a dark alley adjacent to Alabama Street and jammed the long steel pin into his eye. Peloncito told Casper he decided on a less up-close-and-personal approach. He said he shot a couple Norteños as they stood at the corner of Silver Avenue and Alemany Boulevard.

The accelerating pace of violence committed by 20th Street's new booties, which Santini dreaded in the wake of the Polo Grounds confrontation, was in fact happening. Every day the federal investigation continued without arrests of key leaders in the clique was another day someone was more likely to get killed, either a rival gang member or an innocent bystander. The SFPD and the Gang Task Force were obviously overwhelmed and unable to effectively stem the violence.

Still, the federal takedown needed to be conducted strategically and at sufficient scale if the clique was to be smashed beyond its ability to recover. The goal was not to disrupt the 20th Street gang's activities, it was to dismantle and eliminate the entire organization.

CHAPTER 19

Devil Horns Grows

AT THE URGING OF LAURA GWINN, THE DOJ ORGANIZED CRIME Review Section in D.C. now formally accepted the Devil Horns investigation in San Francisco for RICO prosecution of 20th Street as a criminal enterprise. Consequently, a cadre of trial attorneys from the DOJ Gang Unit in D.C. were assigned part-time to San Francisco to work the case, in conjunction with the local US attorney.

In a large and complex federal case such as this, lawyers directed the investigation. They provided guidance to agents in terms of what crimes to pursue, as well as approving sources who were deemed reliable and good potential trial witnesses.

Gwinn's objective now was to identify ten separate crimes of violence committed by 20th Street that might be uncovered in SFPD's cold cases. She divvied up the work reviewing local police files among her team of prosecutors, eventually analyzing nearly fifty cases for their potential as predicate offenses for a RICO conspiracy. The agents on Santini's team were assigned to follow up whatever potential leads had been either missed or ignored by SFPD.

With the help of Santini's new supervisor, Mark Linehan, he recruited a handpicked group of agents for this new, expanded phase of the investigation. They included Brandon Gunn, one of Santini's former trainees, whom he now considered to be a highly effective agent, a short and stocky guy from Michigan with a passion for crime fighting and a keen drive to follow up all investigative leads. There was also Andrew Chang on the new team, an extremely energetic Bay Area native who spoke Chinese better than English. Regardless of his language issues, Chang was a diligent investigator with a never-quit attitude. He had a wife and two youngsters at home, but would spend hours upon hours in the field beating the grass for quality evidence in the case. Also on Santini's "dream team" was John Martin, a new agent fluent in Spanish, who decided to try his luck at federal law enforcement after graduating college with a degree in chemistry.

The group also included Emelda, a top-notch Spanish translator to decipher the dozens of recordings obtained during the investigation, as well as Andre, an intelligence research specialist assigned full-time to the squad to analyze key links between pieces of evidence. A dozen or more other quality agents carefully selected by Santini rounded out the roster. He had started the case with two agents and now had a contingent of over twenty reporting to him under the direction of Linehan.

In the team's conference room, Santini took a step back and gazed at the large, complex pyramid chart he had been developing for three years, illustrating the hierarchy of active 20th Street members along with all their suspected crimes, victims, and locations of key events. At the top of the chart was Tigre. Regardless of how active he was or wasn't, he was still the clique's titular head.

"So," Laura Gwinn began when the team came to order during their first meeting as a group. "What is RICO?"

She proceeded to explain to the assembled agents that for them to be successful with a RICO case, they first needed evidence to establish that 20th Street was an "enterprise," according to the legal definition. "Next, we must prove a pattern of racketeering activity. It must be established that each of the members charged is or was participating in the gang's affairs," she said. This was the most complicated part of the investigation and the main purpose of forming the new team, she explained.

Gwinn believed the majority of the defendants would likely be charged with 18USC 1962 C RICO conspiracy. An important concept for a successful RICO case was establishing an agreement existed between the alleged conspirators. Under the law, if a group of persons agreed to commit a crime but only one of them actually performed the act, they were all still liable if they agreed in advance that the crime should occur. In fact, the crime didn't even have to be committed, just so long as clear steps were taken in the attempt.

Gazing around the room at the assembled team, there finally seemed to Santini to be a clearly attainable goal. Still, it was going to require a lot of pounding the pavement and a higher degree of cooperation from SFPD. It meant Santini's expanded team of agents needed to reinvestigate a large portfolio of unsolved, gang-related assaults and homicides in the city's cold case files.

When Gwinn finished her briefing, Santini stood up before the group. "I can't emphasize enough how dangerous these thugs are," he said. "These aren't just low-level gang members. Many of them are hardened murderers. Some are master manipulators. They are assassins, thieves, and rapists. Officer safety and the safety of the informants are the first priority—over gathering evidence. Any rogue action by any agent to pursue investigative leads is not an option. Everything has to be done above board and Supervisor Linehan and I need to be aware of all investigative activities," he cautioned. "Last, I want to thank you all for joining the Devil Horns team. You are all a valuable part of what may be the biggest case in agency history."

———

Gwinn soon proved she had a keen eye for spotting examples of sloppy police work contained within SFPD's cold case files, quickly convincing Santini's team of agents about the value of following up on shoddy investigations by the city's homicide detectives.

Studying the initial SFPD reports on the attempted murder of a Norteño gang member named Adonis Rupell outside the Palacade pool hall on Mission Street, Gwinn noticed the description provided by an eyewitness who had seen the shooter pull away in a truck. The witness followed the vehicle long enough to get a partial license plate number, but apparently SFPD had never followed up on this critical detail. There was also an eyewitness report about a confrontation that occurred inside the pool hall just moments before the shooting—*also* never investigated.

Sifting through thousands of still frames from multiple video security cameras in the pool hall, special agent Chang identified a man who looked like the 20th Street gang member Kapone. With this evidence and the partial license plate number, the HSI agents visited Kapone's place of work, a vehicle-towing company in San Bruno. Checking for a truck in the company's fleet that fit the witness's description, they found one. When they examined the company's records for the date that Adonis was shot, it showed Kapone had logged the truck out that same day.

Kapone was screwed.

Beyond that, it was clear validation of Gwinn's original thesis that SFPD was regularly dropping the ball on gang-related investigations and that some good old-fashioned detective work could yield solid results. In fairness, the local cops were simply overwhelmed by the sheer volume of cases they needed to process to chase down leads effectively, given their available time and resources.

It was becoming more and more apparent to Gwinn and Santini that murders or attempted murders could well be the main predicate offenses for a federal RICO case against 20th Street.

Santini called Lieutenant Jim Sawyer to request the use of his tactical unit, or Special Weapons and Tactics (SWAT) Team to service a high-risk warrant for search and arrest on Kapone's house, a two-story attached residence in the Hunters Point neighborhood. Early the following Monday morning, the SFPD SWAT team was staged at the front door of Kapone's home. Sawyer was the SWAT commander overseeing the warrant execution.

"Knock notice!" he ordered calmly to the team at the front door.

The first officer in the stack began pounding on the door yelling, "Police! Search warrant! Open the door!" He repeated the warning several times with no response from inside.

The perimeter team called out that they had spotted a Latino male looking out the second-floor window of the residence. They screamed at the man to come downstairs and open the door. He did not comply.

Sawyer called for the breach. His team slammed the door open and both the upstairs and downstairs SWAT units performed a tactical entry. The upstairs team immediately took five persons into custody. The downstairs team moved swiftly through the garage area where they located a living quarters with a locked bedroom door. An officer swiftly kicked the door open, busting the lock and doorjamb.

As the first officer moved into the bedroom, he observed Kapone standing at a sliding glass door that led to an outside deck. He was holding a semiautomatic pistol in each hand and the officer found Kapone's chest area in his EOTech sight. One swing of the hand and Kapone would be shot center mass in the vital organ area. Instead, the thug nervously tossed the guns onto the deck and raised his hands in submission.

Santini was certain Kapone was a drug dealer and murderer. Having him off the street was obviously a form of progress. Unfortunately, the gang had proved it was able to fill personnel voids quickly and the job of dismantling their enterprise was not done yet.

———

Santini raised his right hand and swore to tell the truth, the whole truth, and nothing but the truth. He took a seat on the witness stand and surveyed the group of federal grand jury members. They would be the ones to decide whether to issue RICO indictments against thirty or more members of 20th Street, with Ivan Cerna, aka Tigre, named as the leader of their criminal organization.

Based on his personal experience living in the Bay Area, Santini was worried the grand jury might be comprised of too many "left-wing, granola" types from liberal bastions such as Berkeley. He feared the jury, if they were a bunch of politically correct "progressives," would look at the place of origin and ethnicity of the accused, then take one look at him, Santini, a clean-cut, white federal cop, and decide this was just another case of the establishment persecuting society's disadvantaged.

He tried to read the faces and body language of the jury members for signs of distrust or scorn for police—the obvious gestures or subtle looks of suspicion for power-happy, puffed-up cops. He scanned their hairstyles and clothing, checking for Birkenstock shoes or beaded necklaces on the men, or hairy legs and bushy armpits on the women. They appeared, much to Santini's relief, to be mostly a bunch of average-looking blue- and white-collar folks.

Beginning her presentation to the grand jury, Gwinn walked Santini through an introductory background presentation for the case they rehearsed the day before. As Gwinn led Santini through his testimony, the two settled into a comfortable question-and-answer rhythm. He was impressed and put at ease by her obvious skill at running a court proceeding. The jury appeared to like her style, too. She guided Santini through a concise, twenty-minute synopsis of the 20th Street clique, including its composition, origins, characteristics, areas of operation, transnational nexus, and criminal activities.

After that, Santini's part in the grand jury's first day of testimony was done. He exited the hearing room, since only the prosecutor, jury, witnesses, and court reporter were permitted to be present during proceedings. Waiting outside in the lobby to testify next were two Norteño gang members who had been subpoenaed to give witness testimony about violent attacks they suffered from 20th Street members.

Later that same evening, Santini and Gwinn met for dinner to discuss how things had gone in the proceedings following his own testimony. She told him the Norteños had provided compelling evidence about violent attacks by the 20th Street gang. The jury seemed to be strongly impacted by their stories. So far, so good, Gwinn indicated, and Santini was reassured that she was firmly in charge of the prosecution.

They ordered a bottle of wine with dinner. Gwinn, whose favorite pastime was sailing a thirty-foot sloop on the Chesapeake Bay, also knew her vino. Relieved that the critical grand jury process seemed to have kicked off positively, Santini savored his first sip of a deep red Zin. He was practically giddy over Gwinn's determination to destroy 20th Street, which equaled his own sense of commitment to the mission. She had assumed firm leadership of the case by now, taking a struggling investigation and transforming it into a legitimate racketeering prosecution.

CHAPTER 20

20th Street Power Shift

MANY WEEKS HAD PASSED SINCE THE CONFRONTATION BETWEEN 20TH Street's old dogs and new booties, and the split between the two factions seemed to be on the mend. All the turmoil and unrest associated with conflicting leadership appeared to be behind them.

In September 2007, 20th Street held its first truly cohesive meeting in a long time at Sutro Park, conducted under its new leader, Cyco. Tigre was also present at the meeting and seemingly in good standing with the gang. Perhaps accepting that he was aging out of gang life, Tigre appeared to be resigning himself to a Cyco-led 20th Street. Cyco was an obvious choice for succession as leader. He had committed significant amounts of dirt for La Mara over the years. He also had the backing of the Big Homies now, as well as the loyalty of the newer generation of thugs, who represented the future of the clique.

Cyco was a demanding taskmaster for the youngsters in the gang, and he took the grooming of new members seriously. He conducted regular orientation classes for new and prospective clique members at Peloncito's house on Vienna Street, where he regularly screened a video for the youths titled *Hijos de la Guerra*, or "Children of the War." It was a documentary about the history of MS-13 in El Salvador. Cyco made watching the film mandatory for all new recruits because, he said, it would enlighten them about the origins of the gang and the hardships experienced by the Salvadoran people.

Reports of successful new attacks by 20th Street on the Norteños were circulating regularly back to Santini through Casper. The gang's menacing reputation in the criminal world and its stronghold in the Mission District streets were as firmly entrenched as ever. The 20th Street members were now regularly paying cash dues to the clique, and the Big Homies seemed content with regular visits from MS-13 runners bearing tributes of cash, cell phones, and other merchandise to their Central American prisons, delivered with all due respects and compliments from 20th Street.

Cyco was also ensuring all gangs in the neighborhood were paying a tax to the clique. He was collecting cash-filled envelopes from the Miceros as well as the 11th Street and 19th Street Sureños, keeping 20th Street's coffers flush to purchase guns from Negro in Reno and another more local source, which Santini was unable to identify yet.

Casper was relieved about the lessened strife and turmoil within 20th Street. Like Tigre, he was enjoying a less prominent role in the gang, although lingering suspicion about his cooperation with law enforcement had not completely dissipated. In fact, one of the topics at the Sutro Park meeting of the newly harmonized 20th Street was a developing problem for Casper, stirred up by a gang member named Manuel Umana, aka Lulu. The homie was spreading rumors that Casper was a snitch and couldn't be trusted.

At the meeting, Casper openly objected to Lulu's potentially lethal accusations. Unfortunately for Lulu, Casper and some other veteran gang members already knew he had never been jumped in with MS-13. Armed with this damning knowledge, Casper went on the offensive and argued during the meeting that Lulu's claim of being a full-fledged MS member needed to be investigated. As the clique's new leader, Cyco took Casper's claim seriously, because he was determined to improve the 20th Street's reputation for poor discipline with the Big Homies. He requested that senior gang members in El Salvador investigate whether Lulu was actually a jumped-in member.

The gang's investigation into Lulu's history only confirmed that his brother, known inside MS-13 as Vago, was jumped in with the Amargureños clique in Calle de la Amargura in San Salvador. With no indication Lulu himself ever was, Cyco proclaimed he would be disciplined with a serious beating. After that, the gang would make a final determination on his fate.

When results of the full investigation into Lulu's history came back from the Big Homies in El Salvador, Cyco and Peloncito learned Lulu was paying a bribe to a senior gang member in El Salvador named Gato to provide phony confirmation that he was jumped in. Lulu was green-lighted for death and Gato, a leader of the Amargureños Locos clique in El Salvador, was assassinated by order of the Big Homies.

The threat to Casper from Lulu was eliminated now, but there were still others inside the gang that he needed to worry about, including Casper's duplicitous former girlfriend, Jackie, whom the FBI had by now recruited as an informant.

◦—◦

It was a beautiful, sunny Wednesday morning on the eve of Halloween, 2007, when Peloncito hopped aboard the Metro bus at Palou Avenue, on his way to his job as a carpet installer with a company in Daly City. He was dressed in all black, with Carhartt carpenter pants and a sweatshirt covering his tattoos, wearing nothing blue to signal his MS-13 affiliation. Peloncito moved down the aisle of the bus, walking past some giggling elementary school kids and a sleeping homeless man. He took a seat in the last row.

There were good reasons that Peloncito was widely considered the most vicious hit man for the San Francisco–based clique of La Mara Salvatrucha. Like Kid Twist, a New York mobster in the 1940s who was widely considered the most ruthless killer working at the time for Murder Inc., the Italian mafia's enforcement unit, Peloncito also had a penchant for the lethal use of common household tools. Kid Twist's weapon of choice was the ice pick, which he would ram through his victim's ear straight and deep into the brain. He became so adept at using an ice pick that many of his murder victims were thought by examining coroners to have died of natural cerebral hemorrhages.

Peloncito rode the bus through San Francisco's bustling rush-hour streets, stopping at a crowded corner to pick up a group of waiting commuters. Trailing behind a group of school kids and day laborers boarding the bus he spotted a Norteño homeboy sporting his colors: a red T-shirt and red ball cap, with a red bandanna hanging out his back pocket. He

155

sat in the fifth row on the left, and Peloncito began to size him up. The MS-13 homie's blood began to boil with fury and hatred for the rival gang member who was publicly flying his colors.

Peloncito couldn't take it any longer and decided he would walk the last few blocks to work. As the bus pulled over for the next stop, he stood and moved forward swiftly up the aisle. His senses were buzzing. Sweat began to form on his brow as he approached the chavala from behind, sliding the tool from his inside pocket and gripping it tightly.

As the school kids completed homework answers in their workbooks, Peloncito grabbed the collar of his victim and began thrusting the ice pick manically into his face and head. Over and over he stabbed him, fifteen times. Blood squirted onto his victim's sweatshirt and all over the woman sitting in the next seat, who was overcome and frozen with shock as the chavala's head fell forward, slumping against the back of the next seat forward.

Peloncito moved quickly to the front of the bus and exited before the door closed. He could hear screams as the vehicle started to drive away, then abruptly came to a screeching halt. He dumped the blood-covered ice pick into an alley trash can and walked the back streets to work.

It was going to be a great Halloween.

—⸙—

The Big Homies had something major planned in Central America. Maybe it was a riot, a prison break, or the murder of a prison official. Casper told Santini he didn't know exactly what was going to happen, but he knew it was big. Casper also reported his older brother, the Big Homie named Snoopy, had just contacted him because he could not reach Cyco.

During the call with his brother, Snoopy told Casper he was in contact with the Big Homie named Santos, who called Snoopy from the Ciudad Barrios prison in El Salvador. Santos told Snoopy that all the Big Homies were mandating every MS-13 clique in the United States contribute $300 as a part of a gang-wide fund-raising drive. They required that the payments be received no later than December 1, to fund some sort of large-scale attack being planned.

Snoopy also said he wanted to arrange a three-way conference call with Casper and Santos to go into more detail. During the arranged call, Santos explained to Casper the collected funds would pay for a quantity of guns in El Salvador. Casper agreed that 20th Street should be able to make the required payment, but he recommended that Snoopy and Santos contact Cyco directly to obtain official confirmation, since he was leading the clique now.

As the deadline came and went, no payment was received by the Big Homies from 20th Street. Cyco's leadership may have been consolidating locally, but his deficiencies in cooperating with fellow clique leaders in California and with the Big Homies down south were causing serious problems.

Casper reported to Santini he received another phone call on Saturday, December 8, from his brother Snoopy, who was furious. Snoopy demanded to know why 20th Street failed to make the $300 payment. He complained to Casper that Cyco was failing to answer his cell phone whenever contacts were attempted by the "program" in El Salvador.

During the same conversation, Casper and Snoopy participated in a three-way conference call, this time with Peloncito, who deferred any explanations about the failure to Cyco. Snoopy warned Peloncito heatedly that 20th Street was the only clique that hadn't contributed the required funds yet. Casper attempted to quell his older brother's anger, telling him he believed 20th Street was currently in the process of collecting the money and the funds would be wired to El Salvador no later than December 14.

⌐◦⌐

The delays and excuses from 20th Street were not to be tolerated any longer by the Big Homies, who determined to make an example of the clique's failure to pay up on time. Peloncito received a call from Santos in El Salvador, who ordered that he and Cyco attend an important regional MS-13 gang summit in Los Angeles. Several California-area factions were expected to attend the big meeting to discuss inter-clique cooperation, statewide objectives, and strategic goals of La Mara nationwide, Santos told Peloncito.

Cyco was excited to hear the news. It meant he would be getting an opportunity to represent 20th Street for the first time as the clique's leader in front of numerous peers in the region. He felt like he was finally getting the respect he was due.

A few days later, Cyco, Peloncito, and Soldado drove to Los Angeles to attend the inter-clique meeting, to be held at MacArthur Park in the Pico Union section of the city. The three thugs from 20th Street were excited, and each wore their best blue gangster gear for the occasion. Cyco donned his favorite Southside jacket, while Peloncito wore his blue No. 13 football jersey. Soldado put on his favorite light-blue T-shirt with a matching "20" emblazoned ball cap.

In L.A., the three 20th Street homies first met with an MS-13 member named Lizard at the Los Molcajetes Pupuseria restaurant on Hoover Street, known for its delicious pupusas. Lizard was a fledgling member of the Leeward clique in Los Angeles, which was one of the oldest and most respected in all of La Mara. Even a new member from the Leewards commanded special respect among other MS-13 cliques. It was rumored that recruits for the Leeward crew were all required to kill three people before they were jumped in.

Lizard was young but he also looked hard, like a homie who conceivably could have already killed three people. While loading his pupusas with *curtido*, a fermented cabbage salsa, Lizard informed his three 20th Street visitors they would be required to address the entire meeting that evening.

Cyco was caught off guard to learn he was going to have to answer for the problems inside his clique. Word had traveled to the dark prisons of El Salvador and back to the streets of Los Angeles that 20th Street was dysfunctional and a bad representative of La Mara. Someone would have to answer for their failures.

At dusk, the four homies walked a few blocks together through an upscale neighborhood, past the Park Plaza Hotel, and entered MacArthur Park. At least a dozen Leeward members were waiting, smoking cigarettes, talking on cell phones, and kicking around a soccer ball.

An hour passed and perhaps two dozen more mareros arrived. Members from the Hollywood, Wilshire, Coronado, and Western cliques of MS-13 were also in attendance.

At about 8:30 p.m. the group gathered in a circle and the gang leader Demente addressed them. Cyco, Peloncito, and Soldado were ordered to stand in the center of the ring, back-to-back in a triangle formation, facing the crowd of mareros staring back at them. The encircled trio could see the faces staring at them all around behind the glow of lit cigarettes.

Demente paced around them in a circle.

"You've failed to represent the hood," he said, his voice rising. "You've failed to live up to your sworn oath to serve The Beast. You've failed to pay respect to those who have carried the flag before you. Do we accept failures among us?"

"*No!*" the entire group shouted in unison.

Without being summoned, three mareros walked to the center of the ring, each holding a handgun, which they pressed them against the foreheads of Cyco, Peloncito, and Soldado—long enough to send a message. Suddenly, the three 20th Street members were thrown down and the mob pounced on them, punching and kicking them wildly. Cyco almost lost consciousness before the melee ceased, and Demente leaned over him, pressing his face against Cyco's.

"Correct the 20th Street or the next visit to San Francisco will shine a green light on the '20,'" he said. "Don't fail, homie."

The three 20th Street homies returned to San Francisco, bruised and shaken, the message from the Big Homies to shape up—or else—firmly pounded into their brains. They quickly rounded up the cash for the special collection and forwarded it to El Salvador. From now on, they were committed to running the Mission clique more in line with the ones in Los Angeles and Central America—ultraviolent and more responsive to the Big Homies' demands.

CHAPTER 21

Outside the Lines in El Sal

San Salvador, November 2007

"Buenos días, senore!" Fernando Palacios said.

Santini had not seen Palacios for years, not since he was a rookie border patrol agent just starting his probationary period at Chula Vista Station ten years earlier. Back then, Palacios was a special agent with the border patrol's human smuggling division. Now he was an HSI assistant attaché in San Salvador, responding to the seemingly never-ending flow of requests from investigators all over the United States who were pursuing criminal cases involving Salvadoran nationals.

Santini introduced his traveling companion to Palacios, a special agent named Joseph Sarkinski. Known as Shark to his friends, the HSI agent was in El Salvador with Santini to tie up some loose ends on an MS-13 case he was pursuing in D.C. Shark was looking for additional background information on his primary target, known inside the gang as *Censonate*, or Centipede, accused of killing a rival gang member and his girlfriend in Washington. An informant who had grown up in the same El Salvador town as Centipede was currently in custody with the Policia National Civil (PNC) and Shark wanted to interview him.

Santini had made the trip to El Salvador to find out more about Casper's brother Freddie Zavala, aka Snoopy, a Big Homie and one of the founders of 20th Street. Although he was locked up thousands of miles away, Snoopy continued wielding major influence over the clique's activities in California.

The two HSI agents were also in El Salvador to meet with Salvadoran police members of the FBI's newly formed Transnational Anti-Gang (TAG) joint task force in San Salvador. Known within local law enforcement circles as the CAT house or "Centro Anti-pandillas Transnational," it was a clandestine facility where about twenty specially trained PNC officers and ten analysts assisted the FBI in disrupting transnational criminal networks. Three years of liaison work coupled with offers of generous funding and US visas for Salvadoran officers (otherwise known as sanctioned bribery) convinced the PNC to collaborate and work with the FBI.

Santini had attempted on several previous occasions to work through HSI headquarters to establish a point of contact with TAG, but he had been stymied at every turn. The FBI was extremely keen to learn more about Santini's targets in San Francisco and willing to assist in obtaining information from El Salvador that could benefit Operation Devil Horns. However, the Bureau insisted on becoming full partners in Santini's case in exchange. The agent refused the FBI's demands for cooperation, and so his requests for access to TAG had gone nowhere.

Santini's original opinion of the FBI as the preeminent American law enforcement agency, shared by much of the general public, had deteriorated badly since the start of his investigation into 20th Street. Based on his experience in San Francisco, he believed the FBI functioned more like a rich bully, throwing lots of money and equipment at local law enforcement agencies, then swooping in to steal the glory whenever an investigation was already developed to the point of imminent success. Essentially, Santini thought, the Bureau was functioning the same way with the local police in El Salvador.

Working channels through HSI's international affairs division, Santini linked back up with Palacios, who revealed that their agency had back-door access to the CAT house. The inside source was one of Palacios's Foreign Service National (FSN) employees, who are foreign nationals working overseas for the US government. The FSN, a former PNC officer, had strong ties to several of the officers assigned to TAG. He could access Salvadoran personnel at TAG with little or no notice by the FBI. Santini and his buddy Shark wanted access to the CAT house badly, and now they were very close.

With Palacios as their escort, the three agents rolled unimpeded through San Salvador airport customs and headed toward a government SUV. Inside the vehicle, Palacios opened a hatch in the center console of the truck, exposing a loaded Glock 9 mm pistol.

"It's here," he said. "Just in case."

"I'd prefer something bigger," Shark said, grinning. "Where's the M4?"

At the city outskirts, with the San Salvador volcano looming in the distance, dirt roads cut through row after row of tiny, single-room shanties covered with corrugated metal and plastic tarps. Small children and chickens scampered around squalid homes, watching cars whiz by. Closer to the city, more prosperous cinder-block residences sided with pastel-colored adobe were built onto the hillsides.

Palacios drove Santini and Shark to the US embassy for brief introductions with some staff and to pick up the FSN. After a quick briefing, the four headed to the CAT house, a place so secret it was a mystery even to most people in local law enforcement. Most of the local cops knew CAT existed, but few knew exactly where it was or who was assigned to it. For their personal security, it was critical to keep the vetted officers assigned to the house insulated from PNC street cops, who were often corrupt and easily bought off by gang leaders.

El Salvador was known worldwide as a dangerous place. Including MS-13, 18th Street, and other, smaller criminal groups, there were an estimated thirty-nine thousand gang members thought to be responsible for 27 percent of violent crimes and 40 percent of homicides committed in the country. Some observers of the country argued there were more killings here during the 1990s than there were during the country's previous twelve years of civil war.

The crime situation had only worsened since the turn of the twenty-first century. Statistics from 2005 indicated 56 murders per 100,000 inhabitants in El Salvador, ranking the country as the most violent in the region.[1] In 2002 the country's annual overall murder rate stood at 2,024, rising to 3,182 by 2005. Young men between nineteen and thirty years of age were particularly at risk, totaling some 55 percent of murder victims in the country, according to stats from the PNC and national Attorney General's Office. The average homicide rate for young people was estimated at greater than 90 deaths per 100,000 inhabitants in 2004, while the rate rose to 114 per 100,000 the following year.[2]

The agents drove through downtown San Salvador, past the city center, and headed for the surrounding hills on several winding roads running past dilapidated homes and businesses. The FSN drove cautiously, since it was common for street hoodlums to steal manhole covers and sell them for the melt value of their aluminum. They had already destroyed more than one government car's axles.

Once past the poorer neighborhoods, on the hillsides surrounding the city the shanties and shacks gave way to well-landscaped, upper-class residences surrounded by security gates, walls, and armed guards protecting the wealthy residents and their properties. The agents' vehicle climbed a little higher, then made a quick turn onto a short driveway.

"We are here," the FSN said.

He idled the vehicle in front of a large, ten-foot-high wooden gate set inside even taller concrete walls covered by flowering vines. The FSN beeped his horn three times, then waited. Moments later, a small wooden hatch in the fence opened and a man's face appeared. The FSN spoke briefly to the man on the other side.

After several more minutes, the gate opened and they drove through the entrance, continuing up the driveway leading to a very well-maintained residence, with large columns surrounding a grand entryway. The vast green lawns surrounding the property were mowed and trimmed, adorned with splashing fountains and pink flamingo statues.

Santini, Shark, and Palacios exited the vehicle and were met by a group of five residents of the CAT house. Señora Pineda, the agent in charge, introduced herself first. She escorted them into the foyer of the residence and introduced the Americans to several more officers inside.

The CAT house was just that—a house—a six-bedroom rancher. Its rooms were cleared of residential comforts and filled with low-end office furniture. There were numerous computer workstations installed throughout, enough to accommodate approximately twenty agents. There were lockers and makeshift sleeping quarters, and it appeared as if some of the employees worked long shifts and stayed the night, or perhaps even lived here.

Santini and Shark were whisked to a bedroom that had been converted into a cramped conference space. Here they were given a PowerPoint presentation illustrating the structure of MS-13 in El Salvador and its large network, which extended from Central America through Mexico and into the United States—all controlled mostly by the gang's senior leaders in El Salvador. Santini and Shark were impressed by the presentation and the wealth of information the TAG agents had compiled. Their analysis all checked out with Santini's own understanding of the gang's organization.

When the briefing was finished, Santini provided the Salvadorans with intel obtained through Casper about Flash, the money mule in El Salvador who acted as a conduit from 20th Street to the Big Homies. He gave them everything they needed to know about Flash and where and how he was transferring the money so the Salvadoran police could set up a bust and disrupt the clique's financial network.

As Santini and Shark were leaving the house, they walked past a large, sliding glass entryway. Outside they spied a big inground pool and a lush lawn where several men were kicking around a soccer ball. Their FSN said two of the men were FBI agents assigned to TAG. Santini and Shark found it amusing, in a snarky sort of way. Here they were at the FBI's own CAT house, receiving a briefing, collaborating with officers and analysts, and exiting the premises—all while two Bureau agents played soccer in the sun, completely clueless about the HSI agents in their midst.

They left with a more complete understanding of 20th Street's connections to the Big Homies, including Casper's brother Snoopy, verifying everything Casper had told Santini about Snoopy's exact prison cell location and his ties with other senior gang members.

Santini also made connections with Salvadoran gang experts at the CAT house who might prove highly valuable as subject matter experts in any upcoming trials against MS-13. In addition, he received new information about certain individuals who were making cash withdrawals from Banco Agricola in El Salvador, after deposits were made by gang members at the bank's branch in the Mission.

Santini's expanded ambition for the investigation now was to build a case strong enough to extradite some Big Homies to the United States—which, if successful, would be the first time in history it was done.

CHAPTER 22

Diego Returns

It had been several weeks since ICE shipped Diego back one-way to Honduras, when an agent assigned to Operation Devil Horns poked his head into Santini's office.

"Diego just called me from Honduras," he said.

"Yeah?" Santini said. "What'd he want?"

The agent was still pissed at his wayward informant, who had flaked out on him after such a promising start to his career as a snitch.

"He said he wants to come back and work," his partner said. "He says he's sorry."

Sorry, Santini thought. *Yeah, he's sorry alright.*

But the prospect of getting Diego back into the investigation's mix was too enticing to ignore, even though Casper had worked out great as an informant—more effective than Diego, in many ways. He was better known to the 20th Street clique and had higher-level connections with the Big Homies. But Casper's days as an informant on the street were nearly done. Too much suspicion about him had developed within the clique.

Diego had been a major asset when he was actively providing intel about the clique, as well as facilitating the seizure of guns. He was also purposely detached from clique leadership, to avoid any legal entrapment issues as he provided eyes and ears on the gang's street activities. The streets were where Peloncito and Cyco and their new booties lived, where they killed and maimed, and then frequently bragged about their exploits. If Diego returned to working the street, it could help the operation build a more airtight case against the gang.

The agent went to Nelson Wong at the US Attorney's Office and described the situation, how Diego had called and expressed repentance and was promising to be a reliable informant again, if they let him come back to the States. As one who ultimately would have to try the case in court, Wong understood the obvious value of allowing Diego to return to work. It would likely help obtain additional evidence and make Diego available as a key witness at trial as well.

However, the prosecutor opposed providing any aid to Diego whatsoever in reentering the country. If the informant ever committed a serious crime in the States and it became publicly known that the federal government was responsible for him being intentionally allowed onto American soil, the political fallout could be extreme.

"We could tell him if he shows back up on this side of the border, we'll defer action on his illegal entry," Santini suggested to Wong.

Wong nodded.

"If he makes it across the border," Santini said, "he can call us, and we'll put him back to work. If not, then he's on his own and we just move ahead without him, the way we are now."

The plan was approved by Santini's supervisors, and his partner passed the word to Diego that he had been granted a reprieve—but only if he could get back into the States on his own accord.

It was all Diego needed to hear, and he was on his way north, moving along the shadowy migration corridors from Honduras, through the Guatemalan jungle, and hitching free rides atop the freight trains that rumbled through Mexico to the US border at Tecate. Within a matter of days, Diego snuck back into California and placed a call to Santini's partner.

"It's Diego," he said. "I am in San Francisco."

Now, to keep his handlers happy and remain in the United States, Diego knew he would have to start digging around hard again for useful intelligence. Santini was so furious the last time the two men were together. Diego knew he was skating on thin ice with the agent now.

Prior to the highly publicized case of Brenda Paz, an MS-13 gang member who turned rat and was eventually killed while in protective custody in Virginia, it was not unusual for females to join MS-13 through a group-sex ritual involving multiple homies. (The gang ruled out membership for females altogether after Paz ratted out several members.) Getting gangbanged was an alternative for females to being jumped in through a severe beating with fists and feet, which male initiates were required to endure.

Peloncito's juvenile girlfriend in MS-13, whose gang name was Flaca (Skinny), liked to shave her eyebrows and draw pencil-thin mascara lines in their place. Like a lot of teenagers, she wore tight-fitting jeans. A dark hoodie was her trademark top. She was a disturbed young woman, a lost soul full of confusion and hate. Beyond that, she was dangerously violent. Flaca, sixteen years old, enjoyed the thrill of slashing and stabbing unsuspecting, random victims. She was a perfect partner for Peloncito. Their bait-and-switch attacks on unsuspecting young men played on Flaca's sex appeal and treachery. She'd lure them in, and Peloncito would make them pay.

A typical example of their attack profile: At 24th and Shotwell in the Mission, Jesus Jimenez was grabbing some tacos at Tagueria Guadalajara restaurant when Flaca approached him and asked him for his phone number. He was surprised. She was a little weird-looking, but definitely cute enough for a date. He followed her around the corner into an alley, where a blue Honda stopped abruptly next to them. Peloncito exited the vehicle and walked up to Jimenez.

"Mara Salvatrucha!" Peloncito yelled, and slashed Jimenez in the face with a knife.

Peloncito and Flaca hopped back into the car and drove off, as Jimenez rushed back into the restaurant, bleeding profusely and pleading for someone to call 911. He sat at a table near the window, attempting to control the blood gushing from a four-inch slice on his left cheek, which extended from his left ear to the base of his nose, clear down to the cheekbone.

In another seemingly spontaneous act of random violence, Peloncito and Flaca disembarked from a city bus at Mission and Silver Streets. It was the day after Christmas.

"Hey, cutie!" a young man said to Flaca, flirting, as she stepped onto the sidewalk. The would-be Romeo then noticed an older dude with a mustache and a scar on his face, Peloncito, wearing a black hoodie and a menacing look, step off the bus behind Flaca.

"Whoops!" the young man said, avoiding eye contact with Peloncito, who turned and walked away down the street with Flaca.

A few moments later, Peloncito and Flaca returned and confronted the flirtatious youth and two friends who were with him.

"MS, putos!" the bloodthirsty pair yelled in unison.

Peloncito grabbed one of the male youths and began stabbing him in the neck and back. While the victim struggled to escape, Flaca lunged at the young woman and stabbed her once in the chest. The two attackers then ran away from the scene.

Grievously wounded, the male victim stumbled and screamed, "Help me!" He ran toward Joe's Cable Car Diner across the street and collapsed in the parking lot.

The female victim was taken to the hospital by her boyfriend, while emergency medical first responders tended to the injured male. He was in critical condition from several stab wounds to his neck and chest, requiring several hours of surgery to repair major internal injuries, and he nearly died on the operating table.

⚊⌒⚊

Back at work on the streets, a few days after the bus-stop attack, Diego visited Mission Playground, where Peloncito was schooling a young gang member about the finer points of MS-13's reglos. Nearby, Cyco chatted up a young girl at the Valencia Street entrance to the park. Diego judged the girl couldn't be more than fourteen years old—Cyco had a well-known fetish for underage females.

Peloncito told Diego los puercos (the pigs, or the police), had just taken a walk through the playground, so it would be smart for the homies to take a ride together to a park up the hill.

"Puchica, putos," Peloncito said. (Let's get the fuck out of here.)

Diego and the homies drove several blocks up State Street to a park in Corona Heights, situated at high elevation with great views of the city. Cyco said he enjoyed coming here to watch a herd of wild goats browsing the hillside.[1] The 20th Street crew climbed out of the car and hiked up the hill to some public barbeque pits, where they passed around a fat joint.

In between effusive tokes, Peloncito laughed and bragged about recently stabbing three chapetes on Mission and Silver Streets the day after Christmas. He said that Papa Noel hadn't given him any presents that year, but the opportunity to cut up the chapos was the greatest gift of all.

Eager to report Peloncito's description of the attacks to Santini right away, Diego told the gangsters he needed to phone his wife. He strolled away to make the call in private.

Santini's cell rang as he walked with Gibson through the parking lot of San Francisco General Hospital. The two cops had just finished interviewing a seventeen-year-old female who was stabbed in the chest by a Sureño gangbanger while waiting at a bus stop.

"Michael," said Diego. "I have new information about an attack that Peloncito is bragging about."

"Really, homito?" Santini said. "Junto! Pronto!"

"He is telling about a stabbing he and his girl Flaca did at Silver and Mission."

The hair on the back of Santini's neck stood up. The female victim that he and Gibson just interviewed was attacked at the same intersection. After the attack, SFPD Gang Task Force officers were called to investigate, since the assailants had referred to MS-13 during the assault. A city detective canvassed the area and met with a nearby store's security guard, who provided video footage of the two perpetrators running through a parking lot, making their escape.

Following up the tip from Diego, Gibson showed Jimenez photo spreads of Peloncito and Flaca. The victim affirmatively picked them both out as his attackers. SFPD detectives also showed photo spreads of Peloncito and Flaca to victims and witnesses of the attack at the bus stop. Both were positively identified as the assailants.

Gibson served a search warrant at the residence of Peloncito. The cops knocked on his door late at night and he answered. They searched his bedroom, where they found a black hoodie, a blue hoodie, two knives, two cell phones, numerous pieces of gang indicia including hats, clothing, and jail letters. He was booked for attempted homicide.

Removing Peloncito from the street would change the clique's power dynamics in unpredictable ways. It brought new leaders to the forefront, forcing Santini to track and contain the morphing group as best he could, pulling strings from the outside through his informants.

Flaca was arrested soon after and booked as a juvenile, her identity and case disposition kept confidential. Police later seized about a dozen pages of poems and lists of persons that Flaca wanted dead for one reason or another. The information was forwarded to state prosecutors pursuing attempted murder charges against her.

Mi Vida Loca
by Flaca

Esta vida that I live
Is slowly driving me insane
Extreme paranoia
Always keeping trucha
Living off that dirty feria
Cant trust no one
Not even your own barrio
Sleepin con one ojo open
Stead steppin
Head to toe Sur'ed up
Walkin enemy tierra
Solo on every creep
I'm a one person army
It's me all alone against tu barrio
So fuck the world
Looking every chapa in the eye
Murder is my high
Checkin every Nor puto in sight
Behind bars mi wicked fantasies arise
Wicked in a cell
I know I'm going to hell
Esta vida that I live
I call my vida loca

With probably the single-most homicidal gang member, Peloncito, in custody, Santini turned his attention now to cutting off the other part of 20th Street's two-headed hydra. Cyco was still free on bail pending an illegal firearm charge. His current legal situation was also complicated by a judge's recent deportation order. For the time being, Santini believed Cyco would remain in the States long enough to bust him—hopefully soon—on a more serious federal racketeering charge.

Meanwhile, Casper continued to defy fate by functioning as an informant on the street. Soon after Peloncito's arrest, he was paying a visit to the homies at the little park in the Mission when Patas drove up and asked him to take a ride. The Miceros boss wanted to discuss a volatile situation in the hood. Casper obliged and hopped into Patas's four-door Cutlass.

Casper had always respected Patas. Like Tigre, he preferred working relationships on the street based on mutual respect between the neighborhood's various gangs. Patas avoided unnecessary aggression, as opposed to the preferred style of 20th Street's newest leaders, who tended to spread fear through wanton violence.

Although the Miceros' primary area of operations was Mission Street, between 11th and 24th, Patas had several groups of rovers who intermittently worked different parts of the city. These roving peddlers funneled fake-document customers back to Patas, who controlled the entire counterfeit operation in the Mission, from photo labs to printing and lamination machines.

Patas told Casper that Cyco was demanding a new tax from the Miceros to meet the demand for special funds by the Big Homies in El Salvador. Cyco demanded Patas pay the tax within the next week, or he warned somebody was going to die. Patas told Casper he was not going to bend over for the threat. He also said he knew Cyco was planning to leave the States for El Salvador within the next several days.

After their conversation, Casper walked back to the park and gave Santini a call on his cell phone.

"He's leaving," Casper said.

"Who's leaving, bro?" Santini said. "What are you talking about?"

"Our leader," Casper said. "Cyco is headed south to El Salvador."

"Fuck!" Santini said. "That's bad news, homie."

This revelation that Cyco planned to exit the States shocked Santini and put the wheels in motion for a quick plan to stop him, somehow. The agent couldn't allow one of his investigation's main targets and the current leader of 20th Street to leave the country and avoid prosecution. Santini assigned one of his team's agents the task of ensuring Cyco was put on a leash before he escaped to Central America. While continuing to monitor the airline passenger record system, a ticket reservation for Marvin Carcamo, aka Cyco, popped up for a red-eye flight from San Francisco to El Salvador with Taca Airlines, departing in three days.

A tip from Santini's partner to Bad Boy Bail Bonds about Cyco's plan to flee the country sent the bondsmen into action. Bad Boy had posted Cyco's original $80,000 bond for his pending gun charge. They arrested Cyco at the Taca Airlines ticket counter at San Francisco International Airport in front of his father and brother, Indio.

The San Francisco sheriff's department was adamant they would reset Cyco's bond at only the original amount of $80,000—even though it was clear he intended to flee the United States. Gibson worked through the night, drafting a series of detailed documents for a judge to get Cyco's bail increased to $500,000. The following day, Santini learned that Cyco's family planned on procuring the increased bail amount to get him released. This prompted the HSI agents to contact the local DA's office, which worked with a judge to reset Cyco's bail at $10 million.

Cyco's attorney attempted to argue he was leaving the country and skipping on his bond in a good faith attempt to adhere to the immigration judge's prior order that he leave the country within two weeks. The appeal was dismissed, to Santini's relief. Cyco remained in custody for the gun violation.

Primary target number two for Santini was locked down for the time being, and for that he was grateful. Still, the federal grand jury needed to finish its agonizingly slow and deliberate process before it could deliver any RICO indictments, while violence on the street continued seemingly without relief.

Santini's cell phone rang—it was Casper calling.

"Michael, I have a problem," he said.

"What's up?" Santini said.

"I am under arrest," Casper said.

"For what?!" Santini said.

"They say the car I am driving is stolen," Casper said. "I don't know anything about it. I borrowed the car. I don't know about it."

Santini considered the situation. What did this mean for his investigation, if Casper got locked up for auto theft? Of course, the agent would be losing one of his two main informants, which wasn't good. On the other hand, Casper had been running up against his expiration date for a while. The dumbass might have done himself a favor by getting busted, Santini thought.

"Okay, dog," Santini said. "There's nothing I can do for you right now."

"But I didn't know the car was hot!" Casper said.

"Sorry, man," Santini said. "I can't do anything about it right now. I'll get back to you as soon as possible. Just be cool."

He heard Casper let out a deep sigh on the other end of the line, then the voice of a CHP officer barking an order in the background. He heard Casper's phone rubbing against the fabric of his clothes, and his muffled voice responding to the cop.

He came back on the line. "I have to go," Casper said.

"Okay," Santini said. "I'll be in contact. Good luck, dog."[2]

CHAPTER 23

Norteño War Heats Up

In January 2008, Gavin Newsom was enjoying the overwhelming victory of his second mayoral election just two months before, when he won with 72 percent of the popular vote. The election results weren't much of a surprise to anyone, since Newsom's two main challengers on the ballot were George Davis, a "nude activist" and author of the book *Naked Yoga*, and Michael Powers, owner of the infamous Power Exchange "sex club" in the Tenderloin.

With another four-year mayoral term ahead of him, Newsom was widely considered to already have his eye on the next big thing. And what was the most likely big step for such an ambitious political climber? Why not governor of California, the most populous state in the Union, with an economy the size of a major nation?

SFPD under Newsom's administration still had an abysmally bad record of investigating and solving violent crime. A blue-ribbon panel report released in the middle of his first term exposed a myriad of deep-seated problems within the city's police department, including "leadership failure, communication breakdown, low morale, politics and mistrust."[1] These weren't the kind of crime-fighting creds that would help win votes among the law-and-order crowd in the larger California body politic, especially outside of San Francisco.

Newsom's law-enforcement credentials would require some brushing up if he was going to be taken seriously for statewide office. The field of competitors would certainly be more formidable than a nude activist or the proprietor of a sex club—which is the reason some observers reckoned he picked Kevin Ryan to head the Mayor's Office of Criminal Justice soon after his reelection.[2]

Appointed US attorney for Northern California by President George W. Bush in 2002, Ryan made national headlines as the prosecutor in the BALCO steroids case involving San Francisco Giants homerun slugger Barry Bonds. The Bonds case was characterized by a high degree of self-promotion on the part of Ryan, as well as an ill-conceived prosecution strategy that targeted a small-scale steroids supplier and a handful of celebrity athletes. In the end, the main illegal supplier of the steroids in the case took a walk, in exchange for testifying against Bonds.

Ryan eventually was canned as US attorney in December 2006 by the Bush administration, basically for rank incompetence as the head of DOJ's office in Northern California. In a scathing report released by the Justice Department, Ryan was determined to have presided over an office characterized as "retaliatory, explosive, non-communicative and paranoid." Nevertheless, he was a conservative, well-connected Catholic Republican, reputedly a strong crime fighter who had pursued tough antigang strategies while serving as a prosecutor with the Alameda County District Attorney's Office. All that, apparently, was good enough for Newsom.

Picking Ryan to head up the city's office of criminal justice represented a reach across the aisle in deference to the tough-on-crime crowd from Orange, Riverside, and Los Angeles Counties. Otherwise, Newsom's future political opponents would likely succeed in portraying him as a pantywaist mayor from the City of Gay Pride, who rolled over for thugs and bullies.

While Ryan's appointment to the mayor's administration provided a tough-on-crime veneer, it also allowed someone from the Republican opposition inside Newsom's tent. When a huge public controversy over San Francisco's sanctuary city policy and its negative effect on combating violent illegal immigrant gangs soon sprang to national attention, Ryan's natural political loyalties would only make Newsom's desperate attempts at damage control more difficult.

—~—

By the start of 2008, the Operation Devil Horns team had already started taking the most murderous 20th Street gang members off the street, picking them off one at a time on various state charges with the help of Cabrera, Gibson, and a handful of SFPD cops who occasionally risked their careers. In this way, the thugs could be held in local custody until RICO indictments were nailed down and the gang members could be transferred to federal custody. Peloncito and Cyco were incarcerated now, and so was Kapone. Getting the most violent clique leaders off the street, so the theory went, would also keep the gang disoriented and less likely to organize major attacks.

But being locked up behind bars did not prevent Cyco and Peloncito from continuing to call shots for the clique, a situation that became obvious to the Devil Horns team as they monitored Peloncito's speakerphone address from jail to a meeting of new booties in Mission Playground. During the call, Peloncito expressed to the crew how proud he was of the way they were all taking care of business in his absence. Other tapped phone calls with Cyco and Peloncito while in jail, facilitated by various girlfriends and homies who patched them in through conference-call services, revealed the two homies were still calling shots for the clique.

The main conduit for Cyco and Peloncito to manage gang business from jail now was Slow Pain, who took over as the clique's leader on the streets. Slow Pain was leading the new booties in a campaign to fully oust the clique's old guard—including a ruthless plan to murder Tigre, Joker, Goofy, and Droopy. Based on directions from Cyco, the new booties were also preparing to break off from 20th Street with the support of the PLS in Richmond and to form a new clique based on 80th Avenue in Oakland. Cyco wanted to break out on his own, free from the constraints and baggage of the old 20th Street clique.

Startling incidents of deadly violence in the Mission, committed in plain view of the public, were creating a growing sense of fear in the neighborhood. The rival Norteños were brutal as well, equally capable of attacking and killing, as was proved once again by their fatal hit on an MS-13 marero named Maya. Maya had strayed onto Norteño turf just long enough to grab a quick taco lunch and was gunned down right outside the restaurant where he ate his last meal. It was the first fatal hit on a 20th Street member since Memo was killed, and it couldn't go unanswered.

As a group from 20th Street stood discussing how best to retaliate against the Norteños for the Maya hit, three of the enemy snuck up from behind.

"Hey, you Sureño bitches!" one of the Norteños shouted.

With that, one of them opened up with a semiautomatic handgun, blasting away at the 20th Street crew as they scrambled behind benches and ran for cover. Bullets ricocheted off concrete and brick in the public space where nannies took their children to play in the fresh air and sunshine. Emptying the gun's entire magazine at relatively close range, the Norteño only managed to hit one of the surprised MS-13 gang members, Triste, who was shot in the back. But in hitting Triste, the Norteños had seriously wounded the cousin of Slow Pain, who was furious. He immediately contacted the PLS clique of MS-13 in Richmond and asked them to join 20th Street in getting some revenge on the Norteños right away.

Together as a hunting pair, Popeye and Spooky were among the MS-13 loyalists to answer Slow Pain's call for retribution that night. Driving through the Excelsior District, they were looking for anything that remotely resembled a Norteño, when they spotted Ernad Joldic and Philp Ng sitting together in a parked car. The two of them fit the bill close enough. With Popeye behind the steering wheel, Spooky got out of the stolen white Mitsubishi and walked up to Joldic and Ng.

The pair had just left another friend's house in the 200 block of Athens Street, near where Joldic used to live with his parents. Ng was a San Francisco native and a popular DJ at a nightclub in the city. Joldic was a graduate of Gateway High School, where he distinguished himself as a math whiz. He moved to San Francisco as a young boy with his parents from their native Bosnia, escaping the civil war raging there at the time.

Spooky pulled out a handgun and began firing into their vehicle, killing the young Bosnian immigrant almost instantly. Ng did not expire right away, but survived long enough to be taken to San Francisco General Hospital, where he finally succumbed to his gunshot wounds.

Soon after the shooting, SFPD officer Rodrigo Labson and his partner Brian Hicklin were patrolling the streets of the city's northern district in a squad car and stopped for a red light. Crossing in front of them, they saw a white Mitsubishi with tinted windows and a missing license plate on the front bumper. Labson's partner turned on the patrol car's flashing lights and they pulled right behind the car, which came to a stop at the side of the road.

On the passenger side, Spooky emerged.

"Get back in the vehicle!" Labson commanded.

Spooky acted as if he didn't hear or understand. He turned to look down the street, then took off running.

Labson chased after him on foot, as Spooky sprinted around the corner heading north on Van Ness. Rounding the corner in pursuit, Labson saw Spooky heading down a side alley behind Olive Street and continued chasing after him. Running about fifty feet behind, Labson could see Spooky reaching around for something in the front of his waistband, before he made another quick turn and sprinted down Polk Street.

When Labson got to the corner of Polk, he spotted Spooky down on his hands and knees, fumbling with something on the pavement, his elbows and arms jerking around with the effort. The officer drew his firearm and ordered Spooky down on the ground, but he didn't comply. Labson ordered him again to get down, but Spooky stood up with his empty hands in the air and walked several steps toward the officer, before finally obeying the order.

After putting handcuffs on Spooky, Labson walked back to the spot where he had seen him fumbling around on the pavement. There he saw the grip of a .45 caliber pistol sticking up from a sewer drain, its butt-end slightly too big to fall through the steel slats of the grate. Spooky was out of luck by a few millimeters.

Within moments, SFPD backup arrived to take Spooky into custody, while Labson took photos of the handgun, which was loaded with ammo. He donned a pair of rubber gloves and placed the pistol into an evidence bag.

Back at the patrol car, Hicklin had detained Popeye. When Labson returned, he noticed a couple spots on Popeye's shoes that he suspected might be blood. The footwear was seized and placed into an evidence bag along with a blue bandanna that Popeye had tucked into his back pocket.

At the SFPD's northern station, Labson consulted with his sergeant about the arrest and the strong likelihood they were dealing with gang members. They contacted Cabrera, who showed up to check things out and took custody of Popeye's Mitsubishi and Spooky's handgun. Forensic tests on the gun later determined it was the same one used to kill Ernad Joldic and Philp Ng.

Spooky and Popeye were both initially booked by the city DA on felony weapons charges and for participating in a criminal street gang. Federal prosecutors soon added a charge against Spooky of being an illegal immigrant (from Guatemala) in possession of a firearm.

All charges against Popeye were dropped, however, when San Francisco district attorney Kamala Harris's office concluded there was no evidence Popeye knew the passenger in his car, Spooky, possessed a gun. Popeye was released back to the street. It was a decision that soon would have disastrous ramifications for one San Francisco family after Popeye went straight back to work for the gang.

Even though Operation Devil Horns had disrupted the leadership of 20th Street to a large degree, it clearly was not preventing the clique from regularly engaging in deadly violence on the streets, causing Santini continual angst. With Slow Pain in charge, taking orders from Cyco and Peloncito in jail, the gang was as murderous as ever—even worse. Santini and Gwinn were pushing old cases of violent acts as well as the recent ones through the grand jury in an effort to rope in as many gangsters into the federal indictment as possible. Long, hard days in the grand jury, as the crazy violence continued on the streets, were wearing on them.

With bloody attacks occurring almost daily between the two gangs, Martin Guerra, a twenty-two-year-old Norteño was riding through the Mission with his sister, when he decided to roll through 20th Street territory and taunt whatever MS-13 crew he might come across. It was his bad luck that Droopy, Goofy, and Joker happened to be loitering together in front of the Ritmo Latino record shop on Mission Street.

"Fuck you, scraps!" Guerra shouted at them from the car.

The three MS-13 gangbangers turned and spotted the brother and sister pair as they drove past. They saw Guerra flash the Norteño hand sign and the trio from 20th Street—including Joker, with his paralyzed arm hanging limply—gave chase on foot.

The vehicle came to a stop at a red light down the block. Droopy got there first and began pounding Guerra with his fists through the open passenger's side window. Guerra's sister tried to drive away, but the road ahead was blocked by traffic and she only managed to plow into a parked car, as Droopy continued whaling at her brother's head with his fists.

Goofy reached the piled-up car next, moving between Droopy and Guerra and pulling out a knife. He plunged it into Guerra's gut, then ripped upward all the way to the breastbone, the way a hunter disembowels a deer. If not for the several layers of clothing that Guerra was wearing that day, his vital organs would have spilled out of his abdominal cavity right there in the car, according to surgeons who later sewed him back together at San Francisco General Hospital.

Guerra had the poor judgment that day to piss off the wrong MS-13 crew, who in turn apparently had the lack of awareness to realize the city had recently installed video cameras on that stretch of road in the Mission. The entire attack was recorded, blow by gruesome blow.

With their nearly deadly attempt at enforcing 20th Street's territorial integrity captured by security cameras, Droopy, Joker, and Goofy were now facing serious legal problems. All three were arrested by the GTF and locked up. Gibson was the lead on the investigation.

In addition to attempted murder, Joker was charged with child endangerment, since he abandoned his five-year-old daughter on Mission Street to engage in the attack on Guerra. Surveillance camera video showed Joker's daughter sitting on a bench alone and crying, while her half-paralyzed father tended to gang business down the block. Joker, Droopy, and Goofy would remain in jail until Santini's investigation was complete and they were charged with federal racketeering crimes.

———

"The block is hot!" Sparky told Diego over the phone. "One has just fallen! I have just killed one—right now, homie!"

He sounded winded, like he was running.

Diego immediately conveyed the news to Santini about Sparky's assassination of a Norteño, moments earlier, in broad daylight at Mission and 20th Streets. As soon as he hung up, Santini received another call—this time from Gibson, who confirmed a brutal murder had just occurred at the busy intersection.

Wearing a blue bandanna over his face, Sparky hopped out of a white van and walked up behind one of Patas's minions, a Miceros gang member named Armando Estrada, who was standing in broad daylight at the busy street corner, pedestrians walking to and fro.

Sparky pulled out a shotgun from under his sweatshirt, placed it at the back of Estrada's head and pulled the trigger, nearly decapitating him. Estrada's hideously torn and bloody body lay lifeless on the sidewalk, with a group of passersby gathering around the carnage in a confused daze. Sparky hastily sped away in the van and was already on the Bay Bridge heading to Oakland by the time paramedics arrived to clean up Estrada's corpse.

Soldado gazed at Sparky in the rearview mirror and couldn't help but feel proud of the rookie gang member who had just earned his stripes.

"You are a true soldier now, homie," he said.

Sparky was still in shock and began to hyperventilate when he noticed his sweatshirt was covered in blood and brains.

"Aye, bicho!" he gasped. I've got that fool's cerebro all over me!"

He pulled clumps of flesh from his hair and from the still-hot shotgun at his side.

The crew dumped the van a few blocks from Indio's home in Oakland and ran to their house, making the call to inform Diego about the successful hit along the way.

Upon arriving at Indio's house, Sparky threw his clothes in a plastic garbage bag, while Indio called Slow Pain. Slow Pain in turn contacted Dreamer and asked him to pick up the trio in Oakland and drive them back to Daly City for an after-action meeting and celebration.

Santini told Diego to meet him at his office immediately to make a series of phone calls. The recorded conversations between Diego and 20th Street members provided evidence the clique was mandating a stay-away order on the street in the wake of the Estrada killing. On the phone, the gang members were unanimously giddy that they had caused such a stir in the neighborhood.

During one call, Momia told Diego, "The piñata has been busted wide open—hopefully the fuckers will pay the rent now."

Sending a strong message to the rival gang was 20th Street's intent. The clique would maintain control over the neighborhood by any means necessary and be paid with both respect and tax money—by all rivals in *their* Mission territory.

———

Despite deadly threats from 20th Street against him if he didn't pay the tax they demanded, Patas refused to be intimidated. He believed he and his fellow Miceros had as much right to earn money from the streets of the barrio as MS-13 did, and he wasn't going to be bullied into compliance. It was a brave stance, maybe, but it was also a very dangerous one.

Patas pulled his white 1993 Cutlass Sierra to the curb in front of a driveway at Huron and Laura Streets so he could have a quick toke. He pulled out a king-size, pre-rolled paper from the glove compartment and began to stuff it with the hydroponic bud he had just purchased, legally, from a medical marijuana dispensary on Mission Street called the Green Cross.

When he was a youngster, rolling a good joint took practice; it was all about prepping the weed and the spin technique, the roll of the fingers. These days, anyone could fill a pre-rolled cone. You just bought the weed at a store, instead of copping it on a street corner. The papers came ready-made—just fill and smoke. He lit the monster spliff.

It was almost 5 p.m. when Patas finished his joint and prepared to take a ride to 5th and Market to pick up his girlfriend, who was getting off work at the Bebe clothing store. He cracked open the window to vent the smoke and extinguished the roach in the ashtray.

Patas heard the screech of brakes and a car door slam, saw a shadowy figure approach, and heard a voice whisper, "Que anda, bicho?"

The hooded figure unloaded seven rounds into Patas, shooting him in the neck and back, killing him with a bullet to the head. The assassin then ran back to a silver Honda Civic and slid into the rear seat. The car sped southbound on Huron toward Alameny Boulevard, and out of sight.

When police arrived, they found Patas slumped over to his right, suspended in the seat by the safety belt. Streams of blood and bits of tissue from his head, neck, and back covered the car's interior. Medics attempted to revive Patas on the way to San Francisco General Hospital, but he was pronounced DOA at the emergency room entrance.

———

"I blasted that buster right in the face!" Soldado told Coyote over the phone, laughing.

The stolen silver Honda Civic carrying Soldado was already across the Bay Bridge and entering Oakland on the way to another 20th Street member's home, where Soldado dumped his bloody gray hoodie into the washing machine's hot cycle, with extra detergent.

Soldado was certain that such a high-profile hit would solidify his place as a shot caller in the gang. Even better, if the local homies received the go-ahead from the Big Homies down south to start a new clique in Oakland, Soldado thought he might even be designated *La Palabra* (The Word) for the new clique. He might even have been on his way to becoming a Big Homie!

That evening, when Gibson called Santini to notify him that Juan Rodriquez, aka Patas, was murdered, they agreed that it must have been a hit by 20th Street. Patas was an old-school Mexican *cholo* who didn't have many enemies in the neighborhood, other than the emergent regime of 20th Street's new booties. Santini knew from his informants that the MS-13 gangsters likely had Patas in their crosshairs for months.

The old dogs of 20th Street who were friends with Patas, such as Tigre and Colmillo, were alarmed by the killing. As far as they were concerned, the hit on Patas had not been sanctioned by the gang's leadership and would surely send shock waves through the streets. A few days after the murder, when Slow Pain learned that Payaso, Zapato, and Tigre attended Patas's funeral, he was furious at them for representing the clique there. It only added fuel to the fire for his plan to kill them all.

At Santini's direction, Diego began to dig for information about the Patas murder and he soon started returning info about the hit. Diego reported that Soldado had been bragging about it and that the entire clique of new booties knew who did the killing. He also said Soldado used an old gun for the murder, a pistol in such bad condition it had to be taped together to function.

———

Following the Patas murder, prosecutors Gwinn and Wong were alarmed and convinced that rampaging violence by the insurgent new booties of 20th Street needed to be stymied right away, somehow.

Gwinn and Santini met with Cabrera and Gibson and determined enough evidence existed to meet a threshold of probable cause to obtain a search warrant on Soldado's residence. At the same time, they needed to make certain to keep information obtained from Diego under seal until after the big takedown of the gang. If a defense attorney managed to get hold of the information, the gang would have confirmation there was a rat among them.

Santini had an idea. Maybe they could get a warrant to search Soldado for illegal immigration documents, since he was in possession of a counterfeit green card the last time he was arrested by SFPD. The attorneys decided this was the best course of action to protect their informants.

Santini and a team of GTF officers and HSI agents hit Soldado's house at 949 Connecticut Street in the early evening, just hours after obtaining a federal search warrant. The apartment was in one of the roughest housing projects in San Francisco, an area known as Portrero Terrace or the "Annex." It was a hotbed for gang violence and home to a variety of black, Latino, and Samoan gangs. Even the GTF cops were wary about policing the neighborhood, it was so dangerous.[3]

They served the warrant on an empty house—no one was home when they did the "knock and announce." Legally, the occupants didn't need to be present for the execution of the warrant, so one of the larger GTF cops sprung open the front door with a battering ram. The team quickly cleared the rooms and began their search.

The apartment was filthy. Gibson and Santini were shocked that anyone could live in such squalor. There was half-eaten food strewn about the kitchen and cockroaches dripped from the cabinets as the cops conducted their search.

Santini and an HSI partner entered Soldado's bedroom, decorated with the typical gang paraphernalia including a collection of blue ball caps, jerseys, and belts, as well as gang photos and tribute memorabilia from Maya's recent funeral. Santini's partner opened a closet door and perched on a shelf, in plain view, sat a silver handgun.

As planned, the team locked down the apartment and contacted the US Attorney's Office to request an additional warrant to include firearms. The warrant was granted in just two hours and agents seized the weapon, a Russian-made Makarov 9 x 18 mm handgun. Upon inspection, they quickly noticed a loaded cartridge was taped into the gun with a piece of silver duct tape.

In addition to the firearm, the team seized several counterfeit identification documents. It was ironic, in that Soldado likely purchased the counterfeit IDs from Patas's operation, only to later murder his own supplier. Shortly after the search, Soldado was charged with murder and held in jail—one more 20th Street killer out of commission, as the operation continued driving toward broader RICO indictments.

CHAPTER 24

Drive-By Horror: The Final Straw

A SUMMER EVENING IN THE EXCELSIOR NEIGHBORHOOD, AND FORTY-eight-year-old Tony Bologna slowed his Chrysler Impala to a stop at the intersection of Congdon and Maynard Streets, just a few blocks from his home. With him in the car were his three sons, Michael, 20, Andrew, 18, and Matthew, 16. The family was on their way home from a dinner at Tony's sister's house in Fairfield, around twenty-five miles northeast of the city.

Tony had to get back for his night shift as a manager at Draeger's grocery store in San Mateo, and the boys all had school the next day.[1] His wife, Danielle, who had driven to Fairfield separately, stayed behind to extend her visit a while. She planned to meet her husband and sons at home in the city later that evening.

At that moment, sitting behind the wheel, Tony was simply waiting at the stop sign for another car to cross in front so he could make a left turn toward home.

A gray Chrysler 300 carrying two MS-13 gang members pulled right up beside them. Behind the wheel was Popeye, who had been arrested and released only a few months before with Spooky, who was caught in possession of the gun used to kill Ernad Joldic and Philp Ng. Popeye was released by the San Francisco Sheriff's Department after District Attorney Kamala Harris's office declined to press any charges against him.

With his pudgy face, soft mouth, and fuzzy mustache, Popeye glared at the Bologna family from behind the wheel.[2] He looked amped up and angry, as if he knew and hated the family, although they were actually strangers to him. In the front passenger seat next to him sat Flaco.

Popeye suddenly brandished a 9 mm pistol and pointed it at the Bolognas' car. He opened fire, one round after another. Bullets tore through the safety glass and door panels of the family's Impala, with three of them suffering fatal wounds. Only Andrew somehow avoided being hit in the hail of bullets.

Next to him in the car, Andrew's father and brothers were bleeding and moaning as their blood drained away and they lost consciousness. Tony's foot reflexively pressed on the gas pedal and the car rammed into another vehicle parked at the curb, as Popeye's silver Chrysler sped away on Congdon Street and disappeared over a steep hill. Andrew watched and listened to his father and brothers gasping their last breaths.

━ ～

At first, they told her over the phone it was a serious car accident.

Danielle Bologna grabbed her young daughter and raced from her sister-in-law's house in Fairfield to the California Pacific Medical Center in San Francisco to be by the side of her husband, Tony, and their three sons.

The ride to the hospital was psychological torture for her. Seconds felt like minutes, which felt like hours. All four of them were hurt, but she didn't know how badly. There was nothing she could do for them until she got there.

Tony's sister dropped Danielle at the front entrance of the hospital and she raced inside, panic stricken and fearing the worst. The receptionist directed her to the floor where her sons Michael and Matthew were being treated.

She ran to the elevator and rushed inside, saw her own terrified face in the reflection of the polished metal doors as she was carried up. The elevator doors parted and she hurried out, spinning around in search of the room numbers. Down the hall, she spotted Mike Stasko, Tony's friend and chief of SFPD's homicide division. The two men had coached youth sports teams together through the years.

Stasko saw her rush from the elevator and his stomach sank. *Lord, how was he going to tell her?* It wasn't the first time he had to do something like this, but these were friends of his. And the scale of her loss! It was the worst news he ever had to break to a person.

"Where are they?!" Danielle said.

"Wait," Stasko said.

She read his face, which seemed to confirm her worst fears. Something horrible had happened to her family.

"What?!" she said. "Where are they? Where's Tony? Where are the boys?!"

He did not say the words she wanted—needed—to hear. *It's alright. There was an accident, some injuries, but they're going to be okay. They're strong, they'll pull through. It'll take some time, but time heals all wounds.* Stasko's face seemed to melt more under her agonized stare, a silent plea for reassurance he was helpless to give her.

"Tony's been killed," he said. "Michael, too."

He tried to move closer to her, put his arms around her.

"Nooo!" she shrieked.

She punched him hard in the chest, to keep him away, as if the embrace would seal the horrible truth. Her blow carried all the force of her anguish and fear.

"*This can't be happening!*" she shrieked.

"They were shot," Stasko said. "Matthew is on life support."

Shot?! By whom? How could this be? Her own flesh and blood, her baby, dead? Her man, Tony? Dead?

Inside her gut, the sick, wrenching, unbearable grief began to spark and catch fire. It rose up through her chest and wrapped around her heart. Her breaths came shallow and weak and her head began to spin, as she struggled to fathom what was happening to her, what had happened to her love, joy, and purpose in life.

Then the tears came, wracking sobs of torment and grief. Stasko put an arm around her shoulder and led her, collapsing, to a seat in the waiting area. The energy around her body seemed to vacuum all the oxygen and light from the room like a black hole.

"There is no chance Matthew will recover," the doctor said. "I wish there was something we could do, but there isn't."

"No chance?" Danielle said. "None?"

He shook his head in deep, silent regret. "I'm sorry."

She looked down at her son. His eyes were closed, as they had been for the entire two days since she first saw him lying there hooked up to life support. He would never wake up and speak to her again. She had given birth to him sixteen years ago, fed him at her breast, helped him learn to walk and talk, watched over him as he grew into a young man.

They called him an "old soul," because he seemed to have been born with an innate wisdom. He enjoyed playing cards with his grandmother, Nonna, and his little sister, Sophie. Sure, he was a normal boy with a healthy streak of mischief, but nothing that even approached real trouble. He loved to swim with his brothers at the municipal pool in Ukiah.

All of it was over before he grew into full manhood.

To Danielle, he was still her little boy and the doctors were telling her now that he was already gone, really. She studied the lines of his face and knew they were right. Matthew's soul had already left his body, his beautiful body that had been injured so horrifically by the bullet in his brain. All that seemed left of him was the pain and she wanted it to stop.

She needed to let go. Let him go with his father and brother.

Danielle broke down, sobbing. How could God do this to her? Why? Wasn't it enough that she had to accept her husband Tony and her son Michael were gone forever? That her entire life going forward, whatever broken remnant she could manage to put back together, for the sake of her two surviving children, would always be missing half of its parts? It was as if she just had both her legs cut off; now she had to lose an arm, too.

She had to say the words. She had to say out loud that the doctors should turn off the life support machines.[3]

"Yes," she said. "Go ahead."

The nurses delicately switched off the machines, tiptoeing their way around the bed, wishing they could make themselves invisible. It was a devastating job to have to do. No amount of training or practice could get a person used to it.

Sniffling back her tears, Danielle leaned across Matthew's body, caressed the side of his bandaged head, and whispered into his ear. "It's okay. You can go," she said. "I'll see you one day."

Her tears flowed down her cheeks and fell onto her son's chest.

"I'll see you one day," she repeated.

She kissed him on the forehead.

And he was gone.

⸻

The multiple murders of the Bologna family members would profoundly shake up the entire political context for Operation Devil Horns. Popeye, the public soon learned, was an illegal alien with a history of violent crime as a juvenile in San Francisco. ICE and city officials quickly began a game of finger-pointing and blaming each other for allowing Popeye to slip through the system's cracks and remain free on American streets to commit the horrible killings.

So long as the gang restricted the targets of their most heinous crimes to one another, some more cynical segments of the public and law enforcement viewed every casualty as one less thug to worry about. *Let them kill each other off!* Maybe the problem would solve itself that way. But the gang was more like a malignant tumor left untreated. It grew and spread until it was too late to contain.

The Bologna murders crystallized for the public all the political controversies between left and right surrounding immigration policy, border security, and sanctuary cities. Violent street crime in San Francisco committed by illegal immigrants could no longer be viewed solely through a local lens. By its nature, the problem of MS-13 was national and international in scope. In certain segments of the public mind, the Bologna killings rose to the level of "terrorism"—a random act of violence with multiple innocent victims. The fact they were all members of the same family made the tragedy that more poignant and disturbing.

The American public first became widely aware of MS-13 as a result of the highly publicized Brenda Paz murder case in 2003. She was a seventeen-year-old gang member who agreed to turn informant and provided a wealth of information about gang members and their crimes, including murder. However, when she was accepted into the federal witness protection program, the teen's isolation and loneliness drove her back into the arms of MS-13, and she was eventually murdered in Virginia.

The Paz case generated broader public awareness of MS-13 and focused criticism about how her federal handlers failed to keep her safe. However, her disturbing murder did not inspire the same level of national attention and outrage as the Bologna killings. Paz was, after all, an MS-13 insider, whereas the Bolognas had nothing to do with the gang. Their murders seemed to indicate no one was necessarily safe from the metastasizing scourge from south of the border.

—◆—

Droopy knew he was screwed. Gibson sat him down and showed him video of his near-fatal attack with Goofy and Joker on Guerra, caught in vivid detail.

"You're going into the hole for a long time," Gibson said.

The thug's brain went into survival mode. What did he have that the cops wanted most? It was obvious. The stories about the Bologna murders were all over the news. Droopy knew the cops wanted to solve the case badly. And maybe he had the key: Popeye's car. It matched a witness description of the one carrying the Bolognas' killers.

"What you do for me if I help you find out who killed that family?" he said.

"What family?" Gibson said.

"In the Excelsior," Droopy said.

"You mean the Bolognas?"

"Yeah, them."

The detective looked at his partner, who sat up on the edge of his seat when he heard the family's name.

"You know who killed the Bolognas?" Gibson said.

"What you can you do for me if I give you some information?" Droopy said.

"If you know who killed them, you need to tell me," Gibson said.

"I want a lawyer," Droopy said.

—◆—

Less than a month after the Bologna murders, the producers at Fox News TV persuaded Danielle Bologna to go on air and tell her story.[4] The five-minute spot, hosted by Megyn Kelly, opened with a still shot of Popeye's face with his pudgy cheeks and pencil-thin mustache. The caption at the bottom of Popeye's picture read, "ILLEGAL NOT DEPORTED: NOW TRIPLE MURDER SUSPECT."

Straight into the interview, Kelly began by incorrectly stating the murders had been prompted by an incidence of road rage, when in fact the Bolognas had been mistaken for Norteños by the two MS-13 thugs. Kelly then gave a quick summary of Popeye's history of violent crime in San Francisco as a juvenile, highlighting that he had not been deported because he was never referred by local police to the feds, due to San Francisco's sanctuary city policy.

Danielle Bologna bravely struggled to hold back her tears, the sight of her grief-stricken face on the screen enough to melt even the most hard-bitten viewers' hearts.

"Has there been any acknowledgment by Mayor Newsom or city of San Francisco officials to you of the fact that had they simply reported this guy's illegal immigration status, your husband and sons might be alive today?" Kelly asked Danielle.

Fighting back sobs, Danielle said she had not spoken with the mayor. But, she said, if the government had only done something to prevent violent illegal immigrants like Popeye from roaming San Francisco's streets, she would not have just said final good-byes to half her immediate family.

"Now," Kelly said, "do you want an apology from Mayor Newsom, from the city? What do you want from the city at this point?"

"I want justice!" the grieving wife and mother wailed. "I want the people to see, if my family wasn't safe, what makes you think yours will be?!"

———

Shortly after Danielle Bologna's appearance on Fox TV, two opposing political factions gathered outside the mayor's office building on a sunny Wednesday morning, armed with placards.

On one side were the Minutemen, a group founded in 2004 that patrolled the US-Mexico border as a sort of citizens watch group, augmenting the border patrol's efforts. Here, in front of city hall, they were badly outnumbered. Word of the Minutemen's plan to protest San Francisco's sanctuary city policy and call for Mayor Newsom's resignation had reached activist immigrant rights groups in advance. About two hundred of their ranks showed up now to shout down the Minutemen.[5]

"SANCTUARY CITY MAYORS ARE US TRAITORS," said a placard carried by one of the Minutemen's posse.

"WHO'S THE ILLEGAL ALIEN, PILGRIM?" read an immigrant rights protester's sign.

"NEWSOM, HARRIS & SIFFERMAN ARE ACCESSORIES TO MURDER," claimed another Minutemen placard.

"MINUTE MEN, BORDER THUGS," said another immigrant activist's poster board.

In addition to playing citizen cops along the border, the Minutemen kept a close eye on the efforts of political opponents whom they considered supportive of a porous border policy. Consequently, they had become lightning rods in the political storm surrounding issues of US immigration and border enforcement. The left called them gun-toting extremists, while the right portrayed them as the heroic patriots, just as the group's name suggested.

Arnold Schwarzenegger, while he was governor of California in 2005, said in an interview with KFI radio in Los Angeles that the Minutemen were doing "a terrific job." On another occasion, he stated publicly that the Minutemen would be welcome to patrol the border between California and Mexico, "anytime."[6]

From his mahogany-paneled office overlooking the steps of City Hall, Mayor Newsom had a perfect vantage from which to observe the badly outnumbered Minutemen below. One of the protesters from the political left spit at a sheriff's deputy. He was wrestled to the ground and arrested. Another threw an "unknown liquid" on the City Hall steps, and was also detained.

Pacing the Oriental rug on his office floor, the mayor had a lot on his mind with the fallout from the Bologna murders. National media were covering the tragedy and shining a bright light on the mayor's support for San Francisco's sanctuary city policy as context for the story. On top of it all, the city was facing a $300 million budget deficit and the feds were threatening to cut off funds in retaliation for the city's sanctuary policy. If they followed through with the threat, it would cripple the city government's ability to function.

When asked by reporters to comment on the public disturbance outside, Newsom responded, "It's not the first time I've been asked to resign. It's not the twentieth or thirtieth time since I've been mayor."

"Minutemen," he added, "are not the kind of people I look to for advice or counsel in terms of my performance."[7]

Nevertheless, the political heat on Newsom was enough to force a pivot in the mayor's policy toward illegal immigrant criminals. He couldn't completely abandon the city's sanctuary city policy, of course—that would require an act of the city's left-leaning board of supervisors. He did, however, direct SFPD's chain of command to immediately begin a much higher degree of cooperation with federal police targeting non-citizen criminals.

Santini already had long since figured out workarounds to the city's policy of noncooperation, largely by working through Cabrera and Gibson on the sly. But the mayor's new mandate would grease the skids at SFPD and provide him with easier access to the local police's resources. It was a little late in the game, but better late than never, Santini figured. Santini could now freely receive archive files on gang members that would be valuable for building the RICO indictments. In addition, he could work with Cabrera and Gibson on the street without their constant concern for being disciplined by their management.

CHAPTER 25

Human Hunters Increase the Heat

While held in prison in Honduras, Diego had learned from an older gang member how to ink crude, jail-type tattoos using a sharpened paper clip and shampoo mixed with black ash. In San Francisco, he upgraded his gear to include a used tattoo gun that he bought at a shop in the Mission. Early into his career as a government informant, a 20th Street member named Fantasma, asked him to tattoo an *M* on his right arm and an *S* on his left arm in gothic font, which Diego did.

From Santini's perspective as an agent, the good thing about Diego's role as tattoo artist for the clique was that it gave him more credibility with the gang. Beyond that, it gave him additional opportunities to sit down with individual gang members for extended, uninterrupted periods. During the tedious hours it took to ink a homie with a tattoo design, Diego had a perfect chance to probe the gang member's knowledge of specific crimes.

When the US Attorney's Office in San Francisco first found out about Diego giving a tattoo to Fantasma, the situation raised a big, red flag. In any criminal trial down the road, a savvy defense lawyer could argue that Diego was "creating" gang members by permanently marking them with MS-13 symbols.

It was a fine legal line for Diego to walk between just being "one of the homies," on one hand, and future allegations of entrapment that could possibly torpedo any prosecution on the other. Under US law, two tests existed for determining whether legal entrapment had occurred. The "subjective" test examined whether or not a defendant had a "predisposition" to commit a crime, while the "objective" test scrutinized the government's conduct, judging if the actions undertaken by police or their informants would have caused an otherwise normally law-abiding person to commit a crime.

After reviewing the potential legal pitfalls of Diego inking tattoos on gang members, Nelson Wong, the assistant US attorney working with Santini, advised the agent that Diego could go ahead and ink away. The prosecutor concluded that the 20th Street homies already had a clear predisposition to get themselves tattooed with MS-13 symbols, with or without Diego.

— ◆ —

The night after the Minutemen protests outside City Hall, five 20th Street homies were driving in a car through the Mission, out on a "hunting" trip, including Guerrillero, age seventeen, Momia, eighteen, Demonico, twenty-two, Duende (juvenile) and Pistolito (juvenile). Four hours earlier, Pistolito's uncle was shot as he stood next to the Tonayense Taco Truck in the Mission. The hunters assumed a Norteño had done it.

Somebody was going to pay.

At the corner of Persia Avenue and Lisbon Street, two blocks off Mission Street, they spotted three young Latinos standing together, a female and two males, including fourteen-year-old Ivan Miranda.

A half hour earlier, Miranda had received a phone call from the girl standing next to him, Natalie Linares. She wanted to borrow his iPod. Miranda requested his dad's permission to meet Linares a couple blocks away from their home. His father said he could go, and Miranda met up with Linares, along with her boyfriend, Alejandro Flores.

The five young hunters from 20th Street stopped their vehicle and got out. Guerrillero, Duende, Momia, and Pistolito crossed the street toward their prey, while Demonico stayed near the car, acting as lookout. Pulling out their blades, Momia and Pistolito surrounded Flores, pressing knives against his stomach and back, while Guerrillero and Duende positioned themselves the same way on either side of Miranda.

"What you claim?" Momia said to Flores.

"I don't bang!" Flores said.

"Gimme your player," Momia said.

He pulled the ear buds hanging from Flores's neck and followed the wire to an MP3 player inside his shirt pocket, snatching it away.

Momia started to search Natalie Linares's clothes for valuables. "Where's your cell phone?" he said.

"Get away from me!" she said, pushing him. "I'm pregnant!"

"You shouldn't be checking me!" Flores said to Guerrillero. "I know you!"

"Where's your iPod?" Duende said to Miranda. He reached into Miranda's pocket and snatched the device away.

With a knife held at his back, Flores saw Duende stab Miranda in the arm. Miranda pushed his attacker away and started to run, leaving a trail of blood on the sidewalk as he fled.

Guerrillero pulled out a Japanese sword concealed under his jacket. He and Duende chased after the injured, terrified Miranda. They caught up with him at Madrid Street after a sprint of nearly a hundred yards, with Miranda bleeding profusely all the way.

Guerrillero ran the sword into Miranda's neck once, but it hit something hard and got stuck. He pulled it back out and tried again. This time it went clear through, in one side and out the other. Duende plunged his knife into Miranda's chest.

The victim arched his body. His feet reflexively came together as he stood there upright for a moment, before collapsing to the sidewalk. He closed his eyes as the blood drained from his body, all over the pavement. His breathing grew irregular, shallow, then stopped.

Guerrillero and Duende ran away from Miranda's body to meet back up with Momia and Pistolito. They alerted the homies about what they just did, and the four of them ran away together toward Mission Street, leaving Flores and Linares uninjured. Demonico followed the four escaping homies in the getaway car and picked them up a short way down the road. The hunting party sped away.

Flores and Linares ran up the street to see what had happened to Miranda. They found him lying on the sidewalk, gashes in his neck, blood everywhere. Flores lifted his shirt and saw the chest wound. Linares tried to apply pressure to stop the bleeding, but it was too late.

He was already dead.

As the sun rose that morning, Cabrera received a call about the Miranda killing.

He immediately contacted Santini's team and asked them to put Diego to work to see what he could find out about the murder.

Santini's strategy since fairly early in the operation had been for Diego to maintain distance between himself and Tigre, based on the US attorney's concern that their informant might exert too much influence on the gang's leadership. While the approach somewhat limited Diego's access to the gang leaders, his close contact with younger members, such as the five who attacked Miranda and his friends, made him privy to an alternative body of intelligence from the lower ranks. The HSI agents wired up Diego and sent him to dig for dirt on the Miranda murder.

It didn't take Diego long to find four of the five young hunters hanging at Mission Playground, still amped up from their twisted party the night before. He suggested they all go to Duende's house, so Diego could continue work on the homie's tattoo of a clown holding a gun.

Leaning over Duende's bare back, Diego switched off his buzzing tattoo gun so its noise wouldn't interfere with the hidden wire he was wearing.

"So, what happened?" he said, asking the homies for details about the attack.

"We stabbed the son of a bitch," Guerrillero said. "I had, like, a Chinese-style sword, dog. And I positioned it crazy, and it just slid in, like this."

"And homeboy saw how he looked when he died?" Diego said.

"He looked like this, right?" Duende said.

"Hey, what makes me laugh is how he went down! He even closed his legs, and then dropped dead like this! Look!"

Duende held back his grotesque snickering long enough to mimic the surprised, dying victim, as if he were a slapstick cartoon character or an actor in a campy silent film. He burst into laughter at his own comedic performance.

"On the other guy, on the other guy . . ." Momia blurted.

Momia was talking about Flores and eager to add the details of his own involvement in the glorious revenge attack on the Norteños while the myth was still being formed, lest it be forged into gang legend without his name included in bright lights.

"That knife that I had, crazy," Momia said. "I just went like this and it went in by itself. I just went like this, crazy. Look, I hadn't even, I didn't even do this and the shit went in by itself, dog! And Pistolito turned around and he got him in the ribs."

Diego thought what Momia was telling him was pure bullshit, just a punk trying to get unearned street creds. From what he had been briefed about the incident, Diego knew that Flores had not even been stabbed.

"So the girl recognized you?" Diego said. "The guy that you guys stabbed last night recognized you?"

"This dude—these dudes—fucked up," Duende said. He was talking about Momia and Pistolito.

"Because all they did was take the dude's [MP3 player] and slightly stab him [Flores]. And the guy recognized me. He is out with the narcs right now!"

"The fucker tried to get smart with me, dude," Guerrillero said, referring to Miranda. "I even took his iPod."

"Boom!" said Guerrillero. "I stabbed him. It got stuck and it went in and out here, then this dude stabbed him," he said, pointing to Duende. "Both of us crazy, in and out here, homeboy."

He pointed to his own neck to demonstrate the spot where he had thrust the sword into Ivan Miranda.

"La Mara Salvatrucha rules," Guerrillero said.

"Look here," he added, "I got eighty bucks for the iPod."

———

The youthful hunting party was screwed, having blabbed and bragged about killing Ivan Miranda while Diego's secret microphone was recording every word they said. SFPD detectives soon obtained arrest warrants based on the recordings, as well as eyewitness testimony from Linares and Flores. They rounded up all five and took them into custody, charged with homicide.

Within days, an article was published by Jaxon Van Derbeken, the *San Francisco Chronicle*'s police and courts reporter of several years, providing background on Guerrillero.[1] In the article, the reporter described how Guerrillero basically fit the poster-child profile of San Francisco's sanctuary city policy gone bad.

Like the by-then widely publicized case of Popeye, Guerrillero had been arrested as a juvenile for violent gang activity in the city, stemming from an incident a year earlier. Guerrillero and another MS-13 gang-banger put a sixteen-year-old kid in the hospital. It was the standard MS-13 MO: They approached the unsuspecting victim, asked him what gang he claimed, then beat the shit out of him.

When he was arrested for that earlier attack, Guerrillero, who was from Honduras, pled guilty before a San Francisco juvenile court judge and was put on probation and ordered to live with his parents in Houston. Within a year, Guerrillero was back on the streets in San Francisco, free to kill.

An SFPD spokesperson told reporters the police department thought Guerrillero was in the country illegally now, but the department hadn't reported him to ICE because it would have been a violation of the city's sanctuary policy.[2]

"Ivan was a kid," Miranda's sister, who was known as Little Mejo, told Van Derbeken. "He didn't have anything to protect himself with. If they wanted to take an iPod, why should they kill him? I don't understand that part."

Little Mejo said she knew Guerrillero as a troublemaker at Mission High School, where he was expelled for delinquent behavior. She said that youths like him should be deported from the United States. "They should be arrested," she said. "They are only doing bad things. Ivan was only fourteen years old. They are sixteen, seventeen, eighteen. That's bad! They should be deported to their country!"

CHAPTER 26

Sanctuary City in Panic

GAVIN NEWSOM'S CHIEF SPOKESPERSON, NATHAN BALLARD, WAS A golden-boy spin doctor and a rising star in the Democratic Party's machine in California. He joined Newsom's team in February 2008, not long before the mayor made it public he intended to run for governor.

A graduate of the University of California, Hastings, Law School and former deputy city attorney for San Francisco, Ballard was a handsome, thirty-five-year-old sharp dresser with a bright smile, dark eyes and hair, and a close-cropped beard. Prior to joining Newsom's team, Ballard served in various congressional and state legislative staff positions, as well as with the mayor of Oakland's office and the public defender in San Francisco.

When the public artery exploded after Popeye was arrested for the Bologna family murders, Newsom turned to his young ace Ballard to spearhead the publicity crisis-management effort. Ballard sized up the growing controversy surrounding the Bologna and Miranda murders and moved fast to mitigate the political damage. He e-mailed Kevin Ryan and others on the mayor's staff, requesting they prepare a "simple one-pager" describing how the city was in no way aiding or giving legal advice or aid to "undocumented criminals."

Ryan complained bitterly to Ballard in his reply e-mail the same day. He said in the past two years the Mayor's Office of Criminal Justice, which Ryan only recently took over, doled out $300,000 to three community-based organizations for programs to assist undocumented, unaccompanied, monolingual youth.

"That means that all \$300K went to serve undocumented, juvenile delinquents," Ryan wrote back to Ballard.

What's more, Ryan said, he just told Van Derbeken that the mayor's office now planned on "scrubbing" the program. The move would clearly be perceived as an admission that the youth assistance initiative was a mistake from the start. "Gird your loins," was Ryan's blunt advice to Ballard and the other Newsom staff members copied on his e-mail.

To the circling media, Ballard tried to emphasize that Newsom deserved credit for putting an end to the Juvenile Probation Department's policy of shielding illegal immigrant felons from the feds as soon as he found out about it the previous May. In fact, this would have been around the same time the general public also learned that the city was flying convicted juvenile drug dealers home to Central America on the city taxpayer's dime.[1] In fact, the city had escorted over thirty alleged juvenile felons out of the United States and back to Central America.

The program's presumed motivation had been to preserve juvenile criminals' ability to legally reenter the United States, since official deportation was grounds for refusing future immigration. The secret free-flight-home scheme was discovered by HSI agents at the George Bush Intercontinental Airport in Houston, who stopped and interrogated a San Francisco juvenile probation officer accompanying several convicted Honduran drug dealers that were about to board a flight home. In their hands they held plane tickets paid for by the city of San Francisco.

Responding to this revelation, former San Jose police chief Joseph McNamara, then a fellow at the Hoover Institution, told *San Francisco Chronicle* columnist Debra J. Saunders, "It's just incredible to think they were spending all that money to help criminals evade being deported." McNamara also excoriated federal officials "who were too busy to hold Ramos (Popeye) when they had the chance." In her column, Saunders added, "For a year now, the folks at ICE have been telling me that recent arrests have been the result of concerted targeting of the worst offenders. Yet Ramos wasn't bad enough for them?"

Now, with Van Derbeken's revelations in the wake of the Bologna murders, two more articles appeared in the *Chronicle* that focused attention on the city's sanctuary policy. The reports described the policy in terms of how it allowed an illegal immigrant like Popeye with a violent criminal history to roam free in San Francisco.

A recently retired SPFD captain named Tim Hettrich told the *Chronicle* that SFPD Chief Heather Fong "made it clear that she did not want officers to cooperate with ICE and other federal agencies when it came to arresting illegal immigrants for crimes." It was "common knowledge" throughout the SFPD, Hettrich said. "You were not to do anything with ICE or immigration and illegals, whether or not they committed a crime—even to arrest them—because there will be the perception we are harassing illegals."[2]

The recently retired SFPD captain also said he had numerous conversations about the issue with Chief Fong over the years, whenever he attempted to work with federal authorities investigating the MS-13 street gang. The most recent was about nine months prior to the Bologna murders. "You are not to work with these (federal) people," Hettrich said Fong ordered. "In her mind," he said, "it was always a perception that the board of supervisors will be mad at her, the mayor will be mad at her. She wanted to keep her job—not do her job."

Hours after these incendiary reports hit the newsstands and blogosphere, Ballard swung into full crisis-management mode. He sent another e-mail to Ryan at seven a.m. that Sunday morning on the mayor's behalf, instructing him to prepare a point-by-point rebuttal. Ballard specifically alluded to a news report that quoted Joseph Russoniello, the US Attorney for Northern California, who asserted that certain city programs to assist illegal aliens might be violating federal law.

"What it means to me," Russoniello said, "is they took the concept of sanctuary, and they applied it in a way that it is as close to harboring as I've ever seen."[3] Federal law prohibited anyone, Russoniello argued, from knowingly harboring undocumented immigrants. Yet the city's grant programs relied on young immigrant offenders staying in the juvenile justice system, harbored from federal authorities that might seek to deport them. "Then, they accommodate them by providing all these services to continue their unlawful status," Russoniello said. "The city, in this case, is using taxpayer dollars to basically endear itself to activist groups that need funding for their activities."

Three hours after e-mailing Ryan that Sunday morning and basically ordering him to get on the stick and help generate some rebuttals to Russoniello's assertions, Ballard zipped off another e-mail to San Francisco Sheriff Hennessey. The sheriff was responsible for operating the city's jail system, which had released Popeye to the streets soon before he murdered the Bolognas.

"I just got off the phone with the mayor," Ballard wrote to Hennessey. "He asked me to ask you if you would please provide him with some kind of evidence—a fax receipt? A copy of a form? A fax log?—that he could point to as evidence that you referred Ramos (Popeye) to ICE while he was still in your custody."

No such evidence would be forthcoming.

At the center of the raging game of political hot potato between the mayor and the feds was a recently implemented ICE program known as Secure Communities, which began that same year. For decades, when local police arrested a person they sent his fingerprints to the FBI as a matter of routine. The FBI then confirmed the person's identity and ran a background check for criminal records.

Under the Secure Communities program, there was an additional step whereby the FBI automatically forwarded the fingerprints to ICE. The feds in turn checked to see if the person should be detained or deported for immigration violations, such as having an expired visa, being in the country illegally to begin with, or breaking the terms of a green card by participating in criminal activity. Electing to opt out of Secure Communities, San Francisco had relied on policy statements from ICE (which were later rescinded) to the effect that participation by local jurisdictions in the program was strictly optional.[4]

The feds were trying to stick the mayor and the city with the blame for Popeye's release. Their claim was that the fault lay squarely on local law enforcement. They were the ones who let Popeye go free a few months earlier after he was arrested with Spooky, who was in possession of the murder weapon that killed Ernad Joldic and Philp Ng. There was no record the sheriff had notified ICE of Popeye's impending release.

It wasn't just the feds and the local media who were on Newsom's ass now. Significant national media coverage of the Bologna family murders was taking aim at Newsom as well, just as he was preparing to ramp up his campaign for governor. The timing could not have been worse for the promising young star in the Democratic Party.

While the political pissing match was under way between all the various rivals, yet another San Francisco political player decided to jump into the fray. Jeff Adachi, the city's independently elected public defender, reached out to California attorney general Jerry Brown's office, requesting an investigation into the leak of juvenile criminal records from the public defender's office to the media.

Adachi ran an office of nearly one hundred attorneys and sixty staff members, with an annual budget of $24 million. His office represented an estimated twenty-four thousand individuals annually in San Francisco who were charged with everything from minor misdemeanors to violent felonies. It was Adachi's office, claimed US Attorney Russoniello, that was orchestrating the juvenile court's harboring of immigrant felons. Adachi was seriously upset over the *Chronicle* articles revealing Popeye's and Guerrillero's criminal histories as juveniles.

Adachi also wrote a letter to a state superior court judge seeking an investigation into a breach of confidential information from his office. "What we have here is a consistent pattern of somebody who is leaking confidential information, protected information, from juvenile hall," he wrote. "The legislature has enacted these laws to protect children because juvenile proceedings are not considered criminal proceedings. The laws prohibit disclosure of the identities of juveniles or the circumstances of their cases to the press or anyone else."[5]

With the city's public defender joining the political battle, it seemed like the entire justice system in California was leaping into the bloody mud pit wrestling match over San Francisco's sanctuary city and juvenile justice policies. From the mayor and sheriff to the state's attorney general, to the US Attorney's Office for the Northern District of California, the controversy dug deep trenches between bitterly opposed political factions.

Above the local US Attorney's Office, of course, were DOJ main headquarters and HSI headquarters in D.C., which had a big dog in the fight in the form of Operation Devil Horns, run on the ground by Santini and Gwinn. The pressure was on Santini now to do whatever was necessary to prevent another murder committed by members of 20th Street before the gang's takedown was complete.

In a hostile atmosphere of government finger-pointing and leaks, Santini also worried now the operation might be publicly exposed, somehow. Gwinn still needed to finish working the grand jury process, and to persuade the jurors to issue indictments against nearly three dozen 20th Street homies. Without the indictments, the gang was free to continue its crazy violence on the streets.

CHAPTER 27

Green-Light for Takedown

BOTH IN SAN FRANCISCO AND D.C., LEADERS AT EVERY LEVEL OF LAW enforcement that touched the Devil Horns investigation had arrived at a common conclusion. The case could not be allowed to play out any further, given the media scrutiny and public uproar surrounding the Bologna and Miranda murders. All the decision makers at all the various agencies involved agreed, from DOJ and HSI to the mayor of San Francisco and SFPD. The time to wrap up the investigation and take down 20th Street was now.

There comes a point in cases like this, where the gang's tentacles extend so far and wide, that a decision has to be made about when to pull the trigger and start hacking off its main limbs. Except for some outlying targets left on Santini's wish list, including the 20th Street coke king Chachi and Casper's brother Snoopy, the Big Homie calling shots from his prison cell in Honduras, the clique in San Francisco was thoroughly set up for a full-scale takedown.

Arresting thirty gang members one at a time was not an option, since they would definitely be tipped off and run. On the other hand, simultaneously arresting so many thugs who resided throughout the Mission and across the Bay Area entailed a huge logistical and tactical challenge.

With the assistance of Diego acting as scout, Santini assigned eighteen separate teams of agents, each responsible for arresting a specific gang member, or small group of suspects who lived together. They staked out the thugs' residences, identifying the homes where they slept, what cars they drove, who lived with whom, what cars these other people drove, what times of day the occupants typically came and went, and whether they owned any large guard dogs of concern. The planning and preparation would take many weeks.

From the day that word came down to Santini it was time to wrap up the case, he projected the earliest possible date for the takedown was three months out. All the various police agencies participating needed to be brought on board, briefed, and coordinated. There were hotel rooms for out-of-town special operators to be booked, ten HSI Special Response Teams and several local ones to be thoroughly briefed, armored cars and air support to be requisitioned.

Meanwhile, Gwinn was calling twenty-seven witnesses to testify before the grand jury and working with Santini to present evidence for indictments on all thirty-six suspects.

Adding to Santini's growing anxiety during this time, an article appeared in a local San Francisco newspaper called the *Recorder* that connected the dots between recent arrests of MS-13 gang members in the city, including Cyco, Peloncito, and Kapone.[1] The report surmised a big federal takedown might be imminent, noting the US Attorney's Office for the Northern District of California had filed at least seven separate cases against MS-13 suspects in recent months. Five of the arrests came after the Bologna family murders, and all the cases were being handled by the same prosecutor, Nelson Wong.

Santini knew from hard experience—in particular his blown car fencing sting—that 20th Street members paid attention to media reports. He was worried now that the *Recorder* article might tip them off that the net was closing and they would make a run for it.

Santini gazed out the window of the fixed-wing Cessna piloted by a US Customs agent as the small plane hugged the Pacific shoreline, heading north from San Francisco. Below, the ocean's breaking surf drew a white line north and south, as if tracing the way for the aircraft's hour-and-a-half flight plan along the sandy beaches and rocky outcrops toward Mendocino. To the east, the world-class vineyards of Marin and Sonoma

Counties lay, their fields etched by thousands upon thousands of grape-vine rows undulating across the sloping terrain.

The bird's-eye view encouraged a growing sense of optimism in Santini. Maybe the four-year-long investigation and all the stress and frustration had been worth it. In his briefcase, he carried indictments and warrants for forty individuals that he was bringing for final sign-off from Judge Nandor J. Vadas, one of the most conservative judges in Northern California. Russoniello had identified Vadas as the most likely federal magistrate to give a final stamp of approval. It was the last legal step required before the big takedown of gang members could commence.

Just over an hour after takeoff, the small plane touched down at Little River Airport, a few miles southeast of the Mendocino County seat. From the airstrip Santini headed straight for the courthouse.

Vadas, a former assistant prosecutor with the San Francisco District Attorney's Office, was appointed to the federal magistrate in Eureka, California, in 2004. With gray hair and a close-trimmed goatee, the judge had a highly businesslike manner. Still, Santini sensed right away that Vadas had been affected by reading graphic descriptions in the indictments of violent crimes alleged against the 20th Street thugs.

"We need to put these dirtbags in jail, immediately," Vadas said.

It was just what Santini wanted to hear.

"Pick these goons up, and I'll await the story in the newspapers," the magistrate said.

"Yes, sir!" Santini said.

The agent walked away from the Ukiah courthouse with forty signed search warrants, eighteen arrest warrants, and a grin on his face. The flight back south to San Francisco was even more levitating for Santini's mood than the trip up. He gazed at the sunlight shimmering on the great Pacific Ocean all the way to the western horizon.

There was still some major police work to be done. A massive team of agents and special operators were poised to swing into action, and there were no guarantees that nothing would go wrong before they had all the gang members in custody.

Santini had taken every precaution he could think of to ensure the takedown went smoothly, but this kind of operation always carried with it a degree of unpredictability and risk. The MS-13 thugs had guns. They lived with women and children, some of them. There were neighbors and passersby and dogs and cats and whatever else that could stray into harm's way at just the wrong moment.

And there was still the chance that some of the targets would catch wind of the operation ahead of time, somehow, and scram before the massive sweep occurred.

CHAPTER 28

Zero Hour

MARK LINEHAN, SANTINI'S RECENTLY APPOINTED DIRECT SUPERVISOR, gazed at the three hundred law officers and special operators who filled the hangar at Moffett Federal Airfield, a former Navy base situated near the south end of San Francisco Bay. Blond and blue-eyed with an average build, Linehan possessed a strong ability for organization and administration.

He had recently returned to HSI following a couple years working at Microsoft in Seattle. Quickly realizing the private sector didn't offer the same excitement as law enforcement, he left Bill Gates's employ to get back into the mix. No sooner had he rejoined the agency than he found himself responsible for managing all the complex logistics for the big takedown of 20th Street, while Santini was mostly preoccupied working with Gwinn, nailing down all the necessary indictments.

Located between southern Mountain View and northern Sunnyvale, Moffett was far enough out of the way to avoid attracting attention with such a large buildup of personnel and equipment, but close enough to the city to provide a good launch point. Standing atop a small makeshift stage, looking past the milling crowd of cops and Special Response Team (SRT) members through the hangar's open doors, Linehan watched a Eurocopter AS-350 A-Star helicopter—one of several choppers assigned to the operation—touch down lightly outside.

The special operators assembled for the mission had taken over an entire hotel near the airport in South San Francisco. During the previous few days, pairs of SRT leaders from across the country arrived ahead of their squads to conduct undercover surveillance and site surveys on their assigned targets.

The nearby parking lot was jammed with dozens of large vehicles for transporting sixteen separate raid teams comprised of around twenty operators each. Their vehicle fleet included three MRAPs—huge armored trucks commonly used in combat environments. Inside the vans and trucks were a formidable arsenal of firearms, ammunition, flashbangs, radios, and protective body armor. While the MS-13 homies might possess a few powerful guns themselves, they were about to experience an overwhelming paramilitary force, which presumably enjoyed the element of surprise as well.

"Alright, everyone. Let's bring it in close now for a few minutes, please," Linehan announced through his bullhorn. The men stopped talking and turned to face him, moving in tighter.

"First of all, on behalf of the Special Agent in Charge for Northern California, I want to thank each and every one of you for assisting with this very important mission. We couldn't do it without you all. Special Agent Michael Santini, who has led this investigation for over three years, asked me to personally thank all of you as well. He wanted to be here very badly, but he is tied up with other critical aspects of the case right now."

The operation was set to launch in less than twelve hours and HSI's Special Agent in Charge insisted on this pre-op briefing, specifically so Linehan could reemphasize the agency's Use of Force policy to all the team members involved.

The SAC was especially concerned that such a large-scale sweep, targeting more than twenty residential locations across the bay area, could result in someone getting hurt. Especially if a noncriminal was inadvertently injured or killed, which wasn't difficult to imagine given the amount of amassed firepower and the gang's penchant for violence, an otherwise successful takedown would almost certainly be overshadowed by tragedy. The blame would be aimed squarely at federal authorities, who already faced regular accusations of cruelty and harassment against the immigrant community from activists in San Francisco.

"I realize you are all aware of our use of force policy, but we need to keep it at the forefront of our minds going into tomorrow's operation,"

Linehan said. "I want to remind everyone how we are to conduct our-selves tomorrow morning by reading a few key elements of the policy."

He looked down and read from his notes. "'If feasible, and if to do so would not increase the danger to the officer/agent or others, a verbal warning to submit to the authority of the officer/agent shall be given prior to the use of force. If a particular situation allows for the issuance of a verbal warning, the officer/agent should: (a) have a reasonable basis to believe that the subject can comprehend and comply with the warning; and (b) allow sufficient time between the warning and the use of force to give the subject a reasonable opportunity to voluntarily comply with the warning.'"

Linehan paused to let the message sink in. He was right, they had all heard it before and presumably internalized the Use of Force rules through untold hours of training. Nonetheless, an overt reminder about the importance of avoiding unnecessary violence couldn't hurt. Training was one thing, but making real-life, split-second decisions was another. Even the most experienced special operator on any given day could pull the trigger in a situation where it might be avoided.

"You all have your assignments and know what you need to do," Linehan said. "I'm confident all of you will perform as the true profes-sionals you are. This will be one of the largest single takedown operations in the country's history. The news media will be all over it—depend on it. So, please remember the agencies you represent and be aware of your surroundings before, during, and after the operation. We all want to make our colleagues proud. And one last thing—and I don't need to tell you this—take care of one another. Watch each other's back. We're one team. Okay?" He scanned the faces across the hangar. "Thank you all, and good luck tomorrow!"

They gave him a polite round of applause before separating back out into their respective teams and heading for the vehicles. The sun was just beginning its descent over the Pacific horizon. There was enough time left in the evening for a good meal and fitful rest at the hotel. Three hours before sunrise, a majority of the task force's three hundred members would regather at the Cow Palace in Daly City for final instructions and to gear up and roll.

Just under the official seal of the Department of Homeland Security were six large flat-screen TVs affixed to the wall. The new command center at HSI in San Francisco had never been used to oversee such a large operation as the one in progress now. At a significant cost to retrofit, the SAC was excited to see it put to the test.

The TV monitors would display real-time video of the operation, show target lists, search warrant locations, and status of warrant executions. There were eighteen target posters, with photos and biographical data on all the thugs that were to be arrested affixed to a large wall. The communications station would monitor all radio comms between almost two-dozen teams preparing to affect arrests and seize evidence.

It was 3:30 in the morning when Santini arrived at the command center. He hadn't slept much, and, while nervous, he was excited to get the ball rolling. Soon after he arrived, the guests began to pack in. Present were the director of HSI, Marcy Foreman, and her staff from D.C.; the local SAC and HSI management; the DOJ attorneys, including Laura Gwinn and Nelson Wong; the gang unit captains from CHP and SFPD; and tactical supervisors from the SRT and SWAT teams.

The command center slowly filled with agents and officers from participating agencies, all with specific assignments. There were agents in charge of operational command, communications, enforcement status and updates, records checks, and roll-over warrants. Everything was well organized and although early in the morning, everyone was wide awake and excited with anticipation for a big bust.

As 6 a.m. approached, the operations command began to receive final "ready" reports from teams in the field. The units were all on standby, waiting for the "go" signal. Although Santini couldn't be in the field with the troops, management knew he at least needed to ceremonially ring the starting bell. At 5:55 a.m., he was handed the command radio and given the thumbs-up from his SAC. Santini smiled and leaned into the mic, pushing the comms button.

"All teams, all teams . . . get ready," Santini said with a monotone delivery. He paused and checked his watch. "And . . . Execute!!!" The order was given and the large-scale multiagency enforcement operation was under way.

The South San Francisco police department's SWAT team was ready to go, anxiously awaiting the deployment signal from the team leader at the head of the stack. The armored vehicle's air conditioner churned heavily, flushing body heat from the crowded truck. They had been crammed inside for what seemed like an eternity.

Fifteen special operators rigged with sixty pounds of gear each, including AR15 assault rifles, molle packs loaded with magazines and .556 ammo, ballistic helmets, level-four plates, flash grenades, specialty impact munitions, chemical agents, breaching tools and shields. They had completed final radio checks and zeroed in their red-dot EOTech rifle sighting systems.

Now they were in the "zone," ready to execute a dynamic entry on Tigre's house, a small, single-story structure located at 815 Hemlock Avenue, where he lived with his wife and two young children. It was a quiet neighborhood just a few miles south of Candlestick Stadium.

At 6 a.m. on the nose, the radio chirped with the "go" signal and the truck began creeping down Sister Cities Boulevard at ten miles an hour. The team members shifted and stretched as best they could in the tight space, ensuring their bulky gear wasn't caught on a seat or a fellow operator as they poured out of the truck.

A quick left on Irving Street, then a right on Hemlock. Ten houses up on the left, the team leader shouted an order to the truck's driver, who sped up briefly then came to an abrupt stop two doors down from Tigre's, a small yellow rancher.

"Execute!" the team leader shouted. "Execute!"

They streamed out of the rear door and stacked seamlessly into a line formation, rifles pointed in the direction of Tigre's house as they made their approach. When they reached a small gate at the walkway, the team systematically split into smaller groups, the way they had rehearsed countless times. The entry unit approached the front door while the perimeter units broke both left and right to cover the sides and rear of the house.

The breaching element of the stack broke to the left and took a position to smash open the front door.

"Police with a warrant!" one of them shouted.

"Open the door!"

Just as the breacher lifted his ram to bust the lock mechanism, the door swung open from the inside. A sleep-dazed woman, Tigre's wife, was overtaken by the entry team racing past her and into the house.

"Police! Police!" the team members shouted as they cleared the rooms.

"Police with a warrant!"

The heavily armed squad cleared every room in the house while Tigre's wife and two young daughters cowered in fear, hugging one another on the living room couch. They watched in terror as Tigre was dragged from his bed and handcuffed.

His double life as gang leader had finally caught up to him. This time he would not get off so easily, the way he had dodged repercussions from previous violent crimes he committed in San Francisco over the years. The force and might of the heavily armored arrest team was a portent of the weight of federal RICO laws about to come crashing down on his head.

Outside the house, the team's perimeter elements closed in, as the entry team operators returned to the personnel carrier to remove their heavy armor.

"Code four," the team leader said into his radio. "We are clear at Hemlock. Primary target Cerna in custody. Beginning search."

"Copy, team seven," Santini responded into the radio. "Code four at Hemlock."

The special agent sat down at the command center's conference table with a big smile on his face. Although disappointed he couldn't be there in person, Santini was overwhelmed with a sense of relief now that Tigre was in custody. If anyone was going to run, Santini thought, it would have been Tigre. But the thug was sound asleep in his bed when the long arm of the law came knocking on his door.

The search of Tigre's residence yielded significant evidence of MS-13's criminal organization including letters from the Big Homies. Agents also discovered a bulletproof vest in the backseat of Tigre's car. Apparently, he had taken the gang's rumors that he'd been green-lighted for death seriously. If Tigre needed to worry about keeping himself alive now, it was going to be fellow prisoners behind bars he had to fear.

From across the table, Gwinn noticed Santini's joyful relief. She knew exactly why he felt the way he did. She heard the dispatch from Team Seven and knew how important it was for Santini to have the top dog in custody.

"We did it!" Santini said, catching Gwinn's smile.

He wanted to pick her up and squeeze her in a big bear hug. She had been so pivotal in the success of the investigation. She was smart and tough and uncompromising in her determination—equal to his own—to put the 20th Street thugs behind bars.

"No, Santini," Gwinn said. "You did it. We all just came along for the ride."

He knew Gwinn was being overly modest. It took a team of dozens of dedicated lawyers, special agents, police officers, detectives, intelligence analysts, and linguists to achieve the degree of success they had. And Gwinn—she was the chief architect of the complex legal strategy. Absent her experience and hard work, Santini knew, there was no telling how the Devil Horns investigations might have evolved—or not—in the byzantine halls of DOJ.

Simultaneously, the same dynamic-entry scenario that occurred at Tigre's house was played out in twenty-three other locations throughout the Bay Area and in Reno. In addition, nineteen search and arrest warrants were served at eight correctional facilities for fifteen gang members currently in custody on other charges, including Cyco, Peloncito, Droopy, Kapone, and Joker.

Agents also took eleven gang members into custody on federal immigration charges. They were all "hooked and booked." Forty-two MS-13 gangsters and associates were arrested that morning, effectively dismantling 20th Street. Two suspects wanted on outstanding murder warrants related to the Ivan Miranda homicide were also arrested on state charges by SFPD.

In total, the enforcement operation cost nearly $1 million and entailed almost four hundred HSI personnel, including nine HSI Special Response Teams to conduct high-risk arrests and six local police SWAT teams to execute warrants at other locations.

—◦—

At a news conference in San Francisco later that day, the US attorney for the Northern District of California, Joseph Russoniello, and ICE's director of investigations, Marcy M. Forman, took the stage to trumpet the success of Operation Devil Horns and gloat about the biggest takedown of MS-13 in agency history.

Behind them were three posters that Santini had produced, serving as backdrop. There was a "gun" poster with photos of several of the high-capacity firearms seized during the case. There was a "drug" poster, which displayed photos of the bricks of white crystal and coke purchased, and there was a "warehouse" poster that showed photos of the interior and exterior of the undercover stolen car operation in Richmond.

"There can be no doubt that the greatest threat to the peace and well-being of so many of our communities in this district and throughout the country, for that matter, is the lethal cocktail of drugs, gangs and guns," Russoniello said. "And among the gangs we in law enforcement are determined to bring to heel, none is more vicious, dangerous and indifferent to the rule of law than MS-13. They may see themselves as heroes, may try to recruit members by emphasizing their 'machismo' and terrorize the community by engaging in acts of wanton violence, but they are neither invisible nor invincible. This coordinated effort by federal, state and local law enforcement agencies is but one more steady step in the process of taking back our communities and giving young people the chance to make meaningful good long-life choices . . . alternatives to the often short-term gratification that membership in a gang at best, offers."

"This investigation and the ensuing arrests," added Forman, "have dealt a serious blow to what is arguably one of the most ruthless gang cliques currently operating in the Bay Area. As this case shows, transnational gangs like MS-13 thrive on violence, violence that is often fueled by profits from their illegal activities. Left unchecked, these activities threaten the welfare and safety of our communities. Our goal in targeting these dangerous street gangs is to disrupt their criminal activities and ultimately to dismantle the entire organization."

———

Two days after the big takedown, Santini attended the arraignments for twenty-four defendants arrested and indicted on federal charges stemming from Operation Devil Horns. Due to the large number of accused, the judge overseeing their cases decided to handle all the initial court appearances in one big proceeding. This was the first time Santini came face-to-face with most of the characters he targeted from behind the scenes over four years.

Seated in the back of the courtroom with all the agents from the gang unit, he watched as marshals brought in the accused, one-by-one, handcuffed, to meet with their individually assigned defense attorneys. Santini could stare each one down including Tigre, Cyco, Peloncito, Slow Pain, and all the rest.

The gang members looked befuddled, their facial expressions glazed. Santini sensed they were trying to act tough in front of their fellow clique members, but the agent detected general fear and confusion. They were clearly stunned by the severity of the charges levied against them. The defendants' faces grew paler as their potential sentences were read aloud—"twenty-five to life," or "punishable by the maximum sentence of death."

On the way back to his office from the courthouse, Santini received an "all agency" text, which headquarters used to communicate with agents in urgent situations such as an active shooter or fire at the building. "All Agents, use the rear entrance for ingress/egress to the HSI office due to anticipated protests."

Santini grinned as he read the message. Although not surprised that there was a protest, he was shocked at just how quick the liberal masses in San Francisco could coordinate a civil protest. Arriving at the building, he walked from the parking garage and decided not to avoid the protest. He wanted to check out the crowd of over three hundred that were expressing such anger over the Devil Horns case.

He trod cautiously through the milling activists, mostly Latino men and women, holding signs reading "No Human Is Illegal!" and "We Are All Immigrants!" There was also an old man wearing a "Homies Unidos" T-shirt, screaming "Sí se puede!" or "Yes we can!" over and over in a call-and-response with the agitated demonstrators. The media was on hand too, interviewing protesters and filming the chaotic scene.

Santini was both perplexed and amused. He wondered why these people weren't relieved that HSI had just taken dozens of drug dealers, car thieves, and murderers off the city streets. After reinvestigating fifteen unsolved murders in SFPD's cold case files, the federal team had identified and put away seven killers. But the protesters were enraged over an alleged anti-immigrant sweep targeting "innocent" Latino males.

Despite all the negativity, the agent felt confident the thugs were where they belonged. Behind steel bars where they could quietly sit, worshipping the Beast. He threaded his way politely through and past the mob, and entered the front door of the federal building. Time to work on trial prep—and perhaps a new gang investigation.

EPILOGUE

SEVERAL MONTHS AFTER THE BIG TAKEDOWN, THE *SAN FRANCISCO CHRON-icle* reported a notably steep drop in violence on the city's streets. All forms of violent crime had fallen by 20 percent compared with the year before, while homicides were down an impressive 60 percent. When contacted for comment about the plummet in crime, Mayor Newsom replied, "Sometimes these things are inexplicable. It could just be good luck."

Four months later, the *Chronicle* reported not a single case of homicide had occurred yet in the Mission District, whereas thirteen murders had occurred during the same period two years prior, and nineteen in the immediately previous year. Responding to a reporter, SFPD lieutenant Jim Sawyer said the reduction in violence was the result of the Operation Devil Horns takedown of 20th Street.

With the presidential inauguration of Barrack Obama in 2008 and his subsequent appointment of Eric Holder as US Attorney General, Joseph Russoniello was replaced as head of DOJ's Northern California District office in San Francisco. A federal grand jury investigation into possible violations of federal law related to the shielding of felons from deportation by the city's juvenile probation office subsequently faded away.

Heather Fong retired as the city's chief of police in December 2008 with an annual pension of $250,000, based on her final year's salary of $500,000, which included pay for saved-up vacation and sick days (a standard tactic for government employees, jacking up their lifetime benefit packages). Ironically, she later became the assistant secretary for local law enforcement at the US Department of Homeland Security in 2014.

In April 2009, Gavin Newsom announced his intention to run for governor of California in the upcoming election. During the course of the campaign, Newsom polled badly, consistently trailing the Democratic

front-runner candidate, Jerry Brown, by more than twenty points. Newsom soon dropped out of the race. Five months later he announced his
candidacy for lieutenant governor, and proceeded to win his party's nom-
ination for the seat as well as the general election.

In 2009, the San Francisco board of supervisors overturned Newsom's policy that required local police to contact ICE whenever they
arrested a juvenile on felony charges whom they suspected to be in the
United States illegally.

Inspector Mateo Salcedo of the Honduras National Police, who
had been one of Santini's main points of contact there, was assassinated
in Tegucigalpa as he walked to work on the morning of June 9, 2009.
Surrounded by three armed gang members, Salcedo drew his weapon
but was outgunned from multiple directions and hit with approximately
seventeen rounds. Santini suspected that Salcedo's association with US
law enforcement might have been a motive for the killing.

Kamala Harris, San Francisco's district attorney, announced her intention to run for the office of California attorney general in November 2008.
During her campaign, Harris announced she would not seek the death
penalty against Popeye for the murder of the Bolognas. The decision "outraged" Danielle Bologna, according to a family spokesperson. In November
2010, Harris won the race for attorney general of California and took office
in January 2011. In 2016, she was elected as a US senator from California.

In February 2010, Judge Charlotte Woolard of the San Francisco
Superior Court ruled the city couldn't be held liable by Danielle Bologna
for any crimes Popeye had committed after he was released from jail. The
judged based her ruling on an argument that the city had no information
that Ramos posed a specific threat to the Bolognas. The sanctuary policy was intended "to improve immigration controls," not prevent crime,
Woolard ruled.

Beginning a series of convictions for the 20th Street gang members
taken down by Operation Devil Horns, Demonico and Momia pleaded
guilty in November 2010 to murder in the aid of racketeering for the
killing of Ivan Miranda.

Just as the first round of jury trials for another group of gang
members were set to begin in early 2011, Diego revealed to prosecutors

some previously unknown, critical aspects of his own criminal past in Honduras.

Slated to be a star witness in the upcoming trials, Diego unexpectedly confessed to committing eight homicides in Honduras, mostly involving the killing of bus drivers. These were crimes he had not disclosed to Santini prior to signing on as a government informant, six years earlier. Nor had the Honduran police discovered any evidence in this regard when contacted by Santini. Diego's startling admission meant he could not be put on the stand by prosecutors. He was a completely unreliable witness.

As a result, Diego faced felony charges for lying to investigators. He was cut loose from government financial support and personal protection and forced to make it on his own in America, a known rat to MS-13. Claiming the government failed to hold up its end of their bargain with him, Diego unsuccessfully sued to obtain damages and compensation.

Scrambling to reformulate their trial strategy without Diego, federal prosecutors still had Casper to put on the stand as a witness. Additionally, another gang member, Casper's nephew Goofy, decided to accept a plea deal in exchange for cooperating. Goofy was facing life in prison on gang conspiracy charges, including attempted murder. He decided to flip on his homies only after they falsely accused him of being a rat while he was held in Santa Rita Jail.

Assessing the witnesses and evidence stacked up against him, Cyper pleaded guilty in January 2011 to conspiracy to commit murder, receiving ten years of incarceration, rather than face a trial and possibly a steeper sentence. Three days later, Indio made the same calculation, also pleading guilty to RICO conspiracy and conspiracy to commit murder in aid of racketeering. He received a sentence of life in federal prison. Fantasma pleaded guilty to RICO conspiracy and conspiracy to commit assault with a dangerous weapon in aid of racketeering, receiving a twenty-year sentence.

With rats jumping from the ship all around, Tigre, the first-named defendant in the case, chose to plead guilty to murder conspiracy and illegal firearms charges. In doing so, he avoided the possibility of a death sentence, but received twenty-five years in federal prison.

Goofy, testifying on the stand against Sparky, Cyco, Peloncito, Slow Pain, Spooky, and Soldado, proved to be a more engaging and effective witness for the prosecution than Casper, according to some courtroom observers. While Casper came across as "snide," Goofy was "composed, straightforward, and, every once in a while, unintentionally funny." When asked on the stand why he didn't ride the bus to attack gang members, Goofy replied, "Because the bus stops, like, every two blocks."[1]

During the trial, defense attorneys attempted to portray accused gang members as victims of illegal entrapment, claiming that Santini's two main informants—Casper and Diego—were the real masterminds and ring leaders of the clique. The two tools of the government had taken a disorganized bunch of hapless homies—"a gang that couldn't shoot straight"—and whipped them into shape, orchestrating their criminal activities, the defense argued.[2] After all, it was Diego who had inked-up numerous homies with MS-13 tattoos, the defense lawyers argued. Diego was a menacing presence among the gang, intimidating those who broke clique rules or refused to do "work," they claimed. Cyper testified he got a tattoo and generally did whatever Diego told him to do because he was afraid he'd be killed, otherwise.

After a five-month-long trial, the jury didn't buy the six homies' entrapment defense. In August 2011, Sparky, Cyco, Peloncito, Slow Pain, Spooky, and Soldado were all convicted of racketeering conspiracy and murder in aid of racketeering. A few months later, all six were sentenced to life in prison.

Two months later, in a separate trial as a sole defendant, Dreamer was convicted on one count of violent crime in aid of racketeering conspiracy.

In February 2012, still awaiting sentencing for his own gang-related crimes, Goofy made another appearance as a star witness in the trial of Popeye, his brother-in-law, for the murders of the Bologna family. Goofy testified that Popeye was a known member of the 20th Street clique and that he helped with the group ass-kicking that originally jumped Goofy into the gang in 2000. Popeye was convicted in May 2012 for the murders of the Bologna family and sentenced to three consecutive life sentences, without possibility of parole.

Three months later, Wilfredo Reyes, aka Flaco, was apprehended by HSI in North Carolina and charged for his role as Popeye's accomplice in the Bologna murders. During his own trial, Popeye fingered Flaco as the actual shooter in the incident, claiming he himself had only been acting as the driver.

In May 2013, Diego Mendoza, head of the Honduran National Police's gang unit, whom Santini had met during his visit to Tegucigalpa, was shot and killed by gang members. Mendoza sat watching a soccer game in the city's La Granja neighborhood when several MS-13 thugs surrounded him and shot him in the back of the head, killing him instantly.

The San Francisco board of supervisors adopted a resolution in 2013, essentially re-embracing the city's sanctuary policy of fundamental non-cooperation with federal immigration law enforcement.

That same year, Casper was granted credit for time served and released as a free man in America. Santini attended the hearing where Casper walked out to start his life with a new identity provided by the federal witness protection program. The agent reminded Casper he still owed him a plate of carne asada, which he had promised when they first met in a San Francisco jail six years earlier when the gang member agreed to turn rat.

In July 2015, three years after his arrest, Flaco accepted a plea deal in the Bologna murder case that carried a ten-year prison sentence. A spokesperson for Danielle Bologna told news reporters that the emotionally drained widow was relieved there would be no second trial in the case.

For his role as the case agent of Operation Devil Horns, Santini received a Distinguished Service Award from U.S. Attorney General Eric Holder. Other recipients of the award included Ricardo Cabrera, Sean Gibson, Laura Gwinn, and Nelson Wong, among several other special agents from the investigative team. Following conclusion of the 20th Street case, Santini continued his career as a special agent with HSI for several more years in various posts in the United States and overseas.

Notes

Chapter 2
1. Culiche actually had been nabbed by the Texas Highway Patrol for illegally attempting to cross the US-Mexico border.
2. Jessica Vaughn and John Feere, *Taking Back the Streets: ICE and Local Law Enforcement Target Immigrant Gangs*, Center for Immigration Studies, September 30, 2008, https://cis.org/Report/MS13-Resurgence-Immigration-Enforcement-Needed -Take-Back-Our-Streets

Chapter 5
1. "Mayor Mourns a Victim," *San Francisco Chronicle*, June 29, 2004.
2. "Playground under Siege," *San Francisco Chronicle*, February 5, 1999.
3. "SFPD Dead Last in Solving Violent Crime," *San Francisco Chronicle*, May 19, 2002.

Chapter 9
1. Ismael Moreno, "Has 'Social Cleansing' of Gang Members Spread to Honduran Jails?" *Envio*, no. 282, May 2003.

Chapter 10
1. Dreamer had set Casper up, planting the gun in the car Casper was driving and tipping off his SFPD and FBI handlers.

Chapter 11
1. Harris was elected California attorney general in both 2010 and 2014 and was widely rumored in 2018 to be positioning herself to run for the White House in the next election.
2. Pat Murphy and Luke Thomas, "Police Ethics Panel Reveals San Francisco Law Enforcement Stymied by Leadership Failure, Communication Breakdown, Low Morale, Politics and Mistrust," *Fog City Journal*, June 5, 2006.
3. Ibid.
4. Susan Sward, "Commissioner Slams Police Panel: Sparks Describes Numerous Failures, Quits Key Position," *San Francisco Chronicle*, May 26, 2006.

CHAPTER 12

1. As a criminal informant, Casper was prevented from acting as a leader in the gang. Otherwise, defendants in any future prosecution could claim the government had orchestrated the entire criminal enterprise from the top down, negating a successful RICO case.

CHAPTER 13

1. What Peloncito didn't share was that he had skimmed off enough cash from the clique's treasury to buy himself a used car.

CHAPTER 21

1. Supreme Court of El Salvador, Forensic Statistics Unit, *Boletín sobre Homicidios*, Año 2, no. 1, January 2006.
2. Mo Hume, "*Mano Dura*: El Salvador Responds to Gangs," *Development in Practice* 17, no. 6 (2007): 739–51.

CHAPTER 22

1. In fact, the city parks department had pastured some domesticated goats to eat brush growing out of control, which was creating a fire hazard.
2. Casper's ex-wife Jackie was actively trying to out him as a rat, sending a letter to the Big Homies in El Salvador, saying she had found FBI agent business cards among Casper's belongings. The cards had actually been given to Jackie by the agents, since she was acting as a Bureau informant.

CHAPTER 23

1. Pat Murphy and Luke Thomas, "Police Ethics Panel Reveals San Francisco Law Enforcement Stymied by Leadership Failure, Communication Breakdown, Low Morale, Politics and Mistrust," *Fog City Journal*, June 5, 2006.
2. Sarah Phelan, "Public Safety Adrift," *San Francisco Bay Guardian*, February 11, 2009.
3. Nearby Soldado's apartment, in 2005, SFPD officer Isaac Espinoza had been shot and killed by a West Mob gangster with an AK-47, a crime for which Kamala Harris refused to pursue the death penalty.

CHAPTER 24

1. Nina Martin, "No Sanctuary for Danielle Bologna," *San Francisco* magazine, October 21, 2011.
2. "Surviving Son Testifies in 2008 Bologna Family Killings," CBS SF Bay Area, January 25, 2012.
3. Vivian Ho, "S.F. Killer Confronted by Victims' Widow, Mother," *San Francisco Chronicle*, June 5, 2012.
4. "Murder in San Francisco," Fox News, July 23, 2008.

5. Heather Knight, "Minutemen Protest S.F.'s Sanctuary Policy," *San Francisco Chronicle*, July 31, 2008.
6. Peter Nicholas and Robert Salladay, "Gov. Praises 'Minuteman' Campaign," *Los Angeles Times*, April 29, 2005.
7. Knight, "Minutemen Protest S.F.'s Sanctuary Policy."

CHAPTER 25
1. Jaxon Van Derbeken, "Suspect in Boy's Slaying Avoided Deportation," *San Francisco Chronicle*, November 14, 2008.
2. Ibid.

CHAPTER 26
1. Some observers questioned whether all the homies flown home were in fact juveniles—definitively confirming the Central Americans' ages was often next to impossible due to lack of birth records.
2. Phil Matier and Andy Ross, "Illegal Immigrant Arrested 5 Times before Feds Told," *San Francisco Chronicle*, August 3, 2008.
3. Jaxon Van Derbeken, "S.F. Fund Aids Teen Felons Who Are Illegals," *San Francisco Chronicle*, August 3, 2008.
4. Elise Foley, "ICE Confirms Fingerprint-Sharing Program Secure Communities Is Mandatory," *Florida Independent*, December 14, 2011.
5. Bob Egelko, "Federal Probe into S.F. Sanctuary City Policy," *San Francisco Chronicle*, October 4, 2008.

CHAPTER 27
1. Evan Hill and Dan Levine, "Killings Spur Federal Effort against Gang" *Recorder*, September 8, 2008.

EPILOGUE
1. Lauren Smiley, "A Rat's Life: MS-13 Snitches Run Wild while Turning State's Evidence," *SF Weekly*, April 27, 2011.
2. Ibid.

Index

About the Authors

Michael Santini is the pen name of a career special agent with Homeland Security Investigations. He previously served as a border patrol agent in San Diego, California. For his work as lead case agent on Operation Devil Horns, Michael received a distinguished service medal from the U.S. Attorney General.

Ray Bolger is a journalist with over twenty years of experience covering business, technology, finance, government, and crime. His published articles have appeared in many leading outlets including *The Baltimore Sun*, *The Philadelphia Inquirer*, *The Hill*, and *Forbes* magazine.